KT-221-885

The Complete Handbook of **Fruit Growing**

The Complete Handbook of Fruit Growing

Roy Genders

TREASURE PRESS

First published in Great Britain by Ward Lock Ltd

This edition published by Treasure Press
59 Grosvenor Street
London W1

ISBN 0 907407 52 8

Printed in Hong Kong

Contents

List of Colour Illustrations

1 Planning the Fruit Garden

The latest figures of Britain's Department of Agriculture show that more than a quarter of a million acres of the United Kingdom are planted with orchard crops and soft fruits. Yet this acreage is fast disappearing. Land is sold for high prices for building, a situation that is probably paralleled throughout most of western Europe and in the USA, while with the high cost of labour it has become uneconomic to tend fruit trees and to gather the crops. The result is that more amateur growers are needed to maintain the amount of fruit grown each year and to keep prices at a reasonable level.

Many choice varieties continue to disappear from the catalogue of specialist growers, possibly because they do not crop as heavily as others, or because the fruit, while highly flavoured, may be of unattractive appearance. So for some years now the public have been given the choice of only two or three commercial varieties of each fruit. Many others, highly thought of little more than a decade or so ago, are now but happy memories of an older generation. Who remembers that delicious late apple, the 'Claygate Pearmain'? Not even the highly respected 'Cox's Orange' can equal its flavour when removed from the tree, the fruit ice cold with early morning dew, the flesh crisp and aromatic and full of juice. Or 'Coe's Golden Drop' plum, admittedly difficult to grow in certain soils like most good fruits, but without a peer among plums. When removed from the tree, its straw coloured skin with its cinnamon 'bloom' warmed by the late September sunshine, its flesh exuding the rich flavour of the greengage, one of its parents, it is one of the most delicious of all fruits, worthy of a place in every garden. Only by growing them ourselves can the best varieties be preserved and their fruits appreciated.

Planting for Succession

By careful planning (by which every part of the garden is brought into use) and planting for succession, it is possible for the smallest garden to produce enough fruit to feed the household for almost the entire year, beginning with forced rhubarb in January and February, then early strawberries under cloches, and continuing with a succession of fruit until the autumn fruiting raspberries and the remontant strawberries finish fruiting towards Christmas time, again beneath the protective warmth of cloches. Early strawberries are followed by the first gooseberries, then come raspberries and blackcurrants, blackberries and early apples with later varieties to follow, and then those maturing last of all, to store for winter use.

Where space is at a premium, cordon apples and pears may be planted alongside a path; and beneath standard trees, strawberries and gooseberries may be grown, for both enjoy partial shade. Whereas few vegetables will do well in part shade, there are a number of fruits which will flourish.

Against a warm wall of a house or out-house,

An apple, before and after winter pruning

dessert pears may be grown in espalier form, or plums trained as fan shaped trees. Against trellis, possibly used to divide one part of the garden from another, the loganberry and Japanese wineberry may be planted, the crimson canes of the latter providing cheerful winter colour.

For a hedge, the vigorous Himalayan or the Oregon thornless blackberry may be grown, their long sturdy shoots being tied in along galvanized wires fastened to strong stakes at intervals of 12 feet. One may alternate the planting with the earlier fruiting 'Bedford Giant'; this also bears its fruit on both the new and old wood. The blackberries need little pruning apart from the removal of dead wood, and in two years will make an impenetrable hedge. The Worcester berry, too, may be used as a hedge, training its arching shoots along wires.

To train over trellis or against the wall of a house, tying in the canes to wires fixed so that they are 1 inch away from the wall, the Japanese wineberry will be so much more rewarding than an ivy or Virginia creeper; its handsome canes, covered in crimson hairs, will attain 10 feet or more in a season, and the delicious amber coloured fruits make excellent jam. It is thornless, too.

The Use of a Courtyard

The ever-increasing cost of food should encourage the housewife to grow all the fruits and vegetables she may need. This may be done even where there is no garden in the recognized sense, but merely a courtyard, possibly enclosed by a high wall. Here, against the wall of the house, may be planted an espalier pear. One of two tiers (with two pairs of arms) will cost about £2 and, by retaining the leader shoot, it may be trained to any height.

For a wall which receives only a limited amount of sunshine plant one of the hardy, early ripening varieties such as:

Beurré Bedford	Fertility
Beurré Hardy	Marguerite Marillat
Clapp's Favourite	William's Bon Chrétien

Both 'Fertility' and 'Marguerite Marillat' have an additional attraction: besides bearing heavy crops, their leaves turn a brilliant scarlet colour in late autumn. The leaves of the later maturing but temperamental 'Seckle' turn deep crimson purple, but do not plant this variety (or 'Louise Bonne') with 'William's Pear' for they will not pollinate each other, and though many pears are self-fertile and will set quite good crops with their own pollen, they will usually prove more prolific if two varieties are planted together. On a sunny wall, plant a later maturing pear which in Britain will need all the sun it can get to complete its ripening. And do not plant pears on a wall which is beset by draughts and cold winds. 'Conference', 'Bristol Cross' and 'Doyenne du Comice', however much the sun shines down upon them, are especially fallible in such a position.

Around the sides of a courtyard, quick-cropping bush apple trees–which on Malling IX or XXVI rootstock will come into bearing when only two years old–may be planted in tubs or in large earthenware pots, one to each, with strawberries around the side. If it is required to grow mostly 'Cox's Orange', then remember to plant one 'James Grieve' to every five or six 'Cox's' to act as a pollinator. This hardy apple, excellent in its own right, will also act as a pollinator for the best of all cooking apples, 'Bramley's Seedling'. For tub culture, however, 'Arthur Turner' and 'Annie Elizabeth' are more reliable culinary apples.

Those who have only a small courtyard or veranda on which to grow their fruit may enjoy a long succession of the finest varieties by growing several family trees in large tubs. These trees, on which five or more varieties are grafted, are obtainable on all the more popular rootstocks. One tree of cooking apples and one dessert varieties, whether for northern or southern gardens, will produce fruit for picking from August until Christmas. Pears and plums are also available so that just four tubs will give a selection of the finest varieties.

As the apple is the last of all fruits to bloom, it is only rarely that it is damaged by frost. And is there any lovelier sight than an apple orchard in full bloom against a clear blue sky? Several varieties are more handsome in bloom than others, and they are most ornamental when growing in pots or tubs in a courtyard. Two russets, 'Brownlee's' and 'Merton Russet', have deep carmine pink blossom which is especially striking against the whitewashed walls of a courtyard, but even more beautiful is the blossom of those two excellent cookers, 'Arthur Turner' and 'Annie Elizabeth'. 'Arthur Turner' bears its blossom before it is in leaf, the flowers being deep pink with the petals opening flat to reveal the fullness of their beauty. That of 'Annie Elizabeth' is deepest carmine veined with crimson; though it ripens its fruit early, it blooms late, and may be planted in those gardens troubled by frosts. Nor should the striking *Pyrus eleyi* be omitted where blossom is appreciated. A crab apple of compact habit, its long arching branches are clothed in purple tinted leaves, and in spring it bears clusters of deepest crimson flowers. These are followed in autumn by crimson black fruits which hang like cherries and make a delicious preserve.

Apples of excessive vigour like 'Blenheim Orange', and the tip bearers such as 'Worcester Pearmain', are not suitable for growing in containers but there are a number of others of compact habit which may be expected to yield heavy crops under such conditions:

Lady Sudeley	August
Devonshire Quarrenden	September
Egremont Russet	October
Cox's Orange Pippin	November
Acme	December
Adam's Pearmain	January
Claygate Pearmain	February
May Queen	March–May

Though 'Lady Sudeley', which bears the most handsome fruit of all apples, is often classed as a tip-bearer, it bears its fruit on very short twigs (rather than on spurs like 'Cox's Orange') and so may be said to come halfway between the true tip and spur bearers. It is a very suitable variety for tub or pot culture and has the advantage over 'Beauty of Bath' and other early apples in that it does not drop its fruit before it is ripe. Robert Thompson, keeper of the Horticultural Society's garden at Chiswick a century ago, described it as being 'crisp, rich and sweet, an excellent summer apple'. Of 'Devonshire Quarrenden', Lindley wrote in 1830 that 'cultivated as a dwarf and laden with fruit, it is more ornamental than most fruit trees'.

Pears may also be grown in tubs or pots, and if so should be given the sunniest position in the courtyard. The pure white blossom and dark brown anthers, and the rich autumn colourings of the foliage, combine to make the pear a most ornamental plant quite apart from its fruit. To grow in pots or tubs the following are suitable:

Laxton's Superb	August
Beurré Bedford	September
Dr Jules Guyot	October
Conference	November
Glou Morceau	December
Roosevelt	January
Winter Nelis	February
Bergamotte d'Esperen	March–April

In each case, the month given denotes when the fruit is at its best for dessert; the later maturing kinds should keep until the time mentioned.

Strawberries may be planted around the side of tubs or in window boxes which may be fixed to a sunny wall by means of angle iron brackets; or the boxes may be placed at the foot of a sunny wall. Two varieties should be grown, an early one such as 'Cambridge Favourite', possibly the best all-round strawberry ever introduced; and a late one such as 'Talisman' or 'Montrose' which will fruit

when the earlies have finished. Or plant the autumn fruiting 'Hampshire Maid' which will crop from August until November.

At one time, every Georgian basement courtyard had its fig tree growing against a sunny wall, but the equally durable vine is to be preferred and it will bear quickly and heavily if treated as a cordon, producing bunches of large juicy grapes in its second season. Its culture in this way is extremely simple. Lateral shoots are allowed to form all the way along the cordon stem and these will bear fruit. Afterwards, the shoots are pinched back to a single eye or bud from which will appear the next year's fruiting shoot; this, too, will be cut back to a single eye after fruiting.

In this way at least two or three vines may be grown against a sunny wall. The ancient 'Royal Muscadine', which bears generous bunches of sweet, richly flavoured grapes which ripen to deepest yellow, is ideal for growing as a cordon on an outside wall and the best black for cordon culture is 'Hâtif Noir de Marseilles'.

The self-fertile peach, which does not need the companionship of a pollinator, may also be grown against a sunny courtyard wall. Fan-trained trees are the most suitable for wall culture, likewise with plums, of which 'Victoria', 'Kirke's Blue' and 'Oullin's Golden Gage' crop profusely in this form. In peaches, 'Hale's Early' or 'Peregrine' are reliable. On the sunless side of the courtyard, dessert gooseberries may be planted in narrow beds of soil at the base of the wall surrounded by an edging of brick or stone to retain the soil. Gooseberries prefer cool conditions and a moist soil, and here they should be planted in the cordon or double cordon form when they will bear large, richly flavoured fruits resembling plums if eaten from the plants when fully ripe. Among the best to grow in this way are 'Leveller', 'Broom Girl', 'Bedford Yellow' and 'White Lion'.

The 'Brunswick' Fig–ideal for growing against a courtyard wall

Rhubarb, too, may be grown in a ground bed or in deep boxes painted green on the outside and placed in a corner. Established plants should be covered with another box or a large pot early in spring, to force the sticks so that they grow tender and succulent.

Planted with various fruits, the smallest of courtyard gardens will be a place of interest and beauty almost the whole year through. What is more, one may be able to enjoy some of those choice fruits which are now rarely to be obtained from greengrocers, who have to rely on importations which for flavour are rarely the equal of home grown fruits.

Fruit Tree Requirements

The small garden can be made productive only by careful planning. All too often, fruit trees are planted merely because a certain variety appeals by its appearance. For instance, 'Golden Delicious' apple, with its even shape and unmarked skin, is much in demand by supermarkets; this apple, so lacking in flavour in comparison with many others, has become well known to a multitude of shoppers, and with the 'Cox's Orange Pippin', the other favourite, is now being planted in gardens with little thought as to pollination or to the soil and climate in which they will grow.

Much may be learnt of the climate requirements of a fruit tree from its place of introduction. One of the finest dessert apples for the colder regions is 'James Grieve'; 'Sturmer Pippin', reared from a seed of 'Ribston Pippin', matures so late that it should be confined to gardens where it will receive the maximum amount of late summer sunshine. It is the longest keeping of all apples and will not be at its best until 'George Cave' or 'Lady Sudeley' are ready to harvest the following year. 'Cox's Orange' grows to perfection in alluvial soils; 'D'Arcy Spice' crops well in a warm, dry climate but its dull russet colour and irregular shape does not recommend it to the supermarkets, and few gardeners know of its existence, let alone its delicious flavour.

Another apple which crops well even in cold, clay soil, and when entirely neglected, is 'Herring's Pippin'. Its aromatic perfume and spicy flavour make it a delicious Christmas dessert, to enjoy with a vintage port.

A chalk laden soil may be made more productive by green manuring, sowing rape seed and digging in the plants and their fibrous roots when the rape is about two inches high; or by heavily manuring. The addition of material from the garden compost heap and clearings from ditches will help to add humus to the soil and make it less liable to dry out in summer. A limestone soil, usually a hot dry soil, is not suitable for pears or plums, but cherries grow well in such a soil as do several of the more vigorous growing apples which are able to tolerate such conditions. The most important of these are 'Barnack Beauty' and its offspring 'Barnack Orange'. Another is 'Gascoyne's Scarlet', which makes a big spreading tree. These apples are tip bearers and are not suitable for growing as cordons. 'Charles Ross', too, is of vigorous habit and also does well in a limestone soil. It bears a handsome dual-purpose apple which cooks almost as well as 'Bramley's Seedling'. These are the best apples for a limestone soil to give a succession of fruit:

St Everard	September
Charles Ross	October
Gascoyne's Scarlet	November
Barnack Orange	December
Barnack Beauty	January–March

Few plums grow well in a limestone soil. They prefer one of a heavy nature, but several may be expected to give reliable crops under such conditions:

River's Early Prolific	July–August
Greengage	September
Marjorie's Seedling	September–October
Pond's Seedling	September–October

A thin, limestone soil may be made suitable for growing soft fruits more easily than top fruits, by green manuring and incorporating plenty of humus such as peat or leaf-mould and digging it in as deeply as possible.

Strawberries may be troubled by botrytis (grey mould) and mildew. For this reason, it is advisable to plant mildew-resistant varieties such as 'Cambridge Sentry', 'Late Pine', 'Gorells', and 'Red Gauntlet'. But the best strawberry for a predominantly limestone soil is 'Cambridge Vigour'.

Though plums do not like a dry limestone soil, damsons flourish under such conditions provided they are planted in an area of high rainfall. Plums prefer a heavy soil, one containing a high percentage of clay provided it is well enriched with humus by way of shoddy or farmyard manure. There are several apples that are tolerant of cold, clay soil, in which 'Cox's Orange' should not be planted. Of particular value is 'Adam's Pearmain', one of the hardiest of dessert apples and of which Lindley wrote 'its merit consists in it being a healthy, hardy sort, a free bearer, extremely handsome, a good keeper . . . acid and sugar being so intimately blended as to form the most perfect flavour'. Added to which is its tolerance of a cold clay soil and an exposed garden. 'Herring's Pippin' does equally well under such conditions and its handsome green and red fruit may be used either for dessert or for cooking. 'Newton Wonder' is also tolerant of a clay soil and is one of the most handsome of all apples, while 'Pott's Seedling' will crop well in a heavy soil and in an exposed garden. 'King of the Pippins' is also tolerant of cold conditions, being a heavy bearer in a clay soil.

Plant these apples for succession in a cold, clay soil: (C)=Culinary:

Sowman's Seedling (C)	August
Pott's Seedling (C)	September
James Grieve	September–October
King of the Pippins	October–November

Lord Derby (C)	November
Herring's Pippin	November–December
Newton Wonder (C)	December–February
Sam Young	December–February
Adam's Pearmain	January
Edward VII	January–June
Brownlee's Russet	March–April
Laxton's Rearguard (C)	March–May

For a wet soil, and this does not mean a heavy, clay soil but one where the ground is low lying and not too well drained, those varieties prone to scab should be avoided. In areas where heavy rains are common at all times of the year and where the roots of fruit trees are often submerged for several weeks at a time, 'Grenadier' will thrive. 'Lord Derby' and 'Monarch' are others tolerant of a wet soil. Two dessert apples for those conditions are 'Laxton's Superb' and 'Sam Young'.

Apples which are highly resistant to scab and which may be planted in areas of unusually high rainfall are:

Hereford Cross	September
Ellison's Orange	September–October
Grenadier (C)	September–October
Worcester Pearmain	September–October
Kidd's Orange	October–November
Taunton Cross	October–November
Laxton's Superb	November–December
Monarch (C)	November–December
Claygate Pearmain	December–January
Cox's Orange Pippin	December–January
Gravenstein	December–January

Fortunately, most of these apples will pollinate each other, though all are early flowering and highly susceptible to frost damage. With the exception of 'Laxton's Superb', which seems to be one of those apples that do well anywhere, none is suitable for cold gardens. They are the elite among apples, demanding some care in their culture when they will reward one with fruit of superb quality. Though tolerant of wet, they respond only where the soil is warmed by the early spring sunshine and where the garden is protected from cold winds.

There are a number of suitable apples which are tolerant of cold winters and of below-average rainfall. Outstanding is 'James Grieve' and its equally reliable offspring, 'Lord Lambourne', while 'Acme' and 'Merton Worcester' are new apples to prove their value under such conditions. In cookers, 'Early Victoria' and 'Monarch' are reliable.

These apples should be planted in drier areas:

Early Victoria	August–September
James Grieve	September–October
Lord Lambourne	October–November
Merton Worcester	October–November
Michaelmas Red	October–November
St Edmund's Russet	October–November
Monarch	November
Acme	December–January
D'Arcy Spice	December–January
Tydeman's Late Orange	February–May

Consideration of Frost

Quite apart from general climatic conditions, the question of situation plays an important part in the cropping of fruit trees. Taken generally, apples are certainly the most hardy of all trees, or top fruits, as they are so often called, but even with apples it is most important to give careful consideration to local conditions.

A late frost may limit the cropping powers of such frost susceptible varieties as 'Cox's Orange Pippin' and 'Bramley's Seedling', the finest quality apples in their two respective sections, but both difficult to crop consistently well. As soon as their buds begin to burst, they become liable to frost damage; 'Cox's' especially will prove more reliable if planted in districts where late frosts are not troublesome.

What may be said of frost in general also appertains to individual gardens, those situated in a frost hollow, or near to a river or stream, which tend to be frost pockets. Varieties which may give a good account of themselves in one garden may prove completely disappointing when planted in a garden susceptible to frost, though perhaps situated only several hundred yards apart from each other.

Therefore, if frosts are experienced late in the year, no other consideration should be given to the choice of varieties than deciding whether they will be reasonably resistant to frost. This really means that they will be so late flowering that even the latest frosts do not damage the bloom. 'Cox's Orange' and indeed most dessert apples are out of the question in the frosty garden, though 'James Grieve' and 'Worcester Pearmain', the best all-round apples ever introduced, should prove immune, unless the frost is particularly severe.

Where frosts persist late, but are not too severe, the best early maturing apple is 'Lady Sudeley'. It is possibly the most beautifully coloured of all apples, being of a bright golden-yellow, flushed and striped with scarlet. It should be eaten straight from the tree when it is soft and juicy.

In bloom about the same time and later than most dessert apples is 'Laxton's Superb', probably the best of all mid-season apples. The flesh is soft, pure white and exceptionally sweet, and it remains at peak eating longer than any other apple, from mid-November until early February.

For a late dessert apple, in bloom rather later than 'Superb' and of similar appearance, 'Winter King', renamed 'Winston', is a new apple of great merit. The fruit is strongly aromatic and possesses the slightly bitter nuttiness of the russets. With its neat upright habit, 'Winston' is the ideal late maturing apple for a small garden and does well in all soils.

For cooking apples, three are of value where frosts prove troublesome: 'Newton Wonder', which with its handsome fruit would be the most widely planted of all culinary apples if it did not tend to biennial cropping; 'Annie Elizabeth', almost as good as 'Newton Wonder' and a completely self-fertile variety; and 'Lane's Prince Albert', which makes a drooping little tree and remains in bloom over a longer period than any apple tree though is not quite so late flowering as the other two.

Where frosts persist late and are severe, in a low lying hollow well away from the coast, one may still grow apples. There are four varieties which bloom very late so that they will miss all frosts, however late in the season. One, 'Court Pendu Plat', one of the two oldest apples still grown, makes such a small tree of weak habit as to be little planted now. Of similar habit is 'Royal Jubilee', which is also a weak grower though heavy cropper, but the remaining two, 'Crawley Beauty' and 'Edward VII', would be suitable for a cold, frosty garden. These are two excellent apples, cropping heavily and being at their best from February to Easter; 'Edward VII' will, if correctly gathered and stored, keep until the earliest maturing varieties are ready again in July. Both are suitable for dessert and for cooking. 'Edward VII', which has the excellent 'Golden Noble' for a parent, and 'Crawley Beauty' both crop well in all soils and in all districts.

Where planting the very late varieties, pollination may in some seasons be insufficient to produce a heavy crop, especially if only two or three varieties are grown. It is therefore advisable to plant with them one or two of those apples which bloom over a prolonged period and will be in bloom with them, and which are also resistant to frost damage. These include 'Lane's Prince Albert', 'Worcester Pearmain' and 'Laxton's Royalty', all of which will pollinate those later into bloom.

These apples are particularly resistant to frost:

Annie Elizabeth (C)	Lady Sudely (C)
Claygate Pearmain	Lane's Prince Albert (C)
D'Arcy Spice	Monarch (C)

Edward VII (C)	Pearl
Forge	Royal Jubilee (C)
Howgate Wonder	Sunset
James Grieve	Tydeman's Late Orange

These apples are highly susceptible to frost damage:

Beauty of Bath	Gravenstein
Blenheim Orange	Laxton's Fortune
Bramley's Seedling	Rev. Wilks
Cox's Orange Pippin	Ribston Pippin

Of pears, which bloom before apples, there are several which may be grown in a frost troubled garden. Of these 'Dr Jules Guyot', 'Winter Nelis', 'Catillac', 'Fertility' and 'Laxton's Superb' are most reliable in that they bloom later than most pears; and of plums, 'River's Early Prolific', 'Pond's Seedling', 'Oullin's Golden Gage', 'Belle de Louvain', 'Late Transparent Gage', 'Czar', 'Yellow Pershore', 'Severn Cross' and 'Kirke's Blue' are suitable for planting in a frost troubled garden.

Of soft fruits, it is rarely that strawberries are badly damaged by frost, for their blossom is usually well protected by the foliage. In a frost hollow, however, 'Cambridge Early Pine' and 'Huxley Giant' should be grown. Raspberries bloom late and are not liable to frost damage, but blackcurrants are prone to frost damage and, where late frosts are experienced, 'Westwick Triumph', 'Amos Black' and 'Mendip Cross' are best to plant, followed by 'Seabrook's Black'. 'Boskoop Giant' is highly susceptible to frost damage. In raspberries, 'Malling Promise' should never be planted where late frosts persist; instead, plant 'Malling Jewel' which opens its blossom later and is rarely troubled by frost, however severe.

Protection of Fruit Trees

In this book, which is intended for the amateur grower with only an average sized garden, it is not possible to make suggestions as to the most suitable land on which to grow apples. The selection must be made to suit one's existing garden. No professional grower would plant in a frost hollow, so mention is rarely made of suitable varieties for such land. But though the gardener must do the best with the situation and climate at his disposal, the matter of pollination is all-important, and the maximum of pollination will only take place where the insects are given some protection from cold winds. This is chiefly why fruit trees crop so abundantly in a walled garden where the atmosphere is calm and warm, and much more helpful to bees and other insects than where the trees are continually swept by prevailing cold winds.

So if at all possible, select a position where the trees receive some protection from strong winds, though it is even more necessary for them to receive their fair share of summer sunshine, so essential for ripening the fruit. Plant pears in a position of full sun, for this is more important to growing a top quality pear than an apple, but give the apples as open and light a position as possible. Planting in the almost complete shade of a building, or too close to matured trees which have been planted for wind protection, or for their ornamental value, will cause the fruit trees to become drawn and weakly and they will never bear an abundant crop.

If planting a small orchard in a windswept district, it will be advisable to use the myrobalan or cherry plum, or the damson, for a windbreak. Both are strong growing and their fruit is valuable for preserving. They will not deprive the soil of moisture and nourishment as will the poplar, thuya, or most other hedging plants.

From the shores of the Black and Caspian Seas and from the eastern Mediterranean seaboard, the pear is to be found growing wild and cropping in abundance, and it is from these parts that it reached Italy and Greece several centuries BC, and later Britain, with the Roman invasion. Whereas the apple is European, the pear is of Asiatic origin, coming into bloom before the apple and requiring, as would be expected, a warmer climate. The pear must have its roots in a warm moist soil, and its head in dry sunshine. It may be considered the most difficult of all fruits to grow well. While an English grown apple will stand comparison with any in the world, it is only rarely that an English grown pear will do so.

But the pear may be cropped more satisfactorily than is so often the case if the same rules as to climate are followed as for the apple. The old 'Jargonelle', 'Beurré Hardy', 'Catillac' and 'Durondeau' will all bear quite well at almost 1,000 feet above sea level. In a sheltered position 'Laxton's Superb', 'Dr Jules Guyot' and 'William's Bon Chrétien' may be added provided they are given the protection of a wall. These pears are not only hardy but also flower late, and so miss reasonably late frosts even in the colder districts. Although the pear enjoys a warm soil, a too moist climate will cause outbreaks of scab to which the trees will eventually succumb. Both 'Clapp's Favourite' and 'Pitmaston Duchess', heavy bearers which make large, vigorous trees, may suffer badly from scab in a moist climate.

Whereas there are numerous apples which will yield heavily in a chalky soil, there are no pears which will tolerate such a soil; likewise, in the soot-laden atmosphere of cities, the apple is able to bear heavily while the pear will bear only spasmodic crops. The French have always been masters at understanding the pear, for in their country it grows better than elsewhere.

To give protection from cold winds, interwoven fencing six feet high and creosoted may be used on the side of prevailing winds or to surround the garden as protection against outsiders. The fencing should be fixed to three inch × three inch posts which have also been creosoted and driven at least eighteen inches into the ground. They should be cemented in to guard against wind loosening the posts and panels. Against the fencing panels, all manner of fruits may be grown. In a suitable district, facing south or west, espalier pears may be planted; where the fence faces east, plant cordon apples or blackberries, which may be trained along galvanized wires fixed to strong posts at intervals of eight to ten feet; they will soon make an impenetrable fence which will also act as a windbreak.

An inexpensive windbreak may be erected by extending hessian canvas four to five feet wide along the side of the prevailing wind and fixing it to stakes.

It may be possible to divide one's garden into three parts with a small lawn and flowers nearest the house, fruit in the centre and vegetables at the far end. Vegetables are more demanding in their requirements and must have an open, sunny situation to grow well. Fruit is more tolerant of some shade but less tolerant of cold winds.

Soil and Situation

Soil and situation play an important part in the cropping of all fruits. Those who must grow their fruit in the colder, northerly regions would be well advised to concentrate on late maturing varieties of most fruits, with the possible exception of the gooseberry, which is able to tolerate and actually prefers cool conditions. By planting late maturing fruits, not only will their blossom be untroubled by late frosts, but they will bear their fruit after the mid-summer glut period. For the commercial grower this means a sure crop and satisfactory returns. The amateur who gardens in a frosty district should have a few plants of an early variety covered with cloches to give continuity. Jam and fruit for bottling can be obtained from those which are later to mature.

For the commercial grower, low-lying frost pockets should be avoided; if this is not possible, only the very latest flowering varieties should be planted. Where possible the land should have a slight southerly slope. This will enable it to receive the early spring sunshine so that the soil is warmed and the roots of the plants are stimulated into action without undue delay.

Land with a slight slope will almost always be well drained; this is essential to successful fruit culture, since wet, badly drained land will not only cause rotting of the roots but also fail to warm in time to provide an early crop.

The favourably placed grower who is relying on an extra early crop must harness the absolute maximum of spring sunshine. A delay of but two or three days in the ripening of the fruit may mean considerably lower returns. Not all the land may have a southerly slope, but that which has should be devoted to the earliest crops, though this will be of less advantage the further north one gardens, unless glass protection can be provided.

To obtain the most successful crops, one must always plant those fruits and varieties suited to site and climate. Blackcurrants, now one of the most popular crops, might prove a comparative failure on exposed ground though if some protection from prevailing winds were provided and a late maturing variety such as 'Amos Black' grown, the chances of a satisfactory crop would be greatly improved. Select your crop because it suits your garden or land, rather than because a certain variety may grow well elsewhere.

Soil Textures and their Improvement

The same may also be said about various soils. An early crop cannot be expected from a heavy clay soil which will not readily warm up in the spring. It is the light, sandy loam which produces the early crop. In a stiff clay loam, blackcurrants thrive, whereas only a few varieties of the strawberry will be happy, and then only reasonably so.

A chalky soil will also present difficulties. Certain varieties crop better than others in such a soil, but there is always the danger of chlorosis, the plants being starved of iron in the soil. They turn yellow, become stunted and crop only moderately, finally dying back together. Chalky soils are generally shallow soils, and unless well supplied with humus, plants will suffer from drought and rarely bear the maximum crops.

Different fruits also require different cultural treatment. Blackcurrants, for instance, thrive on a diet of nitrogenous humus, while gooseberries prefer potash, but all soft fruits appreciate a rich, deeply worked soil. A shallow chalk soil, which will almost always be well drained, may first be given additional humus by 'green' manuring. Rape seed should be sown in spring, and when about four inches high should be either dug or ploughed in. The soil may also need a heavy application in the autumn of decayed manure or composted straw augmented by peat or bark fibre; after this has been worked in it will then be ready for planting. Liming will not be necessary with a chalk soil, but may be essential for all other soils except where strawberries are being grown, for they, like potatoes, prefer a soil which is slightly acid.

A heavy, clay soil may be broken up by giving a dressing of caustic (unhydrated) lime, which is incorporated during the early winter months before rains prevent the land being worked. The vigorous action of the lime as it dehydrates will break up the clay particles in the soil and this, together with the action of the frost, will pulverize the soil. If then enriched with a limited quantity of decayed manure, or with peat, or bark fibre in early March, planting may take place at the end of that month, the best time when working a soil of this nature. As a heavy soil may also require additional treatment before it becomes thoroughly well drained, it will be advisable to incorporate coarse sand, crushed brick, lime rubble, or shingle at the same time as the manure.

Heavy land which is also low-lying may require draining by the use of land drains, otherwise crops will become water-logged during period of excessive rainfall, and will never prove profitable. Trenches two feet deep should be made at 20-25 feet intervals, into which the drains are laid, taken across the land so that they can empty into a ditch or wide trench. Poor soil would not warrant the initial outlay but often low-lying land is of a rich alluvial nature, extremely valuable for growing soft fruits, and will be improved by draining.

Land of a light, sandy nature, or a light loam, will present no difficulties, though such a soil often lacks plant nutriment and requires heavier dressings of manure for it to produce heavy crops. It is also necessary to incorporate moisture holding materials, especially in an area of low rainfall. Decayed strawy manure, composted straw, and peat or bark fibre, should all be incorporated to retain moisture. Light land may be prepared early in autumn, and planting may then take place at any time from early November until the end of March, the earlier the better. Exact manurial requirements will be described under the various fruits, for each needs individual treatment, depending upon soil conditions.

When breaking up grassland the turf should be ploughed and disced. When growing on a small scale, double digging should be done, the turf being buried as deeply as possible so that it will not grow again. Newly broken grassland is frequently troubled by wireworm, which will attack the roots of the plants, causing widespread damage. As a precaution, work into the top three inches of the soil an application of Aldrin dust, which will exterminate the pest. This should be done three or four weeks before planting. After the soil has been prepared, always allow it a full three weeks to consolidate before planting, for all soft fruits prefer a firm soil.

Soil of a town garden should be heavily limed before it is manured. Artificial drainage will not be necessary, but such soil will often be sour due to continuous deposits of soot and sulphur. It may also be inert, growing little but ivy and privet unless it is enriched with decayed manures, bone meal, shoddy or spent hops; the last named can be obtained by those living near a brewery. Those living near the sea coast could use chopped seaweed.

Apart from its ability to correct the acidity of soil, lime has the power to release the various plant foods in it, so well manured land will not be beneficial to growing crops unless lime is present to unlock the food content. Again, lime is able to improve the physical condition of the soil by breaking up the clay particles. For a heavy soil an application of caustic lime (unhydrated) will by its vigorous action break up the clay particles more quickly than will hydrated lime. Caustic lime is obtainable from a builder's merchant and must be kept dry. It is applied when the soil is in a reasonably dry condition, being dug well in when the moisture in the ground will cause an explosive action to take place, the clay soil disintegrating with the lime. Without lime, a heavy soil will consolidate with the winter rains and so deprive the roots of the plants of the necessary oxygen. The oxygen will also be cut off from bacteria in the soil which will not be able to fulfil the proper function of converting humus into plant food.

Lime has a tendency to be washed down by rain. When used in hydrated form it should be applied to the surface in mid-winter, after the ground has been dug and the surface left in a rough condition, to be broken down by wind and frost.

The soil of town gardens may contain heavy deposits of soot and sulphur which will contribute to an acid condition. It will benefit from a dressing of hydrated lime before any planting takes place, for no matter how heavily the ground is manured it will not grow good crops unless corrected for its acid condition.

A soil may also be tested for nitrogen, phosphorus and potash deficiency so that the correct requirements of each crop may be supplied in the correct amounts, thus eliminating wastage and saving expense.

To correct nitrogen deficiency, give a four ounce per square foot dressing with sulphate of ammonia for every one per cent deficiency shown on the chart.

To ensure the correct phosphate content, use the solution marked 'phosphorus'; after shaking it up with the soil in the tubs, allow to settle, then take the tin rod, scrape it, and with it stir the solution for 30 seconds. The solution will then turn blue. If pale blue, this will denote a ten per cent phosphorus deficiency and the ground should be given a dressing of superphosphate of lime at a rate of two pounds per 100 square feet.

To check the potash content, use the necessary indicators when a pale yellow solution will denote a two per cent deficiency. To correct this, rake into the surface of the soil in spring, at planting time, two ounces of sulphate of potash per 100 square feet of ground. A deep yellow solution will denote a four per cent deficiency, and double the amount of potash will be required.

If the soil shows a deficiency of each of these plant foods, a compound fertilizer may be made up to the exact requirements and applied in spring, prior to planting. Soil testing can be done quickly on the spot, but as soils may differ from one part of the garden to another it is advisable to make several tests and to make an average of soil requirements before the necessary fertilizers are obtained.

A soil testing outfit may be used over and over again as well as to test the correct alkalinity of mushroom compost, but where it is not thought necessary to obtain the outfit, the District Horticultural Officer will usually provide a soil test.

The Value of Humus

Both light and heavy soils require humus: clay soil so that it will open up and aerate the soil to allow oxygen to penetrate to the plant roots and to assist drainage; sandy soil needs humus to bind it and to provide a moisture holding medium during the dry summer months when plants should be making most growth but will not be able to do so where the soil is lacking in moisture.

Humus may not contain much plant food. It may take the form of decayed leaves, or straw that has been broken down (composted) by an activator. Peat is also useful but slightly acid, so the soil should be given liberal dressings of lime.

Being almost sterile, peat is to be recommended rather than leaf-mould, for with peat there is little chance of introducing either pests or diseases to the soil. Poplar bark fibre may be used as an alternative, but as peat and bark are almost sterile they should be used with artificial fertilizers made to a balanced formula, or with other humus forming materials which contain suitable plant foods. Where these are in short supply, straw composted with an activator will provide both humus and nutriment. To compost straw, obtain a bale and shake it well out in a corner of the garden, preferably where it can be surrounded with boards or corrugated iron sheeting. This will not only keep the heap tidy but will protect from drying winds so that the straw may be more quickly composted. As the straw is spread out, soak it with water, then spread a layer twelve inches deep and sprinkle some of the activator over it. Again, add more straw and more activator, building up the heap in this fashion to a height of about five feet. It will soon begin to heat up, and in ten days will be ready to turn; shake out the straw and activator, give more water if necessary and remake the heap. Allow it to heat up for another ten days before repeating the process and in three weeks the straw will have become dark brown, with a wholesome 'earthy' smell. The bits of straw will have become quite short, so they may more easily be dug into the ground.

An excellent supply of humus can be obtained from the garden compost heap which may be formed alongside the straw compost heap, or made back to back, thus making the most economic use of the boards or corrugated sheeting. Or use a 'bin' of strong wire netting. If correctly made, there will be no unpleasant smell from compost.

Compost making

The compost heap is built up in layers, using any unwanted 'greens' such as pea and bean haulms, tops of carrots and beetroot, and endives which in dry weather may have run to seed–anything except potato haulms and diseased plants which should be burnt, and the stems of sprouts and cabbage which will be difficult to compost.

Cover each layer of garden refuse with soil and give a dusting of lime.

If a small quantity of farmyard or poultry manure can be obtained, add this also, while to bring about rapid and thorough decomposition you should use an organic liquid activator. Lawn mowings may be added, and clearings from ditches and ponds, peat and leaf-mould, seaweed and used hops, in fact anything of an organic nature.

At the end of six months the heap will have been entirely composted and be ready to use on the land; it will be dark greenish brown with the consistency of farmyard manure. Vegetables require ample supplies of both humus and plant food to be successful, hence the achievements of the old cottage gardeners who continuously worked into their land quantities of night soil and rank manure so that the soil was kept well nourished and productive.

There are several chemical compounds which are able to improve the condition of a heavy soil. They are applied to the soil when it is in a reasonably dry condition, being sprinkled over the surface and dug in. Immediately, the compounds begin to break up the colloid matter which causes the soil's clay particles to bind together. Thus a more friable condition is produced.

Into a heavy soil, drainage materials may be incorporated at the same time, using crushed brick or mortar (with its valuable lime content), shingle or coarse sand. If the ground is low lying, an area of top soil should be removed to a depth of three feet and a base of crushed brick provided. Over this, drainage pipes should be laid of sufficient 'fall' to enable the water to be carried away to a ditch or to some other part of the garden where it will do less harm. The soil is then replaced, at the same time incorporating additional drainage and humus forming materials. Gypsum will also help to flocculate the colloid matter of a clay soil and will bind a sandy soil to enable it to retain moisture. It also provides valuable mineral foods such as calcium, magnesium and sulphur, and is inexpensive to use.

Preparing the Ground

No amount of care in the selection of fertilizers and manures will be of value unless the soil is deeply worked and cleared of all perennial weeds which would compete with the vegetables for their food and moisture.

When first bringing the ground into condition, a start should be made in autumn while the soil is still friable and easily worked. The ground must be cleared, the soil drained and aerated, and the lime content increased if need be. The soil should be in a friable condition by the time the first sowings are made in spring. At this stage, double digging or trenching is essential; only by working the soil two spits (spades) deep will it be possible to incorporate the necessary humus and drainage materials and to remove the deep-rooting weeds. When once the land has been deeply worked, trenching or double digging should not be necessary again, but for a number of crops trenching will be done each year to achieve best results. In this way it is possible to concentrate the food requirements of the plants into a limited area so that they are more readily available.

Ground which has not been worked for some years is usually bastard trenched. This means removing the top nine inches or so and placing it to one side of the ground which is being prepared, while the lower spit is treated separately, for this will be soil which has not been subjected to the aerating and sweetening influence of the weather. During this operation, plant foods and

FERTILIZERS AND THEIR FOOD VALUE

Fertilizer	Action	Nitrogen Content	Phosphatic Content	Potash Content
Basic Slag	Slow	15%		
Bone Meal	Slow	5%	20%	
Dried Blood	10%			
Farmyard Manure	Slow	·5%	.25%	·5%
Fish Meal	Quick	10%	8%	7%
Guano	Quick	15%	10%	7%
Kainit	Slow			13%
Nitrate of Soda	Quick	16%		
Nitro-Chalk	Quick	16%		
Potassium-Nitrate	Quick	14%		40%
Poultry manure	Medium	3%	2%	6%
Rape meal	5%	5%	2%	1%
Seaweed	Slow	5%		1.5%
Shoddy (Wool)	Slow	12%		
Sulphate of Ammonia	Quick	20%		
Sulphate of Potash	Medium			50%
Superphosphate	Medium		15%	
Used Hops	Slow	4%	2%	

drainage materials should be incorporated into the lower spit so that it will be in the best possible condition for the plant roots to penetrate. A well drained soil will never become sour.

The Cropping Programme

Where planting a fruit garden, careful thought must be given to those varieties which will crop in certain soils and in a particular district. The amateur may think it advisable to omit biennial cropping apples, those cropping in alternate years, unless other varieties can be planted. True, the biennial croppers make up for this deficiency by bearing more heavily than usual in their 'on' season, but unless there are other varieties to make up for their lack of fruiting in their 'off' season, it will be as well to omit them from the garden. Those apples which are the chief offenders in this way are 'Allington Pippin', 'Miller's Seedling', 'Blenheim Orange' and 'D'Arcy Spice'. 'Blenheim Orange' also takes eight to nine years to come into heavy bearing, and for this reason is rarely planted in the small garden. It also makes a big spreading tree.

The amateur will wish to have his fruit trees in bearing in the quickest possible time, and for this reason, and because of lack of space for standard trees, he will plant those varieties which come quickly into bearing on a dwarfing rootstock. Dwarf pyramid trees will be selected and they may be planted four feet apart (cordons the same distance). They will begin to fruit within two years. Of the dwarf rootstocks, Malling IX and XXVI permit this close planting and come quickly into bearing. Where the soil is light and rainfall low, M.XXVI will prove more successful but it has more brittle roots and will need staking. But it must be said that these rootstocks will not yield more than a bushel of fruit, however long they have been planted, whereas heavy cropping apples such as 'Bramley's Seedling' and 'Newton Wonder' on Malling II will, when established, yield up to ten bushels (400 pounds) in a single season.

From an established pear, growing in a deep loam and with suitable pollinators, about 30 pounds of fruit may be expected from each tree in an average season. The high-yielding plums such as 'Victoria', 'Czar' and 'Yellow Pershore' will give up to 50 pounds of fruit. The delicious but delicate 'Coe's Golden Drop' and 'Kirke's Blue' produce no more than ten pounds from an established tree. Among plums, both these varieties are above comparison in flavour and sweetness.

For pears, Quince C stock is the most dwarf but is not nearly so healthy as Quince A which is now used to the exclusion of most others.

For greengages, the common plum stock is best and, for other plums, St Julien A, which is rather more vigorous and produces a bush or half-standard tree needing twelve feet spacing. Strawberries may be planted beneath. At the East Malling Research Station the dwarf pyramid plum is a recent innovation. Grafted on to St Julien A stock, it crops early and bears regular crops.

The reader may like to know about those apples which come naturally into cropping more quickly than others on whichever rootstock they are worked. These are varieties which make only a small compact tree and so are suitable for the modern garden:

Early Victoria (C)	July–August
Lady Sudeley	August–September
Ellison's Orange	September–October
Rev. Wilks (C)	September–October
Egremont Russet	October–November
Kidd's Orange	October–November
Golden Noble (C)	November–December
James Grieve	November–January
Acme	December–January
Claygate Pearmain	December–February
Golden Delicious	December–March
Laxton's Superb	December–March
Adam's Pearmain	December–April
Crawley Beauty (C)	December–April
May Queen	January–May
Brownlee's Russet	February–April
Edward VII	March–May
Annie Elizabeth (C)	March–June

These varieties are available from specialist fruit growers and will give a succession of fruit for the entire year. Carefully stored, 'Edward VII' apples will have retained their quality until the first of the new season's apples are ripe. These will be those of 'Early Victoria'.

It is usually the most vigorous growers that take longer to come into bearing, and these are not suitable for the small garden; the tip bearers especially come into this category. The selection recommended are all spur forming and so better respond to dwarf treatment.

Remember, when ordering fruit trees, to bear in mind those varieties that do well in a particular type of soil, such as a clay soil, those that do better in drier conditions, and those which prefer a moist climate. There are also especially hardy varieties for places where the plants have to tolerate cold winds in spring and have to ripen their fruit in a much shorter season than elsewhere. Those apples listed as coming quickly into bearing are suitable for the average garden and are tolerant of most soil and climatic conditions, but where the garden is unduly exposed, these apples should be planted:

Ellison's Orange	September–October
Grenadier (C)	September–October
James Grieve	September–October
Herring's Pippin	November–December
Forge	November–January
Christmas Pearmain	December–January

Margil	December–January
Orlean's Reinette	December–February
Crawley Beauty	December–March
Pearl	December–March
Adam's Pearmain	January–March
Laxton's Rearguard	January–May
Edward VII (C)	January–June
Annie Elizabeth (C)	March–June

Pears are more difficult to crop well, requiring warmth and a deep loamy soil, also shelter from cold winds. To provide a succession of fruit for the average small garden, these varieties may be grown as cordons or pyramids and will prove reliable:

Laxton's Superb	July–August
Beurré d'Amanlis	September
Dr Jules Guyot	September
Beurré Hardy	September–October
Beurré Bedford	October
Conference	October–November
Winter Nelis	December–January
Catillac	February–April

Before planting top fruits, check with the pollination tables so that each variety to be planted will bear a heavy crop. Remember that 'Conference' and 'Beurré d'Amanlis' will not pollinate each other; neither will 'Seckle' pollinate 'Louise Bonne'; nor will 'Laxton's Superb' pollinate 'William's Bon Chrétien'. They require a third companion, in bloom at the same time. 'Dr Jules Guyot', a first class pear, will, like 'Denniston's Superb' in plums, acts as a pollinator for most varieties. Also valuable as a pollinator is 'Beurré Hardy'.

Of plums, several may be planted in the small garden. Perhaps the most reliable early plum is 'Czar', followed by 'Victoria'. Both crop well in a heavy clay soil. For later, 'Oullin's Golden Gage' and 'Thames Cross' followed by 'Marjorie's Seedling' are to be recommended. These plums are all self-fertile and, unlike apples and pears, do not need a pollinator. Just one self-fertile plum may be grown on its own with the expectation of its bearing a heavy crop. Here is a selection of the most reliable dessert plums and gages to provide fruit from August until Christmas:

Czar	Early August
Early Transparent Gage	Mid-August
Denniston's Superb	Late August
Goldfinch	Late August
Oullin's Golden Gage	Late August
Victoria	Late August
Count Althann's Gage	Early September
Ontario	Early September
Jefferson	Mid-September
Thames Cross	Late September
Marjorie's Seedling	Early October
Reine Claude de Bavay	Early October

Cherries are now rarely planted in the small garden, for they eventually grow to a great size. Also, because they only crop well as standards and take eight to nine years to come into reasonable bearing, they are best confined to a large garden where two or three may be planted in a shrub border. They will do well in a chalk-laden soil. The three best for dessert are 'Amber Heart', 'Biggareau Napoleon', and 'Waterloo', and they will pollinate each other.

Every fruit garden should have as wide a selection of gooseberries as possible, concentrating on the dessert varieties and planting two of each of five or six kinds. 'Bedford Red' is a neat upright grower and so is the best of green gooseberries, 'Thumper'. At least two white varieties should be grown: 'Langley Gage' or 'Whitesmith' for early fruit and 'White Lion' as a late variety. The yellow gooseberries are the sweetest of all; for an early crop plant 'Bedford Yellow' and 'Broom Girl'.

There should be five rows of raspberry canes, always planting the rows north to south so that the sunlight can reach the maximum number of plants

Mulching a pear tree with manure. Make sure the mulch does not actually touch the stem, otherwise it could cause rot to set in

and all parts of them to ripen the fruits. Plant 20 canes each of five varieties to ripen for succession. Plant four bushes of each of four varieties of blackcurrant, again to ripen over as long a period as possible. Between them and the gooseberries plant rows of strawberries, spacing them 15 inches apart in the row. Plant gooseberries four feet apart and blackcurrants five feet, allowing an extra one foot for the vigorous 'Wellington xxx'. In a corner of the garden, possibly between a greenhouse or frame, plant several varieties of rhubarb, to mature early, mid-season and late. This planting programme of soft fruits will provide the household with dessert fruit from June until October; in these five months blackberries, trained against a fence will be ripening. Top fruits will begin in late July with the first of the apples, plums and pears; there may be apples in store until the following June, when the first gooseberries and strawberries will be cropping.

These varieties will give a long succession of choice fruits:

	Gooseberries	*Strawberries*
Very Early	May Duke	Cambridge Vigour
Early	Broom Girl	Cambridge Favourite
Mid-season	Whitesmith	Royal Sovereign
Late Mid-season	Leveller	Cambridge Rearguard
Very Late	White Lion	Hampshire Maid

	Blackcurrants	*Raspberries*
Very Early	Laxton's Giant	Malling Exploit
Early	Mendip Cross	Glen Clova
Mid-season	Wellington XXX	Malling Jewel
Late Mid-season	Westwick Choice	Malling Enterprise
Very Late	Amos Black	Norfolk Giant

Where one is also contemplating the culture of orchard fruits, soft fruits planted between the trees will yield valuable returns until the trees come into profit. The two fruits most suitable for inter-planting are gooseberries and blackcurrants. Gooseberries will continue to crop well even when the fruit trees are mature, for they will tolerate partial shade. They like potash and are best planted with apple trees, both of which are happy in a heavy soil. Strawberries prefer a light, slightly acid soil and demand the maximum of sunlight. They are not therefore suitable for inter-planting with apples, except during the first two or three years in the life of the orchard. Blackcurrants crop well with plums, for both thrive on an abundance of nitrogen.

Where soft fruit is not to be used for inter-planting an orchard, strawberries and gooseberries, both great potash lovers, and blackcurrants, blackberries and raspberries, all lovers of nitrogen are happy together. So as not to put all your eggs into one basket, the varieties should be spread out as widely as possible. Where growing commercially, sufficient plants of each variety must be planted to give worthwhile pickings, thus making marketing economical.

It must of course be remembered that where frosts prove troublesome, those varieties which bloom and mature early should be omitted, concentration being on the late mid-season and very late varieties. There is now a wide choice of these and they have revolutionized soft fruit growing in the more difficult districts.

Paths should be of concrete flagstones. These will enable a barrow to be moved about with the maximum of ease and will permit the housewife to pick the fruit without getting her shoes dirty. It will be important to make the maximum use of the ground by planting cordon apples or pears alongside the paths. Strawberries and other soft fruits may be grown beneath standard fruit trees. The value of standard fruit trees. The value of standard trees is that they enable full use of the ground beneath them; this will prove both profitable and productive until the top fruits come into full bearing. Rows of cordon apples and pears will also permit the greater use of the ground for soft fruits than when bush or pyramid trees are planted, for these soon spread out with the lower branches only inches above the soil.

Equipping the Fruit Garden

A small greenhouse with benches may serve both the fruit and vegetable garden. Greater use may be made of a warm greenhouse in raising seedling vegetable plants each year. The fruit will be more permanent, and apart from the growing of early strawberries and forced rhubarb beneath the benches, little use will be obtained from a greenhouse or frame for there will be no plants to raise and no hardening to be done. Even the rooting of gooseberry and blackcurrant cuttings will be done in the open ground. Cloches will, however, be an advantage to cover early strawberries.

Thick polythene or glass cloches of the barn type with a galvanized steel frame may be used; the continuous cloches of heavy duty polythene sheeting will be both inexpensive and efficient, and the sheeting may be stored in winter without breakage or the need for much space. The sheeting is held above the rows by steel or wooden hoops. The Vitrone cloches, made of clear vitrone PVC sheeting, are made up in the same way, the hoops being skewered into the ground to prevent the cloches being blown away by strong winds. Six sheets of vitrone to make six cloches 27 inches long × 18 inches wide, together with hoops, clips and ends, retail for about £3. Cloches may be employed throughout the garden year, mostly for early vegetables such as lettuce and tomatoes.

An efficient water supply is vital for growing vegetables but not as essential for fruit. But during a dry spring and early summer, strawberries will need ample supplies, as will gooseberries and other soft fruits when they are swelling. Watering may be reduced to a minimum by digging plenty of humus into the soil and by the liberal use of a mulch given early in summer.

The use of a rotating or oscillating sprinkler for fruit and vegetables will enable the watering to be done without the need for human aid, the swaying action allowing a gentle mist-like spray to fall on the foliage and saturate the ground. Or a plastic hose may be fitted with a finger controlled nozzle, enabling a mist-like spray to be released over a wide area.

A sprayer for the use of fungicides and insecticides will be necessary if trouble free crops are to be grown. Fruits suffer more from pests and diseases than either vegetables or flowers. The sprayer may be either trigger or pump operated, the former being satisfactory for small numbers of plants. A long-reach extension tube fitted to the rubber or plastic tube adjoining the container will permit the spray to reach into the centre of the plants of currants and gooseberries, and high up into the foliage of the top fruits. A variable nozzle instantly adjusts to a fine mist or long jet.

A pair of efficient secateurs will also be needed by the fruit grower. Indeed, they will be constantly in use about the garden, and should be selected as carefully as the professional cricketer chooses his bats. Secateurs of a reliable make will last a lifetime and one should ensure that the 'feel' is right for one's hand and that they are light and comfortable to use. Only then will the pruning of numerous fruit trees and bushes be an enjoyable occupation. Secateurs of poor quality will cause the wood to tear and a clean cut will not be made. This must always be guarded against. Disease will readily enter a badly made cut. The secateurs should be sharp and precision made. To cut through the thick wood of top fruits which may be long established, the adjustable anvil-type secateurs should be used. They will be fitted with a hollow ground steel blade and a thumb-operated safety catch, and will cut through a shoot nearly an inch in diameter.

For reaching tall trees, the tree pruner, with arms 30 inches long, is an indispensable tool. For reaching up to about 7 feet, a 'long arm' pruner has a handle of that length. It is fitted with a cutting knife worked by a lever which is held in the free hand, and is capable of removing branches up to 1½ inches diameter. When using it, care should be taken that the cutter blade is placed firmly against the wood before the lever is used. A lightweight model can be extended to reach up to nine feet with perfect control of the cutting.

To remove the branches from long established trees which may have become neglected, a saw and a ladder are a necessity. A cross-cut saw or a curved pruning saw is suitable and, as with secateurs,

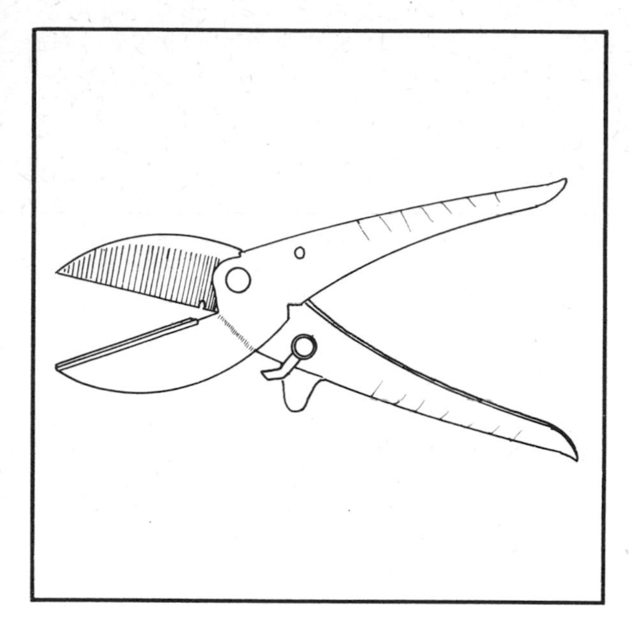

Anvil-type secateurs

Parrot-beak secateurs

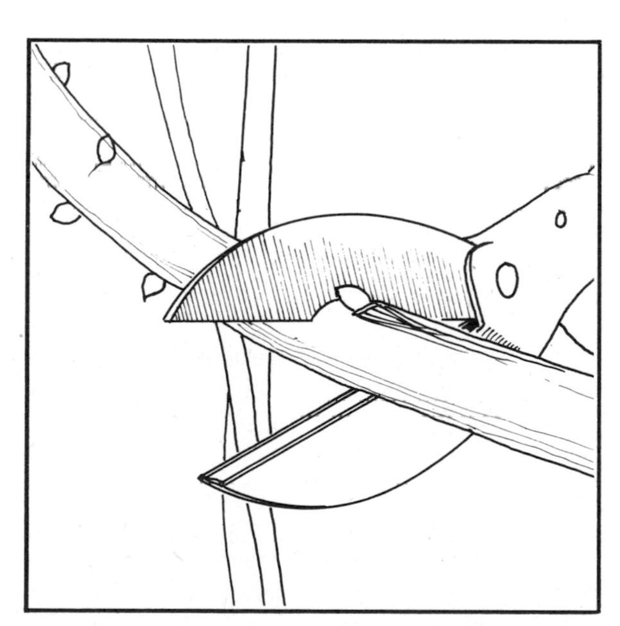

Anvil-type secateurs are used to cut through the thick wood of top fruits

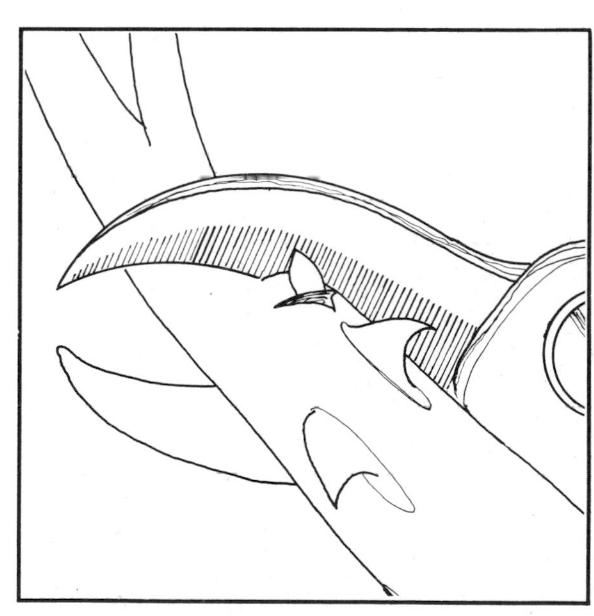

Parrot-beak secateurs are useful for cutting stems of up to $\frac{3}{4}''$ thickness but cannot be used for cutting heavier wood

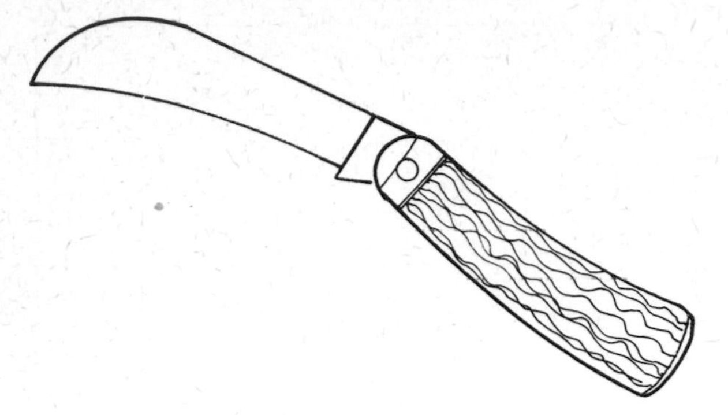

An efficient pruning knife is an essential piece of equipment

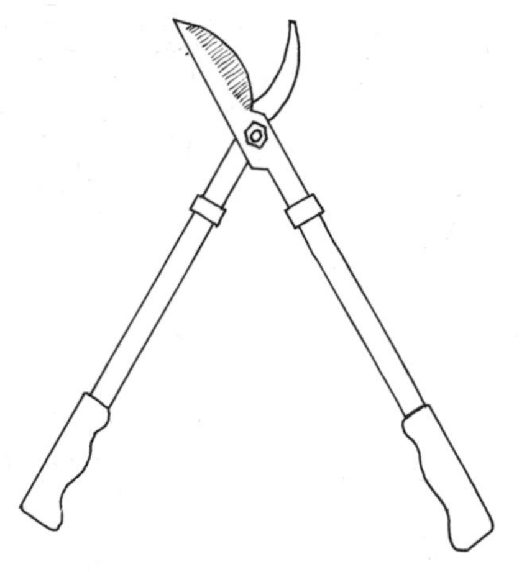

A long handled pruner is designed to cut hard, old wood and the extra length of the handles gives considerable cutting power

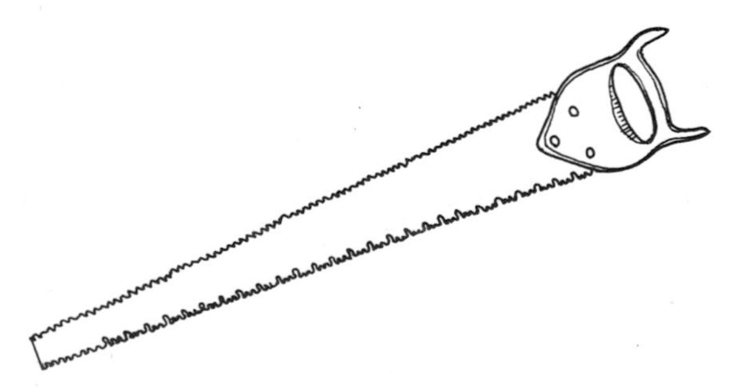

Pruning saw. Note that the teeth on one side of the blade are much coarser than the teeth of the other side. It is thus a dual purpose tool

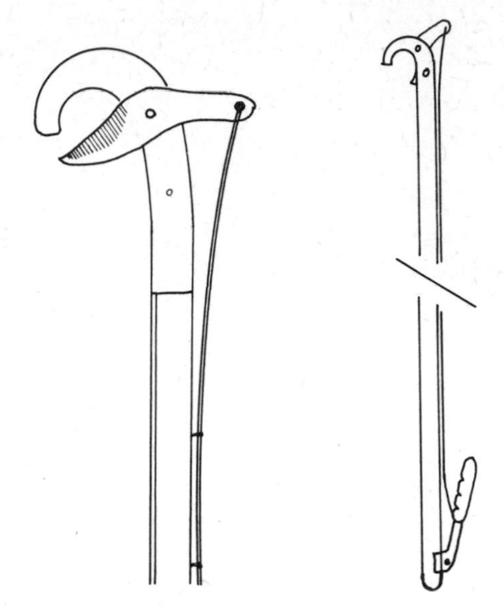

Long arm pruners. These are indispensable tools for removing relatively large branches on taller trees

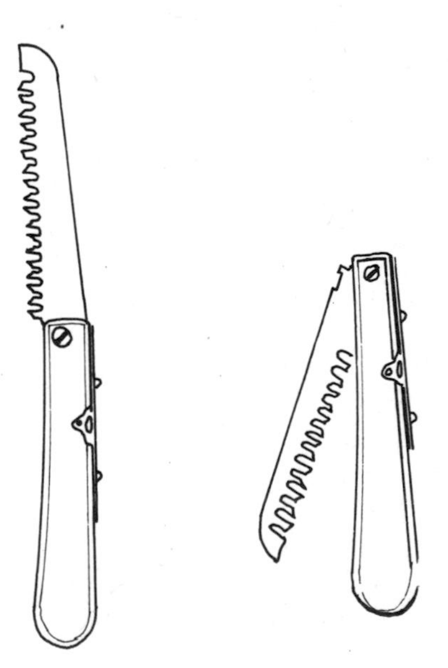

Narrow-bladed pruning saw. These folding types are particularly useful

select whatever is light and comfortable to use. Both saw and secateurs should be cleaned and rubbed over with a fine oil after use, not so much to prevent them from rusting (for they will be of rust-proof steel) but to keep the cutting blades sharp. Look after them well and they will be efficient for a lifetime. A cleanly made cut is essential if the wood is to heal over quickly, and this will not happen if there has been bruising and tearing through using a blunt instrument.

An efficient pruning knife is also important. It will be used for bark ringing and notching and for the removal of suckers (from plums) and in root pruning. The blade must be kept sharp by grinding. Vine scissors with their pointed blades will be of value when thinning the grapes–a difficult operation without efficient scissors.

A ladder made of hardwood or rust-proof aluminium will be a necessity when taking over an established orchard but not, of course, during the first years in the life of a fruit tree. It will be needed for pruning the upper branches and for gathering the fruit. This will be simplified by the use of a tubular alloy fruit picker, the handle being fitted with a wire 'cage' and enclosing an operating wire with spring return action. When gathering fruit it is essential to avoid bruising it, otherwise it will rapidly deteriorate in storage. Shaking the branches of a tree to get the fruit to fall is not to be recommended; with the high retail price of all fruits, you cannot afford to lose a single one through careless picking and storage.

The fruit grower will need a spade which should be of stainless steel to which the soil will not cling and which can be readily cleaned after use. Select the spade for lightness and balance. A spade should not be too heavy. Other necessary tools are a garden fork; a hoe to scuffle the soil between the rows after the winter rains have made it compact; and a stainless steel trowel for planting strawberries. Your tools should always be cleaned after use and kept on a tool rack in the potting shed or garage. Here, too,

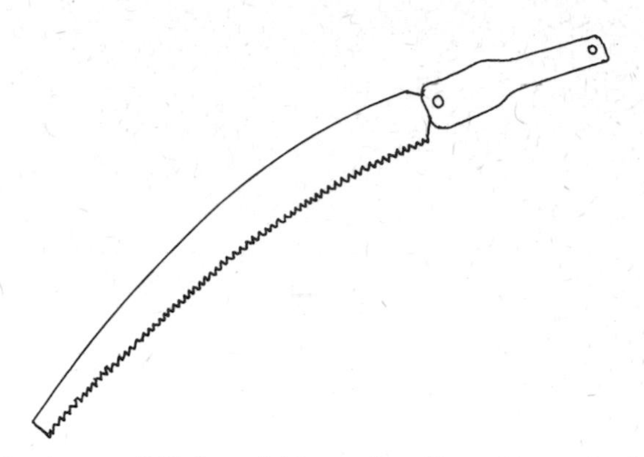

Grecian saw. This is useful for cutting old wood in confined spaces

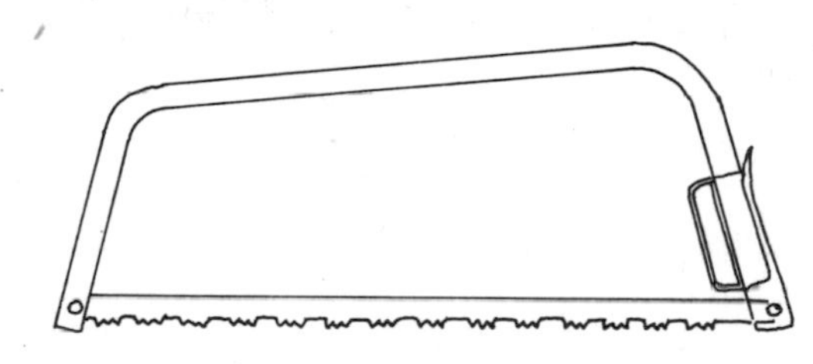

Bow saw. This is essential for removing large branches

Platform steps are necessary for the pruning of taller plants and fruit picking

will be kept a suitable fungicide to paint over the cuts made when pruning or the wounds caused when paring away (with a sharp knife) diseased tissue. There will need to be a high shelf for storing fungicides and pesticides, which should always be kept in their proper container and well out of reach of children. Poisons should never be put in lemonade bottles, as so often happens. Stakes will be required for supporting young standard fruit trees, with suitable ties to which to fasten them.

Of great importance will be a room for storing apples and pear. This may be an airy cupboard fitted with shelves and with ventilators fixed in the door or in a wall; or the potting shed may be used if lined with hardboard and fibre glass insulating material, because frost must be excluded. To give additional protection, the fruit may be placed on a layer of dry bracken or hay. For the connoisseur of dessert apples and pears, the store room, whether it be attic or potting shed, will be the most interesting room of the house. Incidentally, there is no smell more refreshing than that of ripe apples and pears. It was John Kay, physician to Queen Mary Tudor, who advised one 'to smell unto a sweet, ripe apple for there is nothing more comforting to the spirits of man'.

Remember to have the apple store well ventilated. Ripening fruit gives off gases which must be allowed to excape, while at all times there should be a free circulation of fresh air around the fruit.

Small areas of soft fruits may be protected when the fruit is ripening by erecting over the plants square mesh fish netting or wire netting. Protective cages may be left in position the whole year. Steel tubular standards may be used as supports and, together with the top connecting rods, should be coated with green plastic. Bitumen treated netting, which must be of one inch mesh, will have a long life. Permanent cages should be six feet high to allow for ease in cultivating the ground, but special strawberry cages–which are easily removed when picking and when fruiting has finished–need to be no more than two feet high. It will act as a deterrent to birds if netting is placed over the plants when the fruit begins to ripen.

Covering a strawberry bed with netting to prevent the fruit from birds

A deep freeze unit will enable the fruit grower to preserve all surplus fruit and enjoy it in times of scarcity. Raspberries and strawberries freeze particularly well; apples will keep for months when frozen and may be saved in this way where there may be no space to store them in the normal manner. Pears and avocados are the exception; because of their high moisture content they turn darkly coloured when frozen. Most of the soft fruits freeze well, some especially so, and where there is space available for planting for deep freeze, these varieties should be grown:

Apples	Annie Elizabeth
	Arthur Turner
	Bramley's Seedling
	Lord Derby
Apricot	Moorpark
Bilberry (Blueberry)	Early Blue
	Jersey
Blackberry	Himalaya Giant
	Oregon
Blackcurrant	Merton Early
	Tor Cross
	Wellington xxx
	Westwick Choice
Cherry	Early Rivers
	Merton Heart

(Both these cherries act as pollinators for each other)

Damson	Merryweather
Gooseberry	Careless
	Keepsake
Hybrid Berries	Boysenberry
	Loganberry

Peaches	Duke of York
	Peregrine
Plums & Gages	Czar
	Marjorie's Seedling
	Oullin's Golden Gage
	Severn Cross
	Victoria
	Yellow Pershore
Raspberry	Glen Clova
	Lloyd George
	Malling Exploit
	Malling Jewel
	Zeva
Redcurrant	Laxton's No. 1
	Red Lake
Rhubarb	Timperley Early
	Canada Red
Strawberry	Cambridge Favourite
	Cambridge Vigour
	Redgauntlet
	Royal Sovereign

Only the best fruit should be saved for the deep freezer. It should be gathered (especially raspberries and strawberries) before it becomes too ripe and when quite dry. In this way it will remain whole when in the freezer. Do not wash it. Soft fruits are covered with castor sugar after gathering, allowing four ounces of sugar to each pound of fruit. The fruit should be evenly covered and is then carefully placed in waxed cardboard or polythene containers to seal it and prevent dehydration, and to ensure that it is not crushed or bruised. It is then placed in the deep freezer where it may remain almost indefinitely. The sugar coating encourages quick freezing and does much to prevent enzymic change.

Or use a sugar syrup (one pound of sugar to one pint of water) to cover the fruits after placing in a firm greaseproof box rather than a bag.

Peaches require different treatment. First place the fruits in boiling water for about a minute, then cool in cold water and peel off the skin. Cut in half and remove the stone, then place in a plastic bag and put in the freezer.

Apricots, plums, gages and damsons should have the skins left on but the stones removed before placing in deep freeze. Gooseberries are placed in the freezer just as taken from the bush, after topping and tailing. The smooth-skinned varieties are best for freezing.

Apples may be saved in either or both of two ways. They may be peeled and cored and made into a purée, using the minimum of water in their stewing; they are then placed in waxed cartons. Or they may be sliced and left uncooked, but the slices are immersed in hot water for two minutes to blanch them; they are then cooled and drained and packed in the cartons; the slices are not sugared.

Freeze as quickly as possible, with the 'Rapid Freeze' switch at the on position when the fruits are put into the deep freezer. Then maintain a steady temperature; violent fluctuations damage the structure of the fruit cells and cause a breakdown of the solid fruits, so that when thawed they become unpleasantly 'mushy'.

To prevent blackcurrants becoming tough skinned after freezing, place them in boiling water for 20 seconds before placing in polythene bags and freezing.

Remember that 'black' plums can be frozen as they are, while all others should first be covered with sugar syrup.

Rhubarb (pink or red stems) should be cut into 1½ inch lengths before coating with sugar and freezing.

To use the fruits as a dessert after freezing, allow up to six hours for them to thaw slowly and they will be ready to use (if serving without cooking) just before they are fully thawed. If cooking, as with plums and apples, thaw completely before using them.

All fruits must be left in their cartons or polythene bags until ready to use.

2 Tree Fruits

TOP FRUITS

This chapter deals with all tree fruits except stone fruits which have different cultural requirements.

APPLE

This is the most important of all the tree or top fruits in Britain, where it grows and ripens to perfection in the cool, moist climate. Where there is room for only one or two trees, the apple must be given priority; as few as five or six trees will, when established, provide dessert and culinary fruit for several months of the year. The great value of the apple is that, in comparison with the pear and the plum, it will keep in condition for several months, to be used when required. Pears and plums will keep for only a very short time.

Both amateur and commercial growers who plant apples now concentrate on dwarf trees, those budded on to a dwarfing rootstock. This has resulted not only in greatly increased yields per acre but also in the trees rapidly coming into heavy bearing. The standard tree which occupies a considerable area and will take eight or nine years to bear a heavy crop has now given way to the dwarf bush or pyramid tree, both apple and pear, and where 500 bushels per acre was once considered a heavy crop, yields of 1,500 bushels are now quite common. Dwarf trees make for greater ease in tending and gathering the crop, but while standard trees enable other crops to be grown beneath them, dwarf trees do not, so that it is important for the trees to yield as heavily as possible. This means regular attention to pruning and spraying.

British growers have taken a lead from the Dwarf Fruit Trees Association of America in their planting programme of recent years; by using dwarfing stocks, the planting density per acre has increased from about 50 to almost 500 trees, the most popular rootstocks being Malling IX and XXVI and the Malling-Merton (MM) 104 and 106.

Very Dwarf Rootstocks

On the very dwarf rootstocks, Malling IX (Jaune de Metz), the trees will come more quickly into heavy bearing than on any other rootstock. It is the one often used for cordon and pyramid trees, which are required to be of less vigorous habit than bush and standards, but it may also be used for bush trees which may be required for a small garden and which are expected to remain reasonably dwarf and yet come early into bearing. In other words, trees on this rootstock fruit abundantly at the expense of making wood, though they have a tendency to burn themselves out after thirty years fruiting, unless carefully tended throughout their life. This means:

(a) Regular attention to pruning, though this will not present much of a problem with the trees making little new wood;

(b) Care in keeping the ground clean; and

(c) Providing a regular balanced diet.

They also need careful staking during the first years after planting because their root action, as may be expected, is not vigorous, and the trees easily blow over.

Bush trees on this rootstock should be planted from eight to ten feet apart, pyramids seven to eight, and cordons three feet apart, but much depends upon the natural habit of each variety. 'Beauty of Bath', for example, makes a spreading tree and should be given wider spacing than say, 'Adam's Pearmain'; while the more vigorous varieties such as 'Bramley's Seedling', 'Blenheim Orange' and 'Miller's Seedling' should never be planted on this dwarf rootstock. The weight of foliage and fruit would most likely prove too much. Trees on Malling IX, which are planted closer than those of other rootstocks, and come into heavy bearing sooner than any other type, will ensure the largest weight of fruit from a small garden in the quickest possible time. Yet these trees will never yield more than a bushel of fruit (40 pounds) whatever age they reach, whereas 'Bramley's Seedling' and 'Newton Wonder', or Malling II will yield up to ten bushels when in full bearing, and 'Blenheim Orange' and 'Worcester Pearmain' about half that weight.

A more recent dwarfing rootstock is the Malling-Merton, MM 104, which has so far shown a greater resistance to woolly aphid than Type IX, and has also given heavier crops, especially with 'Cox's Orange Pippin' and 'Ellison's Orange'. At recent trials by the East Malling Research Station in Kent, eleven year old 'Cox's Orange' produced 461 pounds per acre on this rootstock compared with 382 pounds on Type MIV, which is similar to MIX.

Another dwarf rootstock, MM 106, gave in comparison only 257 pounds on the same trees, planted in the same heavy loam, but this stock has proved a much heavier bearer when used in light, sandy soil. With its much better anchorage, and being a more satisfactory propagator for the nurseryman, MM 104 looks as if it will supersede all other dwarf rootstocks in the years ahead.

Semi-Dwarf Rootstocks

Malling IV has for some time been the recognized rootstock with a semi-dwarfing habit, and, over a period of the first 25 years, trees will bear larger crops than with any rootstock, but like MIX the trees root badly and require to be staked. This rootstock (and MII) suits 'Cox's Orange' better than any other and is generally used entirely for this purpose, but it is safer to plant in a position sheltered from strong winds. From the latest results of MM 104 it would appear that this rootstock will eventually supersede both MIX and MIV.

Planting distances should be increased by two feet for bush trees where using MIV, as in their first ten to twelve years the trees will make rather more growth than on MIX. Apart from the same need to stake securely, they will prove more suitable for orchard culture, not requiring quite such detailed attention as those on MIX.

MXXVI is also semi-dwarfing, and as a bush tree grows 12-14 feet high and has a similar spread.

More Vigorous Rootstocks

For large garden or orchard planting, MI and II have been successful. Trees on MI will come more quickly into bearing than those on MII, and it has been observed that MI is better suited for planting in a district of high rainfall and soil moisture. It does not suit 'Cox's Orange', and with many varieties in a dry soil it has not resulted in anything like such heavy crops as from trees on MII, on which 'Cox's Orange' does well, and which may be said to be the most successful of all rootstocks for commercial planting. It produces a tree of good size which it builds up gradually, at the same time increasing its cropping so that there is a balanced, long-lived tree, which, over 50 years or more, will bear a heavier weight of fruit than from any other rootstock.

As the trees, especially those of the most vigorous varieties, will require a spacing of 20 feet where the soil is of a heavy loam, this is not a suitable rootstock for a small garden. Much depends upon whether one wishes to enjoy a heavy crop during the first 20-25 years of the tree's life with diminishing crops later, or more regular bearing over 50 years or more.

Trees on MII root deeply and rarely require staking. Being able to search widely for their nourishment, they are good orchard trees, able to withstand drought, and do not require such meticulous attention as to feeding and upkeep. They will, however, require much more attention as to their pruning. Certain varieties such as 'Winston' and 'Sunset', which are of only semi-vigorous habit in comparison with 'Blenheim Orange' or 'Newton Wonder', would find MM 104 more suitable, for these less vigorous varieties will give a greater yield per acre on a less robust tree, and planted half the distance apart than that allowed for MII rootstock.

The amateur can draw his own conclusion, possibly planting six trees ten feet apart on MIX or MM 104, or, on the same area of ground, three trees 20 feet apart of MII or the new rootstock MMIII. But whereas the six dwarf trees may yield around 150 bushels of fruit over the first 30 years of their life, the three trees on the vigorous stock should yield 300 bushels, though the greater weight will be given between 20-30 years of age. For an orchard or large garden, the more vigorous rootstock is to be recommended; for a small garden, the more dwarf rootstocks.

The new MMIII in the East Malling Trials has cropped more heavily than MII, a combination of 'Cox's Orange', 'Jonathan' and 'Ellison's Orange' yielding an average of 348 pounds, from eleven year old trees, compared with 273 pounds on MII. With little difference in the size of tree, it would appear that MMIII will become widely used in future years. It is also remarkably free from woolly aphid.

Most Robust Rootstocks

The two most vigorous rootstocks yet produced are the old MXVI and the new MM 109. The latter may be said to come somewhere between groups c and d for vigour. Both make extremely large trees, as bush or standards, and require planting between 20-30 feet apart. This stock is generally used for standard orchard trees and will take from 15-20 years before coming into heavy bearing. At from 10-12 years of age it bears only half the crop produced by MIX or MM 104 at the same age, and very much less than given by MMIII or MII. These extremely robust rootstocks are of little use for the amateur's garden. But they may be used for those culinary varieties which make rather sparse growth, e.g. 'Lord Derby' and 'Grenadier', and which will respond favourably to the additional vigour.

MM 109 has so far shown a high resistance to drought, more so than either MII or MMIII. No comment can be made on 'Barnack Beauty' or 'Gascoyne's Scarlet', used on MM 109, but one would imagine this rootstock to give heavy crops when planted in a dry, chalky soil.

A new rootstock of great vigour, MXXV has shown that trees will come into heavier bearing at an early age than those on MXVI or MM 109 in spite of it making a large tree. But it has been troubled by woolly aphid, and it is early yet to acclaim it as being an advance over others of robust habit.

All this may sound complicated to the amateur, but it is advisable to consider the part played by each rootstock, not only on the weight of crop, but on the habit of each variety, so that the correct choice may be made for the size of one's garden.

To summarize:

(a) Very Dwarf Rootstocks–MIX, MM 104.

(b) Semi-Dwarf Rootstocks–MIV, MXXVI, MM 106.

(c) More Vigorous Rootstocks–MI, MII, MIII.
(d) Most Robust Rootstocks–MXVI, MXXV, MM 109.

Pollination and Fertility

When planting new fruit trees there is a great tendency to neglect the pollinating factor, with the result that though the stock may be of the best and have been planted with care, nothing but disappointment will be the result. Certain varieties are self-fertile and so will, up to a point, set their own fruit; some are particularly self-fertile, and so will set up a partial crop without a pollinator. These are the diploids which have plenty of pollen. Others called triploids have little pollen. They must be given a suitable pollinator to help them set fruit, while they are not good pollinators for others. The question of providing a suitable pollinator is essential to obtain heavy crops. It is of little use rushing off to post that order for that 'bargain offer' of 'Cox's Orange Pippins', your favourite apple, in the hope that they will bear plenty of fruit without a suitable pollinator. They will not.

Pollination of Cox's Orange Pippin

It was Messrs Backhouse and Crane, of the John Innes Institute, who first discovered that 'Cox's Orange Pippin' would not set its own pollen, a fact still not realized by many gardeners who continue to plant this variety by itself in the expectations of a good crop. Research has shown that even where the blossoms of certain varieties open at the same time as the 'Cox's Orange', it does not mean that a completely successful pollination will result. It has been shown that the pollen of such varieties as 'Stirling Castle', 'Merton Worcester', 'Worcester Pearmain', 'James Grieve' and 'Egremont Russet' ensures a setting of fruit more than twice as high as that of certain other varieties.

A most interesting photograph which appears in *The Apple*, by Sir Daniel Hall and M. B. Crane, shows one half of a tree of 'Cox's Orange' which has been crossed with 'Sturmer Pippin', covered in fruit; the other half, self-pollinated, set only two small fruits. Experiments carried out at the John Innes Institute by those two famous fruit experts resulted in the interesting information that of 11,949 flowers of 'Cox's Orange' self-pollinated, only 92 flowers or 0.76% set any fruit. Yet crossed or pollinated with 'Egremont Russet', 13.4% set fruit; with 'St Edmund's Russet', 14.4%; and with 'Stirling Castle', 15.5%. Where 'Ellison's Orange', 'Worcester Pearmain' and 'Sturmer Pippin' were used separately as a pollinator, the set was just 8%. The results also clearly show that not only is 'Cox's Orange' a poor pollinator for most other varieties, but also where 'Cox's' has been used as a parent. For instance, crossed with 'St Everard', of which 'Cox's Orange' was a parent, the percentage of fruit set showed only 3.3%, though 'St Everard' crossed with 'Beauty of Bath' gave a setting of 10.8%. Of all the tests carried out at the John Innes Institute, the average fertility from cross-pollination showed that ten blooms set fruit out of every 100, yet where varieties were self-pollinated the average of fruit set was only 2.5%.

Suitable 'Cox's' pollinators are:

Allington Pippin	King Russet
Charles Ross	Lane's Prince Albert
Discovery	Newton Wonder
Early Victoria	Peasgood's Nonsuch
Egremont Russet	St Edmund's Russet
Ellison's Orange	Stirling Castle
James Grieve	Sturmer Pippin
Jonathan	Worcester Pearmain

'Early Victoria', 'Charles Ross' and 'Lane's Prince Albert' are excellent cooking apples for a small garden, while 'Egremont Russet', 'King Russet' and 'James Grieve' are most reliable dessert apples to accompany 'Cox's Orange'.

Generally a fair test is to plant, along with the self and partially fertile varieties, another which will be in flower at the same period; it should be planted as near as possible, so that the bees and other insects are able to transfer one lot of pollen to the other without having to travel long distances. For example, with 'Royal Jubilee', which blooms very late and so misses late frosts, plant the equally late-flowering 'Crawley Beauty', or 'Edward VII', or 'Lane's Prince Albert', which has a prolonged flowering season. It is interesting that where several trees of 'Royal Jubilee' have been planted by themselves, they set only 0.9% of fruit; planted with 'Lane's Prince Albert' the percentage was extremely high, as much as 16.1%. So do not blame the nurseryman, or your gardener, if your trees do not bear heavy crops! Gardeners of former times got over the trouble by planting dozens of varieties together, but then they had large gardens to do so!

Biennial Bearing

Again, the question of biennial bearing must be considered. 'Ellison's Orange', a useful pollinator for 'Cox's', tends to biennial cropping, and if this apple is used as a pollinator, another, possibly 'Worcester Pearmain', to take over on its 'off' season, should be planted with it. These apples also tend to biennial cropping:

Allington Pippin	Miller's Seedling
Bramley's Seedling	Newton Wonder
D'Arcy Spice	

The choice must also be governed by climatic conditions. There is also the question of lime sulphur spraying to combat scab and mildew. Here certain varieties are sulphur shy, leaf and fruit drop often being the result. It will therefore be essential to plant together only those apples which are unharmed by lime-sulphur. 'St Cecilia', 'Beauty of Bath', 'Newton Wonder' and 'Lane's Prince Albert' are all sulphur shy, while 'Newton Wonder', a really grand apple, is also inclined to biennial bearing, so it would be advisable to plant several of these apples together. Or plant 'Newtown Wonder'. with 'Lord Derby', which, though tolerant of lime-sulphur, is extremely resistant to scab and mildew, and no spraying may, in any case, be necessary. The two are also excellent pollinators.

Triploid Varieties

It has been found that three suitable varieties planted together will give the largest set of fruit. This is certainly true when planting biennial croppers and the triploid varieties, those which will not cross-pollinate with each other and which are not very good pollinators for others. They must be planted with diploid varieties having plenty of pollen, which fortunately most apples have, and with those which bloom at the same time and are not given to biennial cropping. It is therefore wise to use two diploid pollinators, because there also may be the additional loss of the blossom of one variety through frost damage; in addition, the diploids will pollinate each other. The popular 'Bramley's Seedling' is a triploid variety and should be planted with 'Grenadier', an early cooking apple; and with 'James Grieve' or 'Lord Lambourne', for providing dessert. Those three fine dessert apples, 'Blenheim Orange', 'Gravenstein' and 'Ribston Pippin', are all triploids and should not be planted together. With 'Ribston Pippin' and 'Gravenstein', plant 'Lord Lambourne'; with 'Blenheim Orange', plant 'Egremont Russet', and they will give no trouble, for neither pollinator tends towards biennial bearing. 'Beauty of Bath' is also a suitable pollinator for 'Ribston Pippin' and 'Gravenstein', but is sulphur shy, which the others are not. To fertilize the pollinator itself it is advisable to plant another similar flowering diploid as previously explained.

Building up the Collection

When commencing with apples, most people decide to begin with 'Cox's Orange', the best eater, and with 'Bramley's Seedling', renowned as the best cooker. With them you should plant 'James Grieve', which will pollinate both, and add 'Grenadier', another good cooker, as a second line of defence, for this will also pollinate both. You will then have an early and a later apple for both cooking and for dessert. Then others can be added by degrees. 'Laxton's Advance', a grand early apple, is also a 'Cox's' pollinator, though not so good as 'James Grieve', but since it will also pollinate 'Bramley's Seedling' it may be a much better proposition in the wet districts. Then add 'Laxton's Superb', also a reasonably good 'Cox's' pollinator, though it inclines to biennial cropping and so should be assisted with 'Laxton's Advance', or with 'Worcester Pearmain', or 'Fortune'. And so on.

Of those that are very self-fertile, such as 'Laxton's Exquisite', and 'Epicure', 'Worcester Pearmain', 'St Everard', 'Christmas Pearmain' and 'Rev. Wilks', two only with the same flowering period need be planted together, to be assured of a satisfactory pollen setting. Even though each is self-fertile, it is inadvisable to plant them on their own.

Flowering Times

Flowering times are interesting. Whereas 'Ribston Pippin' and 'Wagner' flower early in the season, they are classed as fairly late dessert apples. In bloom at the same time, 'Gladstone' and 'Beauty of Bath' are the first apples to mature. The average length of time for all apple trees to bloom is about 15 days, spread over a period of about 30 days, the very early flowering varieties being in bloom for the first 14/15 days or so, while the mid-season blooming varieties partially overlap the last few days of the early flowering varieties, and the first days of the late flowering varieties. The very late flowering apples, e.g. 'Edward VII', 'Royal Jubilee' and 'Crawley Beauty', do not come into bloom until the last of the mid-season varieties have finished flowering, with the exception of the very long blooming 'Lane's Prince Albert'. In selecting suitable pollinators, one must be governed by the flowering period of the trees and not by their maturity.

These apples bloom very early, depending upon climatic and seasonal conditions, and will pollinate each other:

T–*Triploid*; P.S.F–*Partly Self-Fertile*; S.F.–*Self-Fertile*; S.S.–*Self-Sterile*.

Beauty of Bath	(P.S.F)
Bismarck	(P.S.F)
Egremont Russet	(P.S.F)
Gladstone	(S.F)
Gravenstein	(T., S.S)
Keswick Codlin	(P.S.F)
Laxton's Advance	(P.S.F)
Laxton's Exquisite	(P.S.F)
Laxton's Fortune	(P.S.F)
Lord Lambourne	(P.S.F)
Miller's Seedling	(P.S.F)
Rev. W. Wilks	(S.F)
Ribston Pippin	(T., S.S)
Rival	(P.S.F)
St Edmund's Russet	(P.S.F)
Wagener	(P.S.F)

These apples bloom early mid-season:

Allington Pippin	(P.S.F)
Annie Elizabeth	(P.S.F)
Arthur Turner	(P.S.F)
Bramley's Seedling	(T., S.S)
Cox's Orange Pippin	(P.S.F)
Ellison's Orange	(P.S.F)
Grenadier	(P.S.F)
James Grieve	(P.S.F)
King of the Pippins	(P.S.F)
Laxton's Epicure	(P.S.F)
Mother	(P.S.F)
Orlean's Reinette	(P.S.F)
Peasgood's Nonsuch	(P.S.F)
Stirling Castle	(P.S.F)
Sturmer Pippin	(P.S.F)
Tydeman's Early Worcester	(P.S.F)
Worcester Pearmain	(P.S.F)

These apples bloom late mid-season:

Blenheim Orange	(T., S.S)
Charles Ross	(P.S.F)
Claygate Pearmain	(S.S)
D'Arcy Spice	(S.S)
Early Victoria	(P.S.F)
Howgate Wonder	(P.S.F)
Lady Sudeley	(P.S.F)
Lane's Prince Albert	(P.S.F)
Laxton's Superb	(P.S.F)
Lord Derby	(P.S.F)
Monarch	(P.S.F)
Newton Wonder	(P.S.F)
Rival	(P.S.F)
Sunset	(S.F)
Warner's King	(T., S.S)
Winston	(S.F)

These apples bloom very late:

Crawley Beauty	(S.F)
Court Pendu Plat	(P.S.F)
Edward VII	(P.S.F)
Royal Jubilee	(P.S.F)

As a general rule, varieties from each section should be planted together to obtain the best results from pollination, though many will overlap–such as 'Lane's Prince Albert', which has a very long flowering period–about 21 days.

Purchasing Reliable Trees

If possible, see the fruit trees growing, which will reveal how they are grown and their quality, before placing your order. Even if no more than three or four trees are to be planted, remember that they will be planted with the expectation that they will bear good crops for at least a lifetime. To lose £2 on a badly grown tree may prove disappointing, but to have those same trees in one's garden for thirty years or more, thereby depriving the small garden of producing home grown fruit, would be even more so. If possible, obtain your trees from the nearest first-class nursery. Trees which have been reared under similar conditions of soil and climate as obtain in your garden may be relied upon to give a good account of themselves when moved only a short distance.

When a particular variety is required, it is only common sense to obtain this from a nursery in the district where the variety was first raised, or first found growing; a particular variety must evidently have proved vigorous where first observed.

It may be that some of the less well known varieties may only be obtained from certain nurseries. Some firms may be specialists in the production of apples and pears, others in the stone fruits. This should be considered before purchasing the trees. And guard against those so-called 'bargain offers'; with the present high cost of labour and land, fruit trees (at any rate, trees of top quality) cannot be produced cheaply, and anything inferior will be money wasted. The very best trees will cost only a matter of 5p or so more than those 'bargains', yet when all other things are considered they will provide a lifetime's pleasure and occupy no more room in the garden than cheap, badly grown trees.

An important advantage of obtaining one's trees within reasonable distance of one's garden is that they may be transplanted with as little root disturbance as possible. They can be moved with a good proportion of soil, while the roots are not exposed to strong winds more than is necessary. Again it is possible either to collect or have the trees delivered just when they are required for planting. If the trees are to be planted during the December to February period, especially in the north, the trees may arrive from a nursery where hard frost is not being experienced, at a time when one's own garden is experiencing a long period of frost and snow. Should this happen, the trees must be placed in a shed or cellar, and sacking or straw should be placed over their roots until the soil is in the right condition for planting.

Soil Condition for Planting

Fruit trees are moved and planted between mid-November and the end of March, depending upon the condition of the soil, and this will be governed by its texture. A light, sandy soil will prove suitable for planting at almost any time during the winter, for it never becomes sticky even following prolonged rain. But to plant in a heavy soil, however well prepared, will be to make it so compact as to cut off the vital supplies of oxygen to the roots, and the tree will be unable to get away to a good start, and so may never flourish as it should.

Where excessively wet soil conditions occur, the trees upon arrival should be placed into a twelve inch deep trough, the straw in which the roots were packed being placed over them. Then the soil is replaced without in any way being made firm. Where planting cannot be done for business or other reasons, the trees should, if possible, be given the same treatment upon arrival, for it is important to prevent the roots from drying out. Again this is where it is advisable to purchase from a firm which has a reputation to uphold, for the trees will be sent out correctly packed in straw and sacking, and despatched either by 'goods' or 'passenger' service at the customer's request, the additional carriage generally being borne by the customer. For a small additional charge, too, the nursery will name the individual trees with a metal name-plate, in place of the usual paper label which will quickly decay. Having the trees clearly and correctly named adds interest to one's garden, and it will be a help with pruning.

It is possible to move fruit trees as late as early April, if lifted with a good ball of soil about the roots and replanted almost at once. This does not mean that this is the most suitable time, of course, for the trees will be coming into activity after the period of winter dormancy, and root action will

Apple trees as they come from the nursery – the roots wrapped in polythene to prevent drying out

have begun. But it is possible that those taking over a new garden may not be ready to plant until early April, say at Easter (if not too late), when the businessman generally does his planting.

Before making the holes to take the trees, correct planting distances should be obtained, so that the trees are in no way deprived of air and sunlight. This may have been done before the trees were obtained, when the ground was being prepared, so that the manures were used without undue waste.

When planting cordons in a row, the best method is to make a trench in which the plants will be placed about three feet apart, wide enough to ensure that the roots do not touch when planted.

Those trees to be planted against a wall will require an additional amount of humus to conserve summer moisture. Decayed leaves, manure or moist peat may be worked in at planting time.

Planting the Trees

The trenches or holes to take the plants should be made before the trees are taken from where they have been heeled in or kept covered from frost. In this way the roots will not be unduly exposed to the air, or to the drying wind so often experienced in early spring. As a general rule, trees for a light soil, especially if it is of a chalky nature, should be planted during November or December. Those for a heavy, cold soil are best planted in March. Equally important is depth of planting.

Failure of the tree to bear well over a long period is often due to either too shallow or too deep planting, and both contribute equally to the various causes of failure. Too shallow planting will cause the roots to dry out during a period of prolonged drought, and especially where the soil lies over a chalk subsoil. It may also cause the trees, where Type MIX rootstock is being used, to fall over even when fully established, especially where planted in an exposed garden.

Too deep planting, on the other hand, will mean that the roots will be in the cold, less fertile subsoil,

Heeling in fruit trees

A 'Conference' pear, espalier. Horizontal line shows ground level

cut off from air and the sun's warmth, and also that the scion, at the point the graft has been made on to the rootstock, will be buried and may take root. Thus the characteristics of the rootstock will play little part in the habit of the tree.

When buying and planting fruit trees, always bear in mind that the roots are as important to the tree, more so in fact, than its shape, and for this reason the younger the tree the more readily is it transplanted. Where planting an orchard, however small, maiden trees, one year old, are not only less expensive but are more readily established, and may be trained and pruned to the requirements of the grower rather than to those of the nurseryman.

Remember that with all trees, the younger they are the more readily will they transplant, though in this respect the exception is the pear, which will readily transplant up to 20 years of age.

The hole or trench is first made to the correct depth, so that the level of the soil will be at a point just above the top of the roots, as near as possible to the same level as the tree was planted when at the nursery. Then a spadeful of a mixture of sand and peat, to encourage the formation of new fibrous roots as quickly as possible, should be spread about the hole. To enable the roots to be spread out correctly, a small mound of soil should be made at the bottom of the hole.

Gardeners of old would place a flat stone on the top of this mound to prevent the formation of a tap root. This may still have its devotees, but the shortening of any large tap root with a sharp knife just before planting should be all that is necessary, at the same time removing any damaged roots, or shortening any unduly long roots. Here again, the experienced nurseryman, whose reputation is built upon the success of the trees he sends out, will see that the trees are lifted as carefully as possible, with the roots undamaged. All too often those 'bargain parcels' arrive almost rootless and take years to become re-established.

The roots should be spread out so that each one is comfortable. All too often trees are planted in holes which are made far too small, with the result that roots are bunched up, and compete with one another for nourishment. A tree badly planted can never prove satisfactory.

When the roots have been spread out, scatter more peat and sand over them, then begin to pack the soil around them. This is best done by holding the tree straight, or at the required angle in the case of cordons (which should be fastened to the wires before the soil is filled in). By pushing in the soil with the feet–a strong pair of boots is the best guarantee of correct planting–the job may be performed by one person. As the soil is pushed into the hole it is trodden firmly about the roots so that there will be no air pockets, which would cause the roots to dry out. Tread the soil in little by little so that a thorough job is done, rather than fill up the hole and tread down afterwards. Where planting against a wall it is advisable to incorporate additional humus materials, as the soil is being placed in the hole to retain the maximum of moisture about the roots. The same may also be done where planting in a light, sandy soil. The planting of a few trees can be much more thoroughly done than when planting in an orchard, and the work should not in any way be hastily carried out. If there can be two people to do the planting, so much the better.

Staking and Tying

Staking is of the utmost importance. Bush trees, pyramids and maidens should require little or no staking, but cordons and espaliers should be fastened to the wires as soon as placed in position. Wall trees in the espalier and fan shape must be fastened to the wall or trellis without delay, using a piece of strong leather for each shoot, which is correctly spaced to prevent overcrowding. It is the full and half standard forms which require careful staking, the stakes being driven into the soil so that there will be about three inches from the stem. If too near they will rub and cause serious damage to the bark. Care must also be taken to prevent similar damage to the base of the stems by boot or spade when planting.

It is advisable to use one of the patented fasteners rather than one which is home made, though an excellent use of old car inner tubes may be made by cutting them into twelve inch strips and twisting between tree and post to prevent rubbing.

After planting and tying, give each tree, or row

Staking is of great importance when planting fruit trees

of cordons, a thick mulch of decayed straw manure, or even of decayed leaves, to prevent loss of moisture while the trees are being established in their final positions.

Training Bush and Standard Trees

Apple and pears are grown and trained in the same way as:

(a) Bush and Standards
(b) Dwarf Pyramids
(c) Cordons
(d) Espalier or Horizontal

If your fruit trees are being purchased as maidens (one year old trees) which is not only the best but also the most inexpensive way, they will require training to form the required shape. And when once this form is accomplished, the trees will require careful pruning, not only to maintain their form but also to maintain a balance between growth of tree and cropping. This will mean the removal of surplus wood which would prevent the necessary sunshine and air from reaching the centre of the tree, not only to ripen the fruit and prevent overcrowding, but also to ripen the new wood as it is formed, on which the future crop will depend. To plant a top quality tree into well prepared soil, and then to allow it to grow away as it likes, will mean that quickly it will make an excess of wood, for the natural tendency of any fruit tree is to grow away as quickly as it can with very little inclination to bear fruit. The result is that before long the tree is just a mass of old wood, the fruiting spurs become overcrowded, and gradually they decay with no new growth to take their place, and with the gradual diminishing of the crop. Frequently quite the opposite is found in private gardens: the jobbing gardener may cut the tree back so hard each year as to deprive it of sufficient wood and foliage to enable it to bear a good crop. But before any serious pruning is necessary, the tree must first take form.

(a) Bush and Standard Trees

These are the most popular forms both for orchard and private garden planting, though for a small garden the most artificial forms are more suitable.

For a standard, what is known as a 'feathered' tree should be obtained. It should be two years old, and may be trained to any length of stem by removing the small 'feathers' or lateral shoots which appear on the main stem. The tree should be allowed to grow away without any check or pruning. Then, when the standard has reached the desired height, it should have its unwanted 'feathers' removed and the head built up in the same way as for a bush tree. A full standard usually has a trunk five to six feet in height while a half-standard has a trunk three to four feet long.

The formation of the head will be by either one of two methods:

(a) The Open Centre Form
(b) The Delayed Open Centre Form

To form a bush on a good 'leg' by the Open Centre Form (a)–the head of a standard is formed in the same way–the maiden tree should be 'headed' back to about three feet above ground level. This will persuade the tree to break into two or three shoots, which will become its framework. Any shoots which break at the lower 15-18 inches of the stem are removed.

The following winter, which is the time when all pruning and cutting of fruit trees is done, the selected shoots are in their turn cut back half way. Those with a more drooping habit, like 'Lane's Prince Albert', are cut to an upward bud.

Next year these so-called extension shoots are likewise cut back about half way, or to about nine inches of their base, at which point they will have 'broken' or begun to shoot. The head of the standard or bush will now have been formed, and henceforth pruning is carried out for fruit bearing, depending upon the habit of each variety, e.g. tip or spur bearer.

The Delayed Open Centre Form (b) is formed

by removing only the very top to six inches of the main stem. Then down the whole length buds are formed, and it is from these that the tree is built up. So as not to interfere with the laterals which will grow from the top two buds, the two immediately beneath should be removed. This will prevent the centre from becoming crowded. With this form it is the spacing that is all important. See that the shoots are facing in the right direction on all sides of the tree, rather than that too many appear together. This is the best form for pear trees, preventing that 'drain-pipe' appearance of pears in the Open Centre Form.

(b) Dwarf Pyramid

This is a form of great value in the small garden. It can be built up into a heavy cropping tree in as short a period as possible. As it is desired to make as much growth as possible at the beginning, and the tree brought into bearing early, bud growth must be stimulated. This is done by making a cut in the bark just above each of the buds on the main stem, taking care to select buds suitably spaced. These shoots may be pruned back to half the new season's growth each year so as to stimulate the formation of fruiting buds, and all blossom buds forming on the leader should also be removed. When once the tree comes into bearing it should be thinned out as for other forms by using one of the proven systems of pruning. Throughout its early life, and until thoroughly established, the main or central extension shoot must be constantly pruned back so that the tree can concentrate its energies on the formation of branches.

(c) Cordons

It is the single-stemmed cordon that is most frequently used. It should be planted at an oblique angle, so as to limit its tendency to grow away. Once again, a dwarfing rootstock should be used, and not a vigorous tree like the 'Bramley' or a tip bearer like the 'Worcester Pearmain'. Likewise only the upright spur bearer of pears should be used. Those apples and pears with a drooping habit do not make good cordons.

The maiden trees should be planted three feet apart, and should be fastened to wires at an angle of 45°. The extension or main stem is never pruned, and in the early years pruning consists of cutting back the laterals during August to six inches from the main stem. This summer pruning will ensure the formation of fruiting spurs as quickly as possible. When the tree has made the necessary growth, the leader may be cut back so that the tree can concentrate on the formation of fruit rather than on extending its form. Henceforth the tree may be kept healthy and the fruit of a high quality by the careful elimination of surplus spurs. A tree with excessive vigour may be curbed with root pruning done every three years. Keeping the stem at an oblique angle will also retard the formation of too much new wood.

Planting apples and pears in the cordon form will allow a much greater variety to be enjoyed. At the same time it will provide better pollination where space permits the planting of very few trees.

Besides the Single or Oblique cordon, the U-shaped form or Double cordon should be understood, since this is occasionally required. Though growing in an upwards direction as against the angle of the single cordon, the bend at the bottom will act as a check to vigorous growth. The U-cordon will be grown against a wire fence as in the case of espaliers and single cordons. Its formation is in fact very similar to that of the horizontal trained tree, the maiden being cut back to twelve inches of stem to two buds facing in the opposite direction. These are allowed to grow unpruned throughout the year. They are fastened to canes against the wires, first at an angle, then gradually to a vertical position.

Pruning consists of cutting back the leaders each autumn to one-third of their new season's growth,

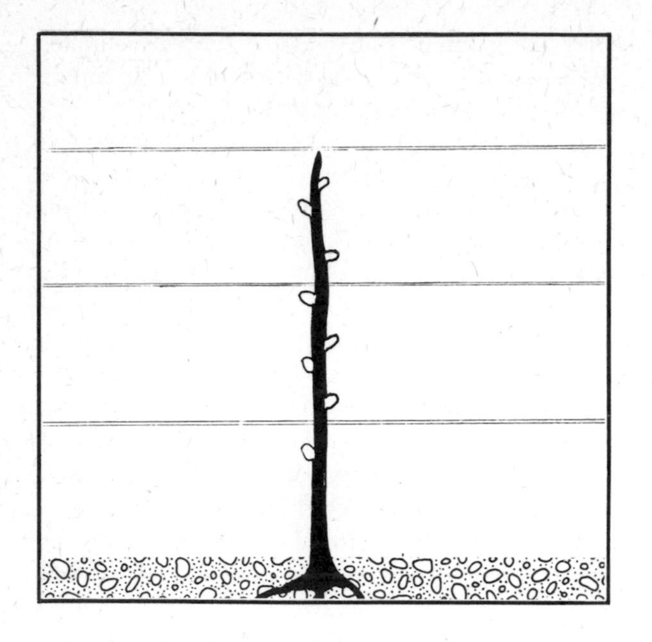

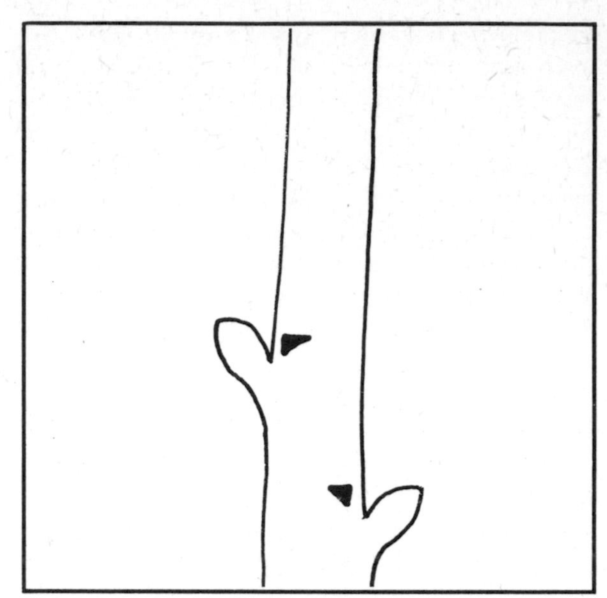

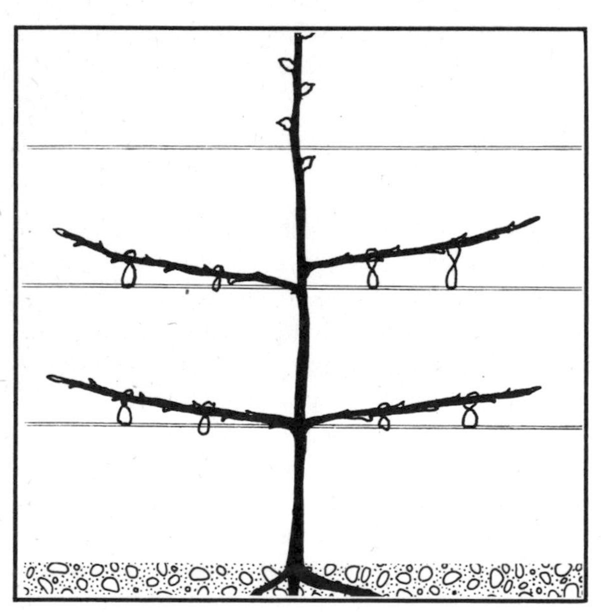

A sequence of six illustrations showing the training of climbers. The first illustration shows the plant in April of its first year after planting, showing where the shoots should be nicked. The second illustration is a close-up showing precisely where the shoots need to be nicked. The purpose of nicking is to make the buds grow out more horizontally than they would otherwise. The third illustration shows the plant having made growth following nicking. The fourth picture shows the shoot being tied down to the supporting canes in April of the second year, and the nicking of the buds

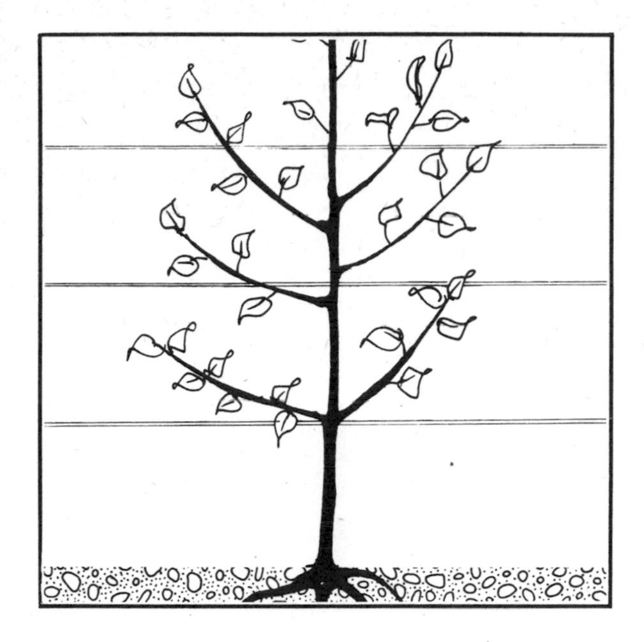

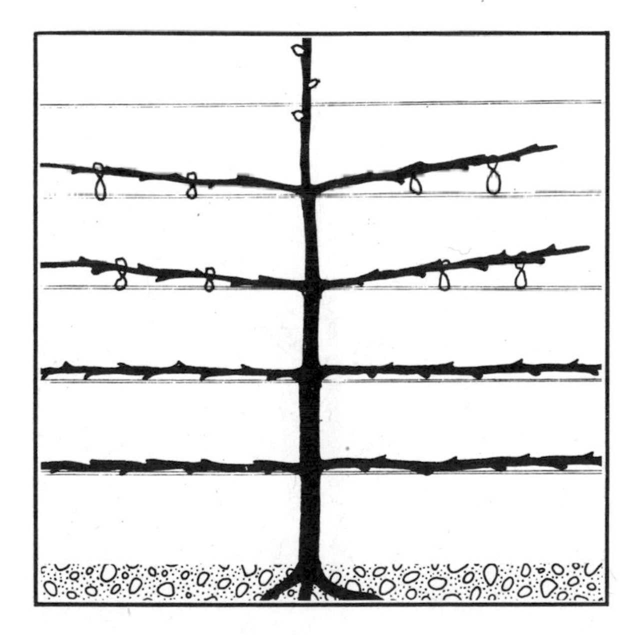

on the new leader. The fifth illustration shows growth made during the second growing season and the last illustration shows a tree being tied down and nicked again in April in the third year after planting

and of pinching out any side growth during August. These side shoots may be further cut back in November to two buds, which will form the fruiting spurs. A variety showing excessive vigour may be root-pruned in alternate years. Should either of the buds fail to form an arm, notching or nicking immediately above will have the desired stimulating effect.

(d) Espalier or Horizontal Form

Trained horizontally along the wires in a similar position as for cordons, there is no more satisfying way of growing apples and pears, adaptable to this form. A maiden should always be planted, the stem being shortened to about 18 inches above soil level, and to a point where there are two buds close together, one on either side of the stem. It is a simple matter to train the tree, the laterals formed by the two buds being tied to the wires to the right and to the left. The extension shoot is allowed to grow away unchecked, until sufficient growth has been made for it to be cut back to two more buds similarly placed and spaced about 15–18 inches above the first to form. To encourage more rapid growth, the laterals should first be fastened at the angle of 45° and only placed in the horizontal position at the end of the first year's growth. Small canes should be used to train them at this angle, otherwise there will be fear of damage by strong winds.

A new tier may be formed each season. When the first tier has been formed, you should encourage it to form fruiting spurs by pruning back in summer all shoots formed on these branches to within five inches of the main stem. This will encourage the plant to form fruiting buds instead of new wood. The work should be done towards the end of July. This is followed by cutting back still further during winter in the usual way. Treatment then consists of thinning out the established spurs, and root pruning if the tree is inclined to make excessive growth. As the side arms continue to make wood, this new wood should be shortened back to one half

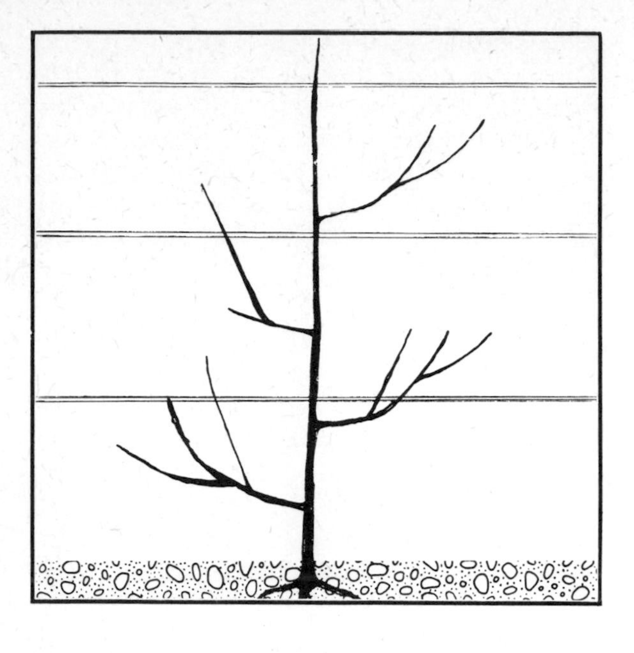

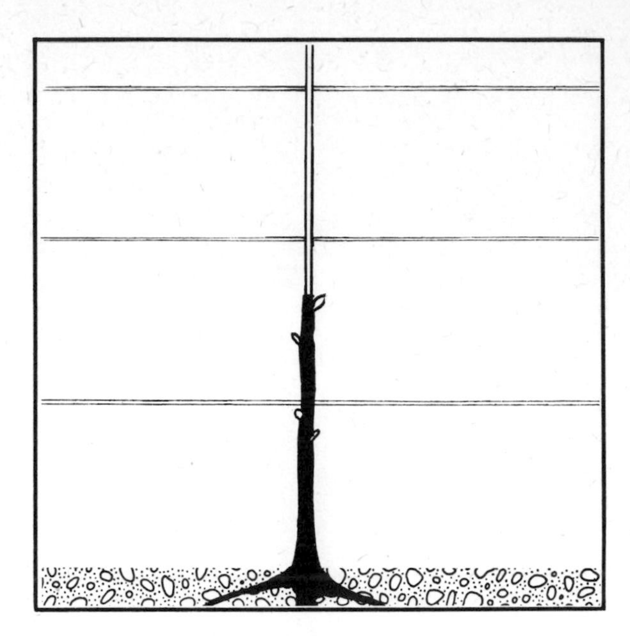

A sequence showing the use of canes in the training of a fruit tree. This can be trained to grow flat against a wall, or on a free-standing espalier, being trained on wires stretched between posts

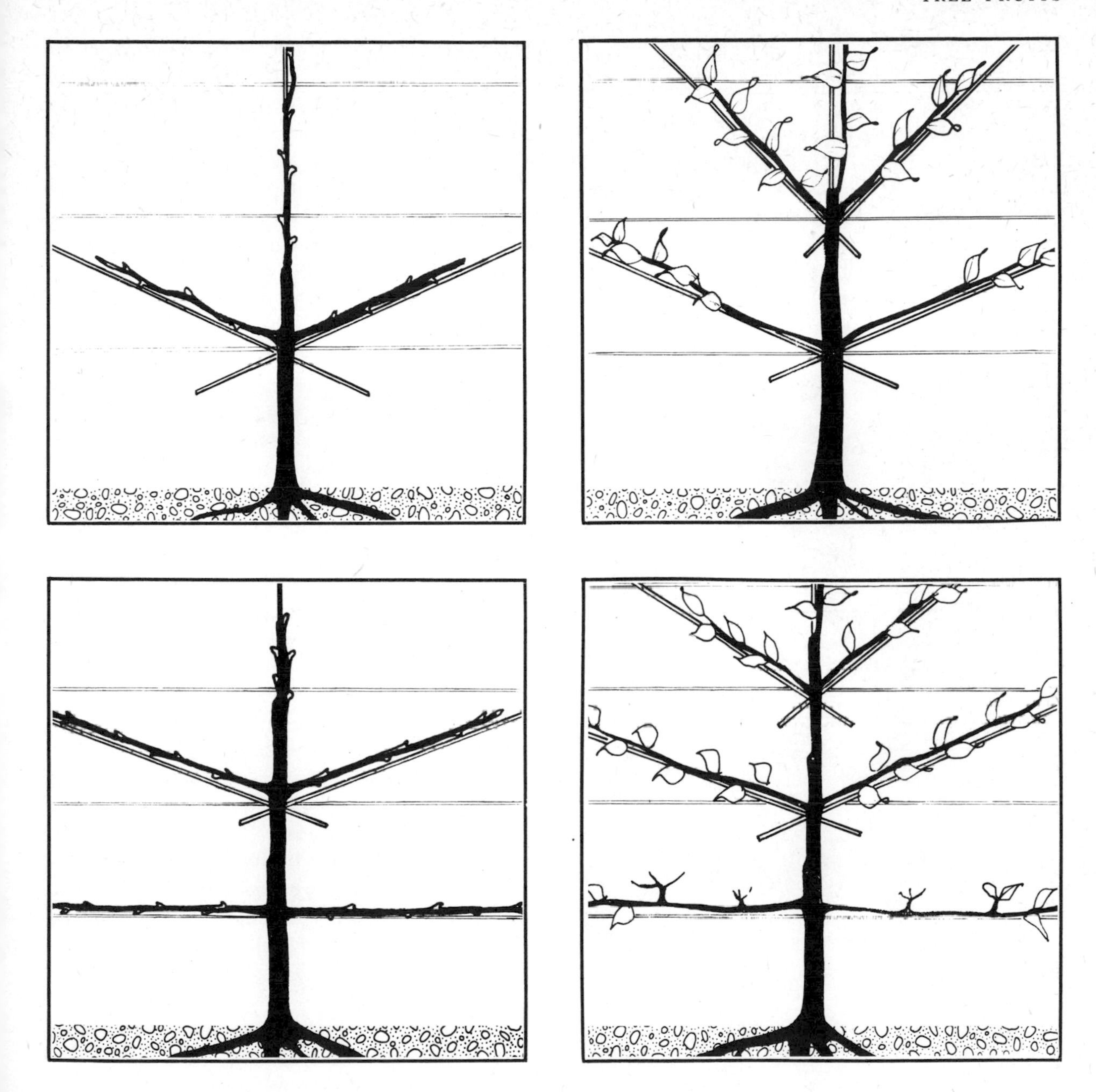

of the newly formed wood each winter, again making certain to cut to a bud which is to form the extension shoot. This may continue for a number of years, until the branches reach the required number. To make for ease in picking and prunning, it is general to allow five pairs of arms or tiers to form the top at a height of about six feet.

Pruning – Making a Correct Cut

It is important to know just how to make a cut before the pruners are taken up. It should be made immediately above a vigorous outward bud, and done with the slope of the cut away from the bud.

Painting a wound on a fruit tree after pruning to prevent infection entering

The remaining wood above the cut will almost certainly die back to the bud. If more wood than necessary is allowed to remain, this may become a source of infection. The cut should be made clean, without bruising or tearing.

It is also important to have handy a preparation for painting over the wounds caused by paring away diseased tissue, or where branches have been severed. White lead paint is satisfactory, and a new liquid fungicide called Medo will do the job even more efficiently.

As soon as a tree has been pruned, the prunings must be cleared up and burnt. To leave them lying about the orchard or garden will only encourage disease, which may be eventually transmitted to the healthy plants from which the prunings were taken. It is preferable to make a small fire towards the end of each pruning day. Burn the rubbish while it is still fairly dry and before the shoots become trodden into the ground.

The Functions of Pruning

Of all jobs in the garden nothing causes so much controversy, or so much worry, as pruning. It would appear that, to the amateur fruit grower, the arts and mysteries of pruning are only to be understood by those who have spent several years at a horticultural college, or as an employee at one of the fruit growing nurseries.

To begin with, there is no doubt that most gardeners carry pruning to excess, cutting back to the old wood so completely that the trees soon become devoid of any new wood at all.

Pruning is done:

(a) So that a proper balance is obtained between top growth and root action,
(b) To enable the requisite air and sunshine to reach the greatest possible portions of the tree,
(c) To maintain a balance between the fruiting of the trees and the formation of new wood.

Removal of an inward branch to keep the centre of the tree open

Plums and cherries do not require anything like so much pruning as apples and pears, chiefly because of their habit of 'bleeding'. This will not only sap their strength, but will make them liable to disease entering through the wound. Instead of pruning the branches, the roots should be pruned. This will slow down top growth and the same result will be achieved without the risk of bleeding. Check the roots and check top growth and vice versa.

What is most important is to ensure the correct balance of the tree, between growth and root action, between the formation of fruiting spurs and the making of new wood. If this is maintained over the years there is no reason why a tree should not remain healthy and bear a heavy crop for a hundred years or more.

Pruning is also done to stimulate growth, to make the necessary new wood which in turn will stimulate root action and enable the tree to search vigorously for its nutriment. This means that, contrary to general belief, it is the slow growing varieties which require the most pruning in comparison with those of vigorous habit like 'Bramley's Seedling' apple. To prune the vigorous grower hard back will be to encourage even greater vigour; then the balance of the tree, the affinity between root action and top growth, may be destroyed.

Functions of Roots and Foliage

There is close affinity between root growth and foliage. The roots supply the raw materials that are to be turned to good account by the foliage, which in turn supplies other substances which are continually building up a more vigorous rooting system; in their turn, the roots search for other nourishment for the foliage to convert. By controlling either roots or foliage, this cycle is halted for a time. But too drastic pruning of either roots or foliage will have its effect in throwing the functions of the plant quite out of tune with one another. It is therefore necessary before doing any pruning to remember the close affinity between foliage and roots. If pruning is done at the wrong time of the year it will cause severe harm to the functions of the plant. If the trees should be pruned while the leaves are fulfilling their functions in summer, the constitution of the tree will suffer; the roots will be searching out for nourishment which cannot be converted by the foliage. The result would be that soon the plant would die back altogether. This is the reason why fruit trees are pruned in winter, preferably between November and early March. A little judicious thinning to allow more light to enter may be in order, as with pinching back of surplus shoots of plums and other fruits. But any severe removal of foliage during the period when the sap is most active will mean a tree of reduced vigour, rather than one of additional vigour if pruning is done while the sap is dormant. Throughout the life of a tree the aim must be kept constantly in mind that it is required first to build up a vigorous tree; next to ensure a bloom of fruit of top quality; and then to maintain a constant affinity between health, vigour and quality. All this is not difficult if we realize just why it is necessary to prune before we take up the pruners.

Pruning is also done to enable air and sunlight to reach all parts of the tree and stimulate that new growth which will gradually replace the old wood. Where air and light are cut off from the tree, a preponderance of old wood forms. This will gradually die back and leave a sparsely furnished tree, one yielding only a small percentage of the fruit that it is able to do.

Renovating old Trees

It often happens that when moving into a new house one may also take over a badly neglected orchard, or even one or two trees which have never been correctly pruned, yet which with some attention will bear good crops.

A ladder and a saw may be necessary to reach the top branches. If the trees are so badly overcrowded as to restrict air and light, then do not hesitate to cut out several large branches, or even to remove a tree in its entirety. But remember that an old tree may die back if too many large limbs are removed at once.

The first operation in renovating an old tree will be to cut out all dead and decayed wood which is playing no part in the life of the tree and which it will be better without. The greatest source of disease will then be out of the way. Then look at each tree again. Where one branch is possibly growing into another tree, causing little light to reach it and obstructing the flow of air around each tree, cut this away also. When removing any wood, whether decayed or green, make the severance right against the main trunk, and in the same way if decayed or surplus wood is to be removed from a small branch. Frequently it is observed that a branch has been removed an inch or even several inches away from the main trunk or branch, with the result that the remaining wood gradually decays and falls a victim to pest and disease, especially brown rot disease, which will attach the remaining parts of the tree and also the fruit.

When removing a large branch it is advisable to give it some support while the cut is being made. This will take much of the weight and prevent the branch from tearing away from the stem, which would cause considerable damage to the bark.

It will be found that a cut made close to the bark will quite quickly heal over and so will be closed against disease. But it is often noticed with an old orchard that certain branches will have been carelessly removed, or may have snapped off leaving several inches of wood which will have decayed and come away, leaving an unhealthy looking cavity on the main trunk, or on a large branch.

To prevent further decay, this cavity should be filled up with cement. If it is only a small opening you can fill it with putty, but if it is left untouched there will be the chance that disease may damage the tree past repair.

Another method of pruning known as de-horning may also be practised. This is a better method where growth has become dense at the centre, and where the removal of a complete branch would not bring about the necessary results.

It is generally the top branches which are dehorned. This consists of cutting them back several feet and possibly reducing them by at least half their length. A sloping cut should be made exactly as when making a cut with the pruners, so that moisture drains away, and the wound should be treated in the same way as when a whole branch is removed from the main trunk. An abundance of fresh new growth will result, and a completely new head may be formed.

As mentioned, any pruning and de-branching of an old tree must be done by degrees. In the first winter, possibly no more than decayed wood and a few small branches overlapping each other will be removed. The following winter more unwanted wood may be cut away: later, if the tree has become excessively tall and straggling, it may be advisable to cut back the main branches to a sturdy young shoot, and so build up once again the lower part of the tree so that it will in time be capable of bearing a heavy crop. But any rejuvenation of an old, neglected tree must be done gradually. If you take out the saw and pruners and cut away right and left during the first winter, there may be nothing but dying trees left. When a tree has been allowed to fall into neglect, there is a great temptation to try to restore its vigour at once, but this must be resisted. It may take four years to renovate an old tree, perhaps longer if the trees are very old.

Pruning Young Trees

When pruning neglected young trees, large branches will not need to be cut away. Instead, thinning and cutting back laterals to form vigorous buds will be all that is necessary. First remove any overlapping wood, taking care to cut back to an outward bud, for the centre of the tree must be kept as open as possible to let in the maximum of light and air.

Then take a careful look at the laterals, which are the shoots growing out from the main stems and on which the fruiting buds are formed. Each season, additional wood is formed and also buds, but if the laterals are not kept pruned they will become longer and longer, and at the same time the buds will become weaker and weaker. Instead of allowing them to remain unchecked, with the result that the fruit will be small, they should be cut back to two or three fruiting buds. Into these the energies of the plant will be diverted with the result that the fruit will develop to a good size.

Cutting back the unpruned laterals to two or three buds should be done before the buds begin to swell, in other words before mid-March, in order that when the sap commences to flow it can be directed at once to the fruiting buds. There is a danger of knocking off the buds if pruning is done when they have started to swell.

Varieties possessing extreme vigour, such as 'Bramley's Seedling' and 'Newton Wonder', would be well able to develop four or five buds. Too drastic pruning will only increase the vigour of the tree to the detriment of fruit.

As a general rule when taking over an established orchard, all outward and downward branches should be left untouched, unless overcrowding each other, for they will receive all the air and sunlight necessary. They also bear the heaviest amount of matured fruit, not only for this reason, but because they are better able to contend with strong winds, having much freer movement than those branches at the centre of the tree, with the result that the fruit is not blown off. It is the centre of the tree that requires the most attention; this should be kept as open as possible.

Restricting the Vigorous Tree

The very strong growing varieties such as the 'Worcester Pearmain' and 'Blenheim Orange', together with those previously mentioned, will require very little pruning, for they do not need any stimulation to make fresh growth. Their growth may of course be regulated by planting a known rootstock of dwarfing habit, but this, of course, is known only where a new tree is being planted. Pruning the vigorous varieties without knowing which they are will only cause disappointment by increasing their wood to the detriment of fruit. No orchard should be touched, except to cut away decayed wood, without first seeing the trees in fruit.

Because hard pruning of a vigorous growing tree will only make it more vigorous, an overcrowded tree of this nature should have a branch or two completely cut away. This will allow the extra light to reach the buds without increasing the tree's vigour. Or it may be restricted by either root or bark pruning. As a rule it may be said that a strong growing tree will form very many less fruit buds than will a slow-growing tree. So with the vigorous growers some method of restricting growth will often be necessary.

Root Pruning

November is the best time to root prune. It is an easy matter to make a trench three to four feet away from the trunk, and to sever the strongest roots, spreading out the more fibrous roots before filling in the trench. The same rule of careful pruning, doing only a little at a time, applies equally to the roots as to the branches, particularly where old trees are concerned. It is therefore advisable to root prune only one side the first year, the other side the following year. Where standard trees are being grown it is not advisable to remove the tap root which is the tree's anchor. If a stone is used at planting time, the tree will concentrate on strong secondary roots which may, if necessary, be restricted by pruning. Nor should severe root pruning be done where the dwarfing rootstocks are used, nor should it be necessary, for their poor anchorage will be made even less secure.

Root pruning should be consistent with the removal of wood to retain the balance of the functions of both roots and foliage. In the cases of vigorous growers, the removal of a branch or of unwanted wood should correspond to the restriction of roots. In dealing with old wall trees which are being root pruned in order to bring them into full bearing once again, the general practice is to prune back the fruiting spurs at the same time as the roots are cut back; this will ensure quality rather than a quantity of fruits of little value. Thus will the connection between roots and foliage be maintained.

Bark Pruning

Bark pruning or ringing is done to curb the flow of sap, with the result that more fruiting buds are formed instead of wood growth. As there is danger that too much bark may be cut away which would not heal over in a reasonable time, ringing should only be done when root pruning has no effect, but it is worth trying with a tree which refuses to bear a crop and is continually making fresh wood even when every known method of restriction has been tried. Instead of making a complete circle round the stem, it is safer to make two half circles, allowing six inches of bark between each. Cutting should be done with a short knife; a pruning knife is best, and immediately the cuts have been made and about three-quarters of an inch of bark has been removed, tape should be fastened and bound securely round the place where the cuts were made. Early May is the best time to do this, and choose a calm day so that the tissue of the tree at the exposed place is not open to drying winds. Cover with tape immediately each tree has been treated.

Grafting

This is an interesting occupation for the amateur who has taken over an old orchard, or where several old trees of a certain variety have not proved a success. Provided the condition of these trees is good and they are free from canker and other troubles, they may be made to change their variety by top-working and frame-working. Top-working is done by removing the lower branches of the tree, and grafting buds of the desired new variety on to the topmost branches. Frame-working is done by allowing the branches to remain, and on to these grafting the new wood.

Grafting is an art that comes only by constant practice. The work is done between early March and early June; the earlier in the season the better for satisfactory results, but the scions or prunings should be removed from the trees during January, for it is necessary to have this new wood in a dormant state at the time the grafting is done. The shoots should be tied up in bundles, named, and allowed to stand in a mixture of moist peat and sand under an open shed and given protection from severe weather until ready for use. There are three main methods of grafting:

(a) The Cleft Method
(b) The Rind Method
(c) Side Grafting

When ready for the operation, the scions are cut at an oblique angle just below two buds; then, by means of a grafting tool, the cuts or clefts are made two, three or four at the end of each branch which has already been cut and trimmed. The prepared scions are then tightly wedged into the clefts, a little moist clay is rubbed in, and grafting wax is poured over each at the point of insertion.

Rind grafting is done by cutting through the bark only, and carefully lifting the bark from the wood of the tree. May and June are the best months for rind grafting and this is the grafting method most commonly used for apples and pears. The scion, prepared in the same way as for cleft grafting, should be inserted between the bark and wood at the point where the cut has been made. The jointing is sealed with wax and raffia. String or tape is used to hold the scion to the tree, leaving the basal bud exposed. The process of 'marrying' soon takes place, and constant watch is necessary, for as soon as the basal bud begins to swell the string or

A cordon apple, showing correct planting angle

raffia must be cut. So much for the two main methods used in top-working.

For frame-working, side grafting is most commonly employed. The lateral shoots are first removed and the tree then worked with side grafts. A cut is made at an angle of about 25° on the selected branches, and into this is inserted the prepared scion which has received a cut at a slightly less oblique angle than for the methods previously decribed. Oblique side grafting is performed by making the cut on the branch at an angle of about 40°, and the scion is inserted in the same way. Grafting wax is poured round the cut and the operation is complete. Nothing could be more simple.

There is one more precaution to take, and that is to provide the grafts with some protection from insect attacks; for these may cause considerable damage by eating the scion buds. Grease bands tied round the trunk below the lowest branch will prevent certain species of weevil from crawling up, and this should be a routine precaution with all fruit trees.

Care of Young Trees

Both apples and pears require similar culture. In the correct treatment and care of a young fruit tree lies its ultimate cropping powers, which include its health, vigour, shape and ability to bear a heavy crop of quality fruit as soon as possible and over as long a period as possible. There is a wide choice of types of tree available; the bush form, standards, cordon, fan-shaped and horizontal trained, and each demands rather different treatment not only in its establishment but also in its subsequent care when established.

In its early years a young tree should not be expected to bear excess fruit at the expense of making a healthy frame; at the beginning, the formation of wood is more important than fruit, for a solid and lasting foundation must be formed.

That prince of fruit growers, Mr George Bunyard of Kent, always advocated that a newly planted tree should be allowed to grow away for a full season entirely untouched. This is to allow it to form ample new wood while the new roots are forming, and so the balance of the tree is left undisturbed. There is then no fear of excessive pruning interfering with the functions of the rooting system while setting in, or while the head or form is being acquired.

The following winter, pruning may commence and one should have then formed an idea as to the system to follow. It will be one of three alternatives:

(a) The Established Spur system, generally carried out for the more artificially trained trees of apples and pears.

(b) The Regulated system which requires the minimum of pruning and which is generally carried out on trees with a vigorous habit, and

(c) The Renewal system which, simplified, means keeping the tree in continuous growth.

The Established Spur System

The value of this system is to allow the tree a greater freedom of growth with the formation of fruiting spurs along the main branches. Wood formed during the summer is cut back during winter to four buds. During the following summer the two top buds will make new growth, while the lower spurs will develop into fruiting buds. From the place above the top buds where the cut has been made, two laterals will have formed during the second season, and these in turn are cut back (B) to two buds.

This method will ensure that while the tree is concentrating its energies on the formation of fruiting spurs at (A), the balance of the tree is being maintained with the spurs forming fruiting buds without having to form new growth themselves.

During the third winter, the fruiting spurs being now correctly formed, the previous year's wood is

Single oblique cordons showing the short spurs on which fruit will be produced

cut back at (C), for its functions are now complete and the energies of the tree can concentrate on the production of fruit at the two spurs (A). Again to encourage the building up of a strong fruiting spur, the laterals should be pinched back during midsummer, reducing them by about a third. In this way a tree is built up to its full fruit bearing capacities in the quickest possible time, bearing in mind the affinity between the rooting system and the formation of foliage, both necessary to maintain the vigour and health of the tree. When once the tree is established, little pruning will be necessary other than to remove any overcrowded branches and to cut out all overcrowded spurs. This method is of course suitable only for the spur bearing varieties such as 'Cox's Orange Pippin', 'Christmas Pearmain', etc., and it is the trained forms which generally respond best to this method.

A word should be said about the necessity to thin out the spurs when once the trees have become established. This is, when they are about ten years old, and those taking over a garden with trees of this age should remember that if no spur thinning is done the tree may soon exhaust itself by forming excess fruit, too much for it to carry in comparison with tree growth. Most gardeners are shy at removing fruiting buds, but in any case too many will cause a reduction in the size and qality of the fruit and especially where this is the habit of the variety, e.g. 'Winston'.

The question of the tip bearers does not come into this system for the buds are formed differently, and in any case they are not suitable for training in the artificial form.

The Regulated System

This system is more suitable for the tip bearers and for bush and standard trees of all apples and pears, for these are the most natural form of fruiting trees. By using vigorous rootstocks like Malling II for apples and Quince A for pears, the tree will not come into bearing as quickly as if the dwarfing rootstocks are used, but it will retain its vigour and its fruiting capacities over a period. With the tip bearers, any excessive pruning will cause greatly diminished cropping, for the buds are borne at the end of the laterals and not in clusters as with the spur bearers. So under this system, cut away as much over-crossing and centre wood as will keep the tree 'open'. Also remove all in-growing laterals as they are observed each season. Any strongly growing branches which appear to be growing away too quickly should be cut back, or de-horned as it is called, to a lateral growing out in a manner that will encourage the shape of the tree. The spur bearers should have their spurs thinned out in the way previously described; though this will not be so essential as with those trees growing on a dwarf rootstock or in artificial forms, overcrowded spurs should be regularly thinned. This system demands just as constant attention in the pruning programme, and a little cutting back should be done

LEFT Cordon trained apple
ABOVE Fan trained apple

ABOVE Fan trained apple in full fruit
RIGHT Espalier trained apple

ABOVE Apple 'Sturmer Pippin'
RIGHT Apple 'Worcester Pearmain'

LEFT Apple 'Cox's Orange Pippin'
ABOVE Apple 'Lord Lambourne'

each year, rather than removing excessive wood in alternate years. These varieties which are excessively strong growing should be root pruned every three or four years; if too much de-horning is done this may only increase the vigour, and the result will be too much wood, to the detriment of the quality of the fruit.

When forming new fruit trees, the less pruning the better, until the fruiting buds have started to form, for pruning tends to encourage excess wood at the expense of fruiting buds. So first allow the trees a full year's growth before pruning, then commence with the bush and standard forms by shortening back the new season's wood of the leaders by a third at the end of every season. Then, as the tree begins to take shape, the leaders will require only tipping each year and possibly occasional de-horning if growth is too vigorous. The laterals too, for spur bearers will require cutting back as described, the tip bearers being left untouched until the time when they become excessive and some wood may have to be cut away.

The Renewal System

This works out exactly as described; it is the continued renewal of old wood by new, thus retaining the vigour of the tree over a very long period without making too much old wood. The idea is to maintain a balance between the production of new wood and fruit buds. It is necessary to build up an open tree with well spaced, erect branches, because it is on these that the new wood is continually formed. Suitable erect growing shoots or leaders which form on these branches are pruned back to form replacement branches which in due course will take the place of the older branches.

The same method takes place with side shoots. These are left to fruit unpruned. They are then cut back to within two buds of the base which will then produce two more shoots. Again, these are left unpruned and allowed to fruit. In turn, each of the two shoots is pruned back to two buds after fruiting, and so the process of the continued replacement of new wood for old goes on.

The proportion of shoots pruned and left untouched will be governed by the vigour of the variety. For 'Bramley's Seedling' a better balance will be maintained if a greater proportion of shoots is left unpruned, for stimulation is not required. But much will depend on the general health and vigour of the variety of tree. If the tree seems to be making heavy weather of life, it will require more pruning of side growth to provide the necessary stimulation. Where a tree is healthy and vigorous, a number of the shoots may be left unpruned for as long as three or four years, thus maintaining a balance between fruit and wood.

Summer Pruning

Those who grow apples and pears in the artificial forms, especially as cordons and espaliers, may prevent the formation of too much new wood by summer pruning. In the case of bush and standard trees planted in an orchard, pruning is done only during winter to stimulate the formation of new growth. Careful attention to the shortening back of wood during summer will provide a check on the action of the plant's roots, which in turn will check the production of new wood.

Mid-July is the time to pinch back any lateral shoots which have made excessive growth, and these should be shortened to six inches of their base. This should be done before the wood has ripened and before the end of the month!

Not only will the effect be to resist vigour; it will also enable new fruiting buds to be formed more quickly than when summer pruning is not carried out, the tree using its energy in this way rather than in the continued formation of new wood.

There is another factor worth considering where summer pruning is done, and that is to enable additional sunlight to reach the swelling fruit; this will ensure more satisfactory ripening of the fruits, especially with pears.

Biennial Cropping

With apples there is a tendency for certain varieties, e.g. 'Blenheim Orange', 'Miller's Seedling' and 'Newton Wonder', to form an extremely heavy crop only in alternate seasons. Some form of regulated pruning is therefore necessary to limit the blossom during the 'on' year, to enable the fruit to retain its size and encourage the tree to bear a certain amount the following or 'off' year. All spurs should be reduced to two buds and all maiden wood must be left unpruned. This will ensure that blossom buds will be numerous for the following season, while during the 'on' year much of the vigour of the tree will be utilized in the formation of new buds rather than on those already formed. Where possible severe frost has damaged the blossom for one year it frequently happens that the tree will produce an excessive amount of fruit the following year, and this may be followed by a lean year. By employing these methods a more regular crop will be assured.

Should a variety be required to make a good sized fruit very early in the season e.g. 'Arthur Turner' and 'Emneth Early' apples or pear 'Doyenne d'Eté' it will be necessary to cut back their laterals more than is normally done. Instead of cutting back only a third of the wood, cutting back two-thirds will ensure a more rapid maturing of the fruit, even if the quantity may not be so high as when given normal treatment.

Branch Bending

Where a tree is making such excessive growth that further pruning may only stimulate more wood, branch or shoot bending will help to restrain this. At the same time, restricting the flow of sap will help to form fruit buds at the expense of new wood. It is the lower branches which are more easily bent; these may be either tied at their tips to the stem of the tree, or may be weighed down with strong stones or bricks fastened with cord to their tips. While this does not really come under the title of pruning it does restrict growth of fresh wood and will also cause these bent branches to bear a heavy crop of fruit.

Notching and Nicking

It often happens that a certain bud is required to be restricted in its growth, while another may refuse to break and so may cause the tree to become mis-shapen. To encourage a bud to break, a notch should be made above it; to retard a bud, a norch should be made on the stem immediately *beneath* it, removing a small piece of bark.

In general it is found that the most vigorous buds are those towards the top of a stem or branch, the vigour diminishing with the buds at the centre and being less vigorous at the lowest point. It may therefore be necessary to stimulate those at the lowest point by notching; this will even out the formation of new branches.

Nicking of the stem has a similar effect. It is generally done where restriction of the extension of lateral growth is required. In addition to the cutting back of the stem, the prevention of an extension by the top bud will ensure that those buds lower down the branch will make more growth; this may be the object when building up a bush or standard tree. The cut or nick should be made with a sharp knife, preferably the pruning knife.

When to Harvest

One great mistake is to remove apples from the trees too early. If allowed to hang as long as possible, the fruit will not only reach that full maturity without which it will not keep; it will also be far happier on the tree than in the best of store rooms, and its keeping qualities will be both lengthened and enhanced. Several of the russets, particularly 'Brownlee's Russet', will shrivel and lose their crisp flavour if picked too soon. And 'Sturmer Pippin'–a grand apple for a heavy clay soil and one which will keep well into May–must be fully ripened or it will keep no longer than February.

We tend to harvest our late maturing apples during the favourable weather of early October, for it can be an unpleasant business if the fruit is allowed to hang until the cold days of early winter. However, many of the late keeping varieties are best left until then. One of the most delicious of all dessert apples is 'Claygate Pearmain', with its green flesh and dull russet-yellow skin, but it is only at its best if removed early in December. Carefully stored, it will then keep until March. If removed in October, when it appears to be ripe, it will keep only until Christmas, when it will tend to become soft and lose its crisp nuttiness. Two others which require the same treatment are 'Cornish Gilliflower' and 'Christmas Pearmain'; with their neat habit, both apples are ideal for a small garden and both crop heavily early in their life.

That pleasantly aromatic apple, 'Duke of Devonshire', is best picked towards the end of October; the same applies to 'King's Acre Pippin', while 'Laxton's Superb' should be removed in early November, when it would seem to have reached full maturity.

Most early maturing varieties show that they are ready for picking by parting from the spur when they are gently twisted, but the keepers hang on tightly, and it is left to one's own judgement when to pick. The one exception to the rule seems to be that good keeper 'Annie Elizabeth', a cooking apple of value which will begin to fall when fully mature and so should be removed the moment it is ripe. The culinary apples, possibly on account of their great weight, do tend to fall when mature, but even so should be allowed to hang on the tree for as long as possible. Fruits of that heavily cropping apple 'Grenadier' can be used for cooking from mid-August, and will remain without falling until late October, but being such woefully bad keepers, they should be used from the tree throughout autumn, and the fruit should be allowed to hang until the last to mature are to be used.

Very different is 'Newton Wonder', one of the most handsome of all apples: it should be allowed to remain unpicked until November, when it will have reached a huge size and be fully mature, and will store in perfect condition until Easter. 'Lane's Prince Albert' requires similar treatment, but it does not keep so well, so the longer it can be left on the tree the longer it will keep in store.

Another apple requiring November picking is the chalk lover, 'Barnack Beauty', which will then retain its good dessert qualities until March. The new 'Bowden's Seedling' will also remain shiny-skinned and juicy until April if allowed to hang until late November.

Several apples are not at their best until they have been up to two months in store. These are the apples which will keep until spring. The dual purpose 'Edward VII' is one. It is removed from the tree a deep green colour, and makes uninteresting eating. But by February the skin is turning a rich golden colour. Do not be fooled by this: leave it until early summer when it will be mellow and deliciously sweet and juicy, then eat it just before 'George Cave' or 'Beauty of Bath' is ready on the tree in July. The new 'Laxton's Rearguard' is similar. It bears a flat fruit which when ripe in early March turns a rich golden colour, flushed with red and russet. It possesses much the same rich flavour as its parent, 'Ribston Pippin', the flavour of which Lindley said in 1830 was 'not to be surpassed'. But allow it to remain on the tree until early December, to ensure that its full flavour and crispness are to be enjoyed in early spring.

Factors Denoting Maturity

There are factors to be considered apart from the characteristics of various varieties. One is the soil, for in soils that are light and sandy, the fruit will not hang as long as fruit on trees growing in a heavy soil, and trees growing in grass also retain their fruits better than where the soil is being cultivated beneath the trees.

Apples growing in the north are, through fear of

adverse weather and frosts, best gathered by mid-November. In the south, the late maturing varieties may be left on the trees for another month.

To find some indication as to whether the late varieties are ready for picking, cut a fruit through the centre; if the pips have become hard and almost black, the fruit may be said to have reached maturity. Removing them from the tree calls for great care; apples are not so easily bruised as most other fruits, but this does not mean that they can be handled carelessly. Bruised fruits will quickly deteriorate. They should be carefully twisted from the trees and placed in shallow baskets for removal to the store room. The question of wrapping the fruits is always a debatable point. Wrapping in waxed paper certainly helps to preserve the fruit by preventing evaporation, but there is always the danger that some fruits will decay without being noticed. It may be preferable to place the fruits on waxed or greaseproof paper, taking care to see that they do not touch one another; then as soon as any decay is noticed the fruit can be used at once.

Storing Conditions

Wherever possible, late apples for keeping should be gathered dry. If wet, wait for a windy day to dry off the moisture. Apples should be stored in complete darkness and kept as cool as possible if they are to last for any length of time. A too dry room will cause shrivelling; a place where there is any undue change in temperature will cause considerable condensation which will also be a deterrent to long keeping. Robert Thompson, in *The Gardener's Assistant,* published a century ago, suggested covering apples with a thin layer of very dry straw to absorb any moisture which arises from the fruit, and this method has been found to be great help to long keeping. 'Edward VII', and 'Crawley Beauty' may be kept until the following summer by placing them on a layer of dried bracken; cover them with bracken, too. On wooden shelves in a stone barn or dry cellar, the fruit keeps almost indefinitely. A dry shed is also suitable but to prevent temperature fluctuations the roof should be either thatched or lined inside.

Pre-Harvest Drop of Apples and Pears

Amateur growers may experience a premature dropping of apples, and sometimes pears, before the fruit is fully mature. This can cause serious damage to the fruit, which will lose its dessert quality and will be useless for storing. Two offenders are apples – 'Beauty of Bath' and 'Gladstone'; and 'Conference' pear. The placing of straw round the trees during June will not only act as a mulch but will also give the fruits some help in breaking their fall. It is, however, possible to use certain proprietary sprays containing napthalene-acetic acid. If sprayed on to the offending trees before the fruit is more than three parts grown, these will restrain dropping, which is often caused by a warm July and August (with cold evening conditions), or merely by strong winds.

It is generally the early maturing varieties which are the worst offenders, but 'Cox's Orange Pippin' is often troubled by premature fruit dropping, where soil and climate do not completely suit it. The trees should be sprayed on or about July 1st. 'Beauty of Bath', one of the most popular of the earliest apples to mature, is most often the worst offender; the new 'George Cave' is recommended as a substitute, chiefly on account of its ability to hold its fruit.

Varieties

Culinary

For July and August

EARLY VICTORIA Also known as 'Emneth Early'. The bright green, irregular shaped fruit is borne in such profusion that in some seasons it may require thinning.

For September

ARTHUR TURNER A vigorous but upright grower,

bearing handsome blossom and large handsome fruit, the polished green skin having an orange flush. The fruit should be used from the tree, but it hangs well and may be removed when required, from late August until November. For this reason it is extremely useful for the small garden.

GRENADIER If only its massive, exhibition quality fruit would keep even a few weeks, this would be one of the finest of all apples, for not only does it make a small, well-shaped tree able to withstand any amount of moisture at the roots, but is also a tremendous cropper in all parts, and is used for pollinating a wide range of apples, including 'Bramley's Seedling', 'Laxton's Superb', 'Cox's Orange', 'Ellison's Orange', and others too numerous to mention. It is a fine apple, being highly resistant to scab and canker, and its fruit is among the best of all for baking, yet it will not keep. It must be used from the tree. But for this, no other apple would be grown for cooking.

POTT'S SEEDLING This is a very hardy variety of excellent culinary value, with the ability to crop well in poor soils.

For October to mid-November

CHARLES ROSS A handsome apple of large proportions, the flesh being crisp and refreshing, the skin deep green, heavily flushed scarlet on the sunny side. It is not a strong grower except where suited, and this has detracted from its popularity of recent years, but it always does well in a chalky soil. It is also somewhat sensitive to lime-sulphur, and for this reason is not now planted as much commercially as at one time. It does not keep too well, becoming rather dry, but if taken from the tree in mid-October and used before the beginning of December there is none better as a dual purpose apple. Pollinated by most mid-season flowering varieties, especially 'Grenadier', 'Ellison's Orange' and 'James Grieve'.

LORD DERBY Another excellent culinary apple. Like all the early cookers, it should be used from the trees. It makes a tree of vigorous growth though of upright habit, and bears heavily in all seasons and in all soils. Like 'Grenadier', it always does well in a wet, clay soil. It bears an irregular green apple, whose flesh cooks to an attractive deep colour, and is especially delicious when sweetened with brown sugar.

REV. W WILKS Yet another famous off spring of 'Ribston Pippin', introduced about 1900, and what a handsome apple it is, making large size and being a universal winner on the show bench. The skin is primrose-yellow, thinly striped with scarlet, the flesh creamy and juicy and quite sweet. Fruits will frequently weigh more than two pounds each. The tree is of neat habit and is a tremendous cropper, but the fruit must be used by the end of November.

WEALTHY This is another dual purpose American apple of handsome appearance. It is cropping well in Britain. It is not a new apple but one which is only now becoming popular. It bears a most attractive fruit with a yellow skin, flushed and striped scarlet and russet. The flesh is juicy and refreshing, and it is delicious eaten from the tree in November; or it is eqally useful for cooking, breaking down beautifully when baked. At its best in November.

For November

MONARCH Though often used in November as harvested, this apple will keep, if stored carefully, until April. It is a useful Cox's pollinator. The blooms are extremely resistant to frost, but the tree often suffers from brittle wood and requires its lower branches to be supported. A most handsome apple with its olive green and pink flushed skin, it is delicious when cooked.

PEASGOOD'S NONSUCH Yet another famous apple which makes a dwarf garden tree, yet bears a reasonable, though not enormous, crop of handsome, golden fruit, with a bright crimson cheek. The tree is very hardy, though it crops well only in a deep, well-drained loam.

For December

GOLDEN NOBLE This fine old apple may be used between mid-October and Christmas, its yellow flesh being soft and juicy, delicious when baked. It makes a compact tree, ideal for small gardens, its fruit being among the most handsome of all, with its orange-yellow skin slightly speckled with grey and brown.

HOWGATE WONDER This is a new cooking apple, now being widely planted commercially. It was raised in the Isle of Wight, is thoroughly hardy, the fruit is ready mid-October, and it keeps until early February. The large apples are of a handsome green colour, striped scarlet, an excellent exhibition variety.

For January to February

BELLE DE BOSKOOP A native of the Low Countries where it is widely planted, this makes a strong growing tree and takes a year or two to come into bearing. The fruit is so valuable for Christmas use that it could well be more widely planted. The fact that it isn't is because its bright yellow fruit with its grey russeting is none too attractive. This, however, will not put off the amateur, for it makes delicious eating either as dessert or when cooked.

BRAMLEY'S SEEDLING One of the richest apples in vitamin C content, making a huge orchard tree and bearing heavily, where the blossom is not worried by frosts, and where the soil is a well-drained loam. It also takes several years to come into heavy bearing; it is a triploid, reqiring a pollinator and yet being of little use itself for pollination. This is not a variety for an amateur's garden, for it is also a biennial cropper. Against all this, it bears the finest of all cooking apples, which should be used from Christmas until Easter.

LANE'S PRINCE ALBERT This makes a dwarf yet spreading tree, with drooping branches, and is most sensitive to lime-sulphur. It requires a rich, deep loam when it will bear profusely a handsome apple with white, juicy flesh.

OPALESCENT A fine all-round apple of American origin; its glossy, almost purple-crimson skin and large size make it one of the most handsome of all apples. Used for dessert during December, it is rich and juicy and will remain so until mid-March. It is possibly second only to 'Bramley's Seedling' as a cooking apple. Add to this its hardiness and its large and regular cropping habit, and it must be considered an apple with a distinct future. Grown well, the fruits reach huge proportions without in any way becoming coarse, nor do they require thinning.

WAGENER Like a number of the dual purpose apples, this is an American variety and an instance of a variety know for more than 150 years only just becoming popular. It makes a small, compact tree and is an abundant bearer, the fruit being the best keeping of all apples. If taken from storage as late as mid-April, the fruits will not contain a single wrinkle and will still be firm and juicy. The bright glossy green skin, flushed with scarlet, makes this a most handsome exhibition apple. It needs a pollinator preferably 'Egremont Russet' or 'Lord Lambourne', to crop abundantly.

WOOLBROOK PIPPIN This is a splendid dual purpose apple for January to February use. It may be used for cooking until Christmas, but afterwards its juicy and aromatic fruits with their yellow and red russeted skin are so delicious as to be worthy of best dessert. It is a vigorous but upright grower, and bears especially well in light soils.

For February to April

NEWTON WONDER With its highly coloured fruit, at its best when grown in grass, its pale green skin flushed and striped with scarlet, this is one of the very best cookers for storing. It makes a large spreading tree, and is definitely biennial, but it blooms late and misses late frosts. Plant with 'Lady Sudeley', 'Charles Ross' or 'Early Victoria'.

NORTHERN GREENING A grand small garden cooker, keeping well until mid-April. It makes only a dwarf, upright tree, yet crops abundantly, the fruit being of a rich, glossy green colour. Ideal for a cold garden, its only fault is that the fruit is small, but against this it never shrivels when stored.

For March to May

CRAWLEY BEAUTY This is a superb apple and quite indispensable in a garden troubled by late frosts. It is in bloom the first days of June. The fruit should be allowed to hang until mid-November, and if carefully stored will keep until April. The skin is deep green, striped and spotted with crimson, the flesh soft and sweet. The tree is resistant to the usual apple diseases and is of upright habit, making it most suitable for a small garden.

EDWARD VII Probably one of the very best of all apples. Like 'Crawley Beauty', it blooms late and makes a neat, upright tree. It is the result of a 'Blenheim Orange' × 'Golden Noble', two splendid apples. Though usually listed as a cooker, 'Edward VII' makes delicious eating if kept until Easter, and it will store until the first July apples are ready. It will then be golden skinned and possess a rich, sweet flavour. The fruit should be allowed to hang as late as possible

UPTON PIPPIN Bearing heavy crops in the worst seasons and making a large apple of exhibition quality is 'Upton Pippin'. The skin is of a pale primrose striped with pink, and the fruit will keep well until Easter. The flesh is crisp and sweet, and it makes perhaps the best baked apple of any, 'Bramley's' included.

For April to June

ANNIE ELIZABETH This apple may be considered one of the very best for a small garden. It makes a healthy, compact tree, and comes quickly into bearing. The fruit, if harvested at the end of November, will keep until 'Early Victoria' is available in early July. It blooms late and bears a handsome ribbed fruit very popular on the show bench.

Varieties

Dessert

To Mature July and August

BEAUTY OF BATH It makes a vigorous, spreading tree and has been widely planted until recently because there is no similar variety that bears highly coloured fruit so early. This variety is usually ready by late July when it should be used, otherwise the fruit will become dry and flavourless. It would appear that 'George Cave' and 'Laxton's Advance' would replace it for commercial planting. It blooms early and may prove useless in a frosty garden; it is tip bearing and self-sterile. Use 'Laxton's Advance' as a pollinator.

DISCOVERY A chance seedling which possibly has 'Beauty of Bath' for a parent. It is a vigorous grower and is a tip bearer, so should be confined to the larger garden. It crops heavily when established and is at its best during August; the fruit is flat and pale yellow, flushed with scarlet; the flesh is white and juicy.

ELTON BEAUTY This is a most handsome fruit certain to become a favourite for the show bench. It is the result of a cross between 'James Grieve' and 'Worcester Pearmain', and bears the better qualities of these two prolific cropping apples. Its green skin is flushed and striped bright scarlet, with an attractive green ring around the centre. This is possibly the best flavoured of all early apples; it matures at the end of August yet keeps until early December, the only long-keeping, early apple. Just right for the late summer shows, and for the late seaside trade, where grown for profit, this is one of the outstanding early apples of the century.

GEORGE CAVE Is this the long-awaited apple to replace 'Beauty of Bath'? The latter has a spreading habit and an inability to hold its fruit until fully mature, but 'George Cave' matures a week before 'Beauty of Bath' and has quite exceptional fertility, its bloom being resistant to frost. The skin is almost as highly coloured as a ripe 'Worcester Pearmain', the flesh being white, firm, sweet and juicy, with almost no core. The next generation of gardeners will plant this abundantly.

GLADSTONE This is the first of all apples to mature, being ready for eating mid-July if grown in a sheltered garden. It makes a large, spreading tree and is a tip bearer; it bears very large, highly coloured fruit which must be used just before it is mature or it will become soft and flavourless.

LADY SUDELEY Like all early apples this one is extremely highly coloured, being of a rich golden colour, vividly striped with scarlet. It makes the best tree of any for a tub or pot, bears heavily and remains free from disease. It comes into use early in August but must be gathered just before fully ripe to obtain its best flavour. Flowering late, it is a valuable early apple for a frosty garden.

To Mature September

CELIA This is proving a valuable late mid-season apple. It was raised from 'Langley Pippin' × 'Worcester Pearmain', and bears a heavy crop of fruit which stores until early December. This is an apple of beautiful shape, with a glossy green skin, mottled and striped reddish-brown, and is ready for eating about September 1st. The flesh is sweet and crisp, and the fruit is well able to stand up to adverse weather. Like 'Elton Beauty', this apple is free from mildew and able to withstand lime-sulphur.

HEREFORD CROSS This has 'Cox's Orange' as a parent; the fruit has the same crisp orange flavour and is of similar appearance. It is ready for eating at the end of September.

JAMES GRIEVE This is usually one of the most reliable of all apples. It should not be over-fed with nitrogenous manures, or it will make excessive growth and crop less freely. It is early to bloom, and should not be planted where late frosts persist. 'Gladstone' or 'Laxton's Epicure' are suitable pollinators, while 'James Grieve' itself is an excellent pollinator for 'Cox's Orange'. Though it is of vigorous habit, it is of upright growth, and as it is a spur bearer it proves suitable for all but the smallest gardens. It crops well and regularly, the fruit being of a rich flavour from the tree early in September, or stored for 3-4 weeks. It is one of the few apples introduced from Scotland.

LAXTON'S FAVOURITE This new apple, with its high colouring and crisp, sweet flesh, is ready for eating towards the end of September. It is a vigorous but upright grower, and so is suitable for a small garden. It crops regularly, the fruit being of an even size and well shaped.

MILLER'S SEEDLING An excellent early September apple, at its best just before 'Worcester Pearmain'. It makes a large tree, yet comes quickly into bearing and crops so heavily that it tends to biennial bearing, requiring a season of rest after one of plenty. It is a handsome apple with pale yellow skin, striped scarlet; the fruit is on the small size and has no outstanding flavour. It will prove reliable in all soils.

TYDEMAN'S EARLY WORCESTER Raised at East Malling, the result of 'Worcester Pearmain' × 'MacIntosh Red', the fruit is mature about ten days before 'Worcester Pearmain', and has the same glossy, crimson skin. The round, medium-sized fruit is at its best about the first week of September.

WORCESTER PEARMAIN Unlike the equally highly coloured 'Gladstone', this apple is generally picked all too soon or as soon as it colours. The quality will be greatly improved if allowed to hang for several weeks, when it will be as crisp and juicy as the best of dessert apples. It is perhaps the best apple of its period, and is widely used as a 'Cox's' pollinator, but it is a tip bearer and makes a large tree, and so should be omitted from the smallest gardens. It is good in all soils, completely hardy, a regular cropper and free from disease.

Ripe in September and Early October

DEVONSHIRE QUARRENDEN Another old favourite, having a brisk, juicy flesh, and a flavour peculiar to itself. It is not too fertile and suffers from scab, but its shining crimson fruits are quite delicious.

ELLISON'S ORANGE Valuable in that it quickly comes into heavy bearing, the large handsome fruit being of 'Cox' appearance, but must be eaten early September, just before it is ripe. If over ripe the flesh is soft and has a peculiar aniseed flavour. It is a good 'Cox' pollinator and extremely resistant to scab, mildew and canker.

LAXTON'S EPICURE Like 'Fortune', this is another apple of excellent qualities from the 'Cox's Orange' × 'Wealthy' stable, and a winner of the Bunyard Cup for the best seedling apple. It is ripe and should be used during September, when it will be found to possess the juicy sweet flavour of 'Cox's Orange'. Like 'Fortune', it is self-sterile and needs 'James Grieve' or 'Worcester Pearmain' as a pollinator.

LAXTON'S FORTUNE Rightly given an Award of Merit by the RHS, this is one of the best apples ever introduced, the result of a 'Cox's Orange' cross with 'Wealthy'. It is early to bloom and is self-sterile, and must be planted with 'Lord Lambourne', or 'Laxton's Exquisite'. The fruit is at its best during October, when it should be used, for it will not keep. It is a strong and regular cropper.

MOSS'S SEEDLING Introduced in 1974 after extensive trials, it was the first apple to be patented under the Plant Breeders' Rights Scheme which guarantees the raiser of all plants a royalty on every one sold. It is an early 'Cox's Orange', being of similar appearance and flavour but in most years it bears almost twice the weight of fruit.

RED ELLISON A bud-sport, one branch only of a tree of 'Ellison's Orange' bearing deep cromson fruits. Besides the distinctive crimson colour, the variety has all the valuable characteristics of 'Ellison's Orange'.

To Mature October and Mid-November

EGREMONT RUSSET For the small garden or orchard this is an ideal variety, for it makes a small upright tree and crops heavily in all seasons. It also makes a fine cordon. It is at its best a little earlier than most russets, in November, and does not need storing to bring out its flavour and abundant juice. With its round, even-shaped fruit, this is one of the most handsome of all the russets, and one of the most delicious for late October dessert.

KIDD'S ORANGE RED This apple was raised in New Zealand between the two wars. It may be said to be the most highly coloured of all late apples, and is now being extensively planted commercially. It has the same high colour as 'Worcester Pearmain', and possesses even better keeping qualities than 'Cox's Orange'; moreover, it is one of those valuable varieties which, like 'Herring's Pippin', will crop well with the very minimum of attention. It may do well when grafted on to cookers. It is resistant to scab and makes a neat, upright tree.

LORD LAMBOURNE Awarded the RHS Cup for the best seedling apple of 1921, it has since then been widely planted commercially. It makes a good sized tree and does especially well in standard form. It is self-fertile and a heavy cropper, but is best away from damp districts, like the similarly coloured 'James Grieve', from which it was evolved. It is ripe in mid-October and remains sweet, crisp and juicy until late in November. A grand apple for a large garden.

MERTON WORCESTER Raised at the John Innes Institute, the result of a 'Cox's Orange' × 'Worcester Pearmain', it ripens a week later than 'Worcester Pearmain', is a better keeper, but has the appearance of 'Cox's Orange', a yellow skin flushed with scarlet and russet. The creamy-yellow flesh is crisp and aromatic. Does best in drier districts.

MICHAELMAS RED Raised at the East Malling Research Station. The fruit is almost a replica of its 'Worcester Pearmain' parent, having the same shiny crimson skin, and matures about a fortnight later. For a small garden this is a better variety than its parent, for it is of less vigorous habit, and is not a tip bearer, so may be grown as a cordon.

RIVAL This is one of the best of all apples for November, being of outstanding flavour. No apple is more juicy. It makes a large, spreading tree, and the handsome fruit has an olive-green skin, flushed bright scarlet on the sunny side. May be eaten from the tree mid-October to mid-November, or may be stored until Christmas.

SHAW'S PIPPIN This is an apple of unknown parentage. It makes a large apple of rich colouring and possesses the flavour of 'Blenheim Orange'. It is ready for gathering mid-October and will keep in condition until the year end. The tree comes more quickly into bearing than 'Blenheim Orange' and is a more suitable variety for a small garden. Although the fruit is large, no thinning is necessary.

ST EDMUND'S RUSSET This is a tip bearer, and a strong grower. It is early flowering and pollinated by 'Beauty of Bath'. To many it is the best flavoured of all October apples, almost equal to a 'Cox's', being juicy and sweet. The skin is bright orange, shaded with russet. Only in size and appearance have russets any bad marks against them; in all other respects they are the most hardy and easily managed of all top fruits, and no apples make for better dessert.

TAUNTON CROSS It is a mid-October maturing apple of most handsome appearance, very similar to 'Charles Ross' though the fruit is flatter, its green skin having a bright crimson flush. The flesh tinged with pink is particularly sweet. Of dwarf habit, the tree is extremely resistant to scab, and crops particularly well in wet districts.

Ripe Mid-October to End November

ALLINGTON PIPPIN Those who enjoy a brisk, acidy apple will find this a welcome change from the rather sweet earlier maturing varieties. It is inclined to biennial bearing and makes a large spreading tree, but growth is more restricted in soils of a dry, sandy nature. This could be said to be a dual-purpose apple, for like all those with a tart flavour it cooks well.

DELICIOUS Also known as 'Golden Delicious', it is an American apple widely planted as a dwarf bush or pyramid. With its even shape and clear golden-yellow skin, it is a favourite with the supermarkets and is now widely planted commercially. It is at its best for dessert during November-December.

HERRING'S PIPPIN It is a most reliable apple for a cold, heavy soil, cropping freely even if entirely neglected. The deep green fruit, flushed crimson on the sunny side, possesses a strong aromatic perfume and spicy flavour.

KING OF THE PIPPINS This is an exceedingly hardy variety which at one time was widely planted commercially. It makes a small, upright tree and bears heavy crops, the orange coloured fruit possessing a distinct almond flavour; the flesh is firm and nutty like a russet. 'James Grieve', 'Beauty of Bath' or 'Grenadier' would be good pollinators. The fruit should be used during November.

KING RUSSET A russet 'sport' of 'King of the Pippins' and, like it, an excellent 'Cox' pollinator. A most handsome apple, its yellow fruit is covered with a golden-brown russet while the flesh is crisp and nutty. It is at its best during October-November.

MOTHER An American variety. The yellow and crimson fruits with their pinky flesh possess a rich, aromatic flavour and are exceptionally sweet and juicy.

For Christmas Dessert

CHRISTMAS PEARMAIN Like 'Claygate Pearmain', it makes a neat, upright tree, is extremely hardy, does well in a cold clay soil, and crops heavily. For an exposed garden it should be included, but though its flesh is crisp and juicy it cannot compare in flavour with others of this section.

CLAYGATE PEARMAIN This is one of the very finest of all dessert apples. Anyone who has gathered the green and grey russeted fruit, covered with the frost on a late December morning, will have tested this apple at its very best. The flesh is also green, deliciously sweet and crisp, and very aromatic. It makes a neat, compact tree, ideal for a small garden. Few know it because it is the vividly coloured imported apple which attracts most attention.

COX'S ORANGE PIPPIN Raised from a pip of 'Ribston Pippin', which accounts for its quality, 'Cox's Orange' not only possesses superb flavour, but is of arresting appearance, which accounts for its popularity. It does however, possess a wide variety of adverse points, which make it one of the most difficult to crop well. The blossom is susceptible to frost, the tree may be termed a weak grower, and is very frequently troubled by scab, mildew and canker in cold soils. It is sensitive both to lime-sulphur and copper sprays. Yet the fruit carries a more subtle blending of fragrance and aromatic flavour than any apple, and nothing has yet been found to take its place, though 'Acme' may do.

GRAVENSTEIN This apple may be included in the previous group for it is ready for eating at the end of October. It will however keep until Christmas, and is of such superb quality that it is a sacrilege to use it before. To enjoy its honey-like flavour to the full, one needs to be able to sit in front of a log fire entirely at ease. It is an old German variety of poor appearance, which conceals its soft, juicy, creamy flesh with its subtle aroma. It makes a huge, spreading tree, requires plenty of room and should be given a warm soil.

MARGIL A very old apple, it makes a very small tree and bears heavily. It is not popular, for its small, flattish fruit is not in any way handsome, being yellow and crimson and covered with splashes of russet, but this matters little, it is what is inside that counts, and the crisp yellow flesh is sweet and juicy and strongly perfumed. With a light sherry this fragrance is brought out to the full, but use it by the early New Year.

RIBSTON PIPPIN Though almost past its best by Christmas, being suitable for November and December, this magnificent old apple has achieved fame as the parent of 'Cox's Orange', as well as for its own delicate flavour. It makes a spreading tree and crops regularly, though sometimes lightly, and must have plenty of moisture at its roots. The fruit is most handsome, being of an olive-green striped and flushed scarlet. Still grown commercially throughout the world, but is now strangely neglected by the amateur. Do not forget it is a triploid.

To Mature December to January

ACME Of all the dessert apples introduced over the past decade, this gives promise of being the most outstanding, and has been named accordingly. It is the first apple to crop on its own roots setting its fruit freely, even in the nursery rows the second season after planting.

BLENHEIM ORANGE One of the great apples of England in every sense of the word. It makes a huge tree, bears a tremendous crop and one of the largest of dessert fruits, at its best from mid-November until early January, useful both for dessert and for cooking, like eating sweet Brazil nuts. It has, however, two disadvantages. One is that it is a triploid, and though being pollinated by 'James Grieve', 'Ellison's Orange', etc. is not able to pollinate them in return. Another is that it takes ten years to come into heavy bearing, and is therefore little planted in private gardens. And like its culinary counterpart, 'Bramley's Seedling', its blossom is most susceptible to frost.

D'ARCY SPICE Does best in a sandy soil and in dry areas. It tends to biennial cropping and its fruit is nobbly, not nearly so attractive as the others mentioned, but it is the nearest apple to nut-like eating, is sweet and aromatic, a grand amateur's apple, and at its best during December.

LAXTON'S SUPERB Like 'James Grieve' and 'Worcester Pearmain', this is a grand all-round apple, making delicious Christmas and New Year eating. Like its parent 'Wyken Pippin', it is extremely hardy, much better than 'Cox's Orange', and yet has the flavour and high quality of 'Cox's Orange', its other parent. Though widely planted as an orchard tree, it crops abundantly in the cordon form, and makes a compact bush tree, ideal for any garden. It is a tremendous cropper, the fruit being slightly larger than 'Cox's Orange', of similar colouring but with pure white, nutty flesh. Carefully stored it will keep until March. Pollinated by 'Rival', 'Worcester Pearmain' and others. Like all huge croppers, often requires a rest season, and is inclined to biennial bearing.
MERTON PROLIFIC This is a late maturing apple, raised by the John Innes Institute. It is a regular and heavy cropper, the almost olive-green skin having a striking carmine-red flush which becomes brighter with keeping. It has 'Cox's Orange Pippin' and that excellent dwarf late cooker, 'Northern Greening', as parents. It makes a neat, upright tree. The fruit should be gathered mid-November and will keep until the end of February.
ORLEANS REINETTE This is possibly the most richly flavoured and sweetest apple in cultivation, grown at least 200 years ago, and originating from the Low Countries, where it has for long been popular. The fruit is flat and of a beautiful golden colour, shaded crimson with a large open eye, rather like a small 'Blenheim Orange'. It is at its best over Christmas, 'as a background for an old port it stands unapproachable', says Edward Bunyard, in his *Anatomy of Dessert*. It makes a compact tree and is extremely hardy and, like all russets, is rarely troubled by disease.
PEARL A really good dessert apple for the Christmas period is Rival, one of the parents, with 'Worcester Pearmain', of this new apple. 'Pearl' blooms reasonably late and is extremely frost resistant, though it is tip bearing and is of vigorous habit. It is a heavy cropper, the conical fruit hanging well and ripening to a deep red colour by late September, the flesh being yellow and with almost a 'Cox's Orange' flavour. It will keep well until the end of January, the flavour improving with storing. One of the best of all apples for the festive season.
ROSEMARY RUSSET This fine late apple's skin is golden, tinged with green and red, and covered with brown russet. It was widely planted at the beginning of the nineteenth century, when it was regarded as the best of all New Year apples. It is a hardy variety, and makes a small tree.
SAM YOUNG For cold, clay soils, this is a most reliable apple, at its best from November until mid-February. Its bright yellow skin is russeted with grey, and spotted with brown, the flesh being green and especially rich and juicy. Introduced from Ireland about 200 years ago, it is also known as 'Irish Russet'.

To Use in the New Year

COURT PENDU PLAT One of the oldest apples in the world, widely planted in Tudor gardens, and still a most valuable tree. Its hard, yellow flesh is pleasantly aromatic, much like 'Cox's Orange', but, unlike that variety, it blooms very late and so misses late frosts. For this reason it was known to Stuart gardeners as the 'wise apple'. Though making only a very small tree, it bears heavily: it is a handsome highly coloured apple.
EASTER ORANGE This is an excellent apple, the fruit, orange flushed with scarlet and russet, being at its best for Easter, the creamy flesh being crisp and sweet. The tree is of quite vigorous growth but, like 'Claygate Pearmain', of neat habit.
MAY QUEEN This is an ideal apple for a small garden, making a very small, compact tree, immune to scab, yet cropping heavily. The fruit with its crisp, nutty flavour is at its best if kept until May.
STURMER PIPPIN It is so late to mature that it should only be planted where the fruit receives the

maximum of late autumn sunshine. It was raised from a seed of 'Ribston Pippin', (surely the best and most prolific parent of all apples). Though green the fruit is handsome, being covered with dark brown russet, the flesh being firm and having a gooseberry like flavour. The fruit will keep until June, and is only at its best early in summer.

To Ripen January to February

BARNACK BEAUTY For a chalk soil this is the best of all dessert apples, and only on such soil does it crop abundantly. It is a tip bearer, and makes a huge, spreading tree. The fruit is very handsome, being of beautiful shape and of a deep golden colour, heavily flushed with crimson. The flesh is yellow, juicy and extremely sweet, at its best during January and February.

To Mature February to May

LAXTON'S REARGUARD This is the longest keeping of all dessert apples, only 'Edward VII', which may be termed a dual-purpose apple, keeping longer. It is an extremely hardy variety, with the same characteristics as its parents 'Court Pendu Plat' and 'Ribston Pippin', both being hardy and of compact habit. The fruit, which has a slightly russeted appearance, is similar to 'Cox's Orange', but is of a more flattened shape. It should be allowed to hang on the trees until early December, and is not at its best until March. It will keep until June.

TYDEMAN'S LATE ORANGE Also raised at East Malling, this variety may be described as a late keeping 'Cox's Orange', storing until April, and being of similar flavour with dark crimson-russeted skin. It is pollinated by 'Grenadier' or 'Charles Ross'. Would appear to crop heaviest and remain more free from scab in drier districts.

To Ripen March to April

PIXIE Its parentage is unknown. It makes a compact tree and crops regularly, the smallish round greenish-yellow fruit, which is crisp and juicy, keeping until the end of March when it is at its best.

WINSTON This is a fine late keeping apple. The fruit is one of the richest coloured of all apples, being bright orange profusely streaked with scarlet; the flesh is sweet and has a strong aromatic flavour. It makes a compact tree, is immune to disease and bears consistently well. It is in fact one of the best apples now grown commercially, and should be more widely planted in private gardens.

For February to April

BROWNLEE'S RUSSET Another fine apple this, which retains its olive-green colour when mature. Its flavour is brisk and aromatic, and it keeps in condition right until early spring without its skin shrivelling. The tree is extremely hardy, of compact upright habit, is very fertile and almost completely devoid of disease. Where the soil is cold and none too well drained this is an indispensable keeping apple. Its blossom is among the most beautiful, being of a rich cerise-pink colour.

CRAB APPLE

Malus domestica is native to the British Isles, and in medieval times was in demand for its fruit to make into conserves and for flavouring, its tartness and aromatic flavour being appreciated when peeled and placed in ale. Today the many varieties are more widely planted for their handsome flowers and ornamental fruits rather than for their culinary value, though for making jams and conserves their fruit rivals that of the sweet cherry.

The crabs make neat, compact trees while their slender branches may be pruned back to maintain almost any shape desired. While *Malus floribunda* and 'Red Jade' are of graceful weeping habit, 'Golden Harvest' and 'Goldsworth Red' make neat, upright trees which are ideal for the small garden; *M. lupehensis,* of irregular branching habit, is one of the best landscape trees for the larger garden. Several retain their richly coloured fruit throughout the winter, and while that of 'Wintergold' and 'Golden Harvest' is deep yellow, 'Knaphill Red' and 'Profusion' bear crimson-red fruit which is in striking contrast.

For making jams and conserves, three are outstanding and, either as standards or bush trees, may be planted in every garden, for they are handsome both in fruit and in flower. These are 'Dartmouth', 'Professor Sprenger' and 'John Downie', their fruit making a clear amber-coloured jelly.

The crabs do best away from areas of heavy rainfall which may cause outbreaks of scab and canker to which many other apples are prone. In favourable conditions the crabs are rarely troubled either by pest or disease, and as they bloom later than most apples their flowers are rarely caught by frost. They are reliable croppers, in most seasons, their branches in October being heavy with clusters of clean, small fruits of about two inches diameter, like the smallest 'Beauty of Bath' which will often fall before reaching maturity.

Tolerant of cold winds, the crabs may be planted in almost any part of the garden. At the back of the shrub border, as standards, they will be colourful for at least nine months of the year. Plant them five to six feet apart, preferably two of a variety, so that there will be worthwhile pickings of fruit to make into jelly.

Allow the fruit to hang as long as possible when it will take on a rosy texture on the sunny side, and the longer it is left on the tree the sweeter does it become. It should be used for conserve immediately after harvesting.

Varieties

DARTMOUTH It does well in all soils and makes a compact, open-branched tree, its fragrant white flowers being followed in October by shining crimson fruit which hangs on short, slender stalks.

JOHN DOWNIE It is one of the best of ornamental trees, being of open, upright habit, its snow-white flowers being followed in early September by clusters of golden egg-shaped fruits.

PROFESSOR SPRENGER Of compact habit, the blossom is pink and white, while the small round fruits are golden-orange.

MEDLAR

This is rarely planted today but has ornamental value and grows well in a heavy, damp soil in which few other fruits will flourish. It does, however, require a sunny situation and protection from cold winds. Where it is established, it blooms profusely in spring and bears heavy crops, both at the ends of the branches and on the old spurs, pruning being the same as for the apple. It is propagated by budding on to pear or hawthorn stock, and this is done in July.

As the fruits form, the trees should not lack moisture, and they will appreciate a mulch of decayed manure or garden compost to supply the necessary nitrogen and to prevent soil evaporation in summer. The fruits should not be removed until early December for, like celery, they should first be frosted. Store eye downwards on shelves in a dry airy room for about two to three weeks until they become soft, when they will make pleasant eating provided that they were not removed from the tree too early. When ripe, they should be consumed without delay. The medlar is considered to be the ideal fruit to have with port.

Varieties

DUTCH OR BROAD-LEAF DUTCH It makes a large spreading top and is a valuable shade and ornamental tree, attractive in blossom and in fruit with large, broad, dark-green leaves. The fruit ripens to russet brown and measures two inches across. It has a reasonable flavour.

NOTTINGHAM Also the common or wild medlar, making a medium-sized straggling tree with little ornamental value, although the russet-brown fruit has better flavour than the Dutch variety.

MULBERRY

In his *Sylva,* the English diarist John Evelyn devoted a chapter to the mulberry. It requires a rich, well-drained soil and an open sunny situation. In the standard form, it will make a pleasant shade giving tree, and it is rarely troubled by pest or disease. Plant between November and March, 25 feet apart, taking care not to damage the roots, neither must they be shortened at planting time for they will bleed if cut or damaged, causing the tree to lose vigour and eventually die. Make the soil firm about the roots, and in spring mulch with decayed manure or garden compost. The trees grow to 40 feet and have a life of several hundred years.

Standard and bush trees will require little pruning, but as the fruit is borne on spurs, nip back the young shoots to four buds in summer.

The mulberry is propagated by cuttings 15 inches long, taken in October and inserted into trenches containing sandy compost. They should be treated at the base with hormone powder before inserting. They will have rooted by early summer. Suckers which may appear around the base of the tree should not be used, as they may be those of the wild white mulberry *Morus alba,* on the leaves of which silkworms feed and on to which the black mulberry is often grafted.

The fruit is gathered when fully ripe and deep red in colour, late in summer, either by hand or by shaking the tree, which should be done with care

Disease

MULBERRY CANKER. This fungus, which attacks and destroys the young shoots, is the only troublesome disease. It usually attacks during cold, damp weather and mostly those trees situated in exposed gardens. Affected shoots must be removed and burnt without delay.

PEAR

Coming from the Mediterranean regions, the pear has never achieved the same popularity in Britain as the native apple. Demanding a warmer climate in which to reach perfection, it is, with the possible exception of the varieties 'Jargonelle' and 'Hessle', best grown in the southern half of England, and there should be given the warmest part of the garden, protected from cold winds. Also, as it blooms about a fortnight earlier than the apple, care must be taken in selecting a garden which is not troubled by late frosts. Frost hollows must be avoided as well as those gardens situated near to a river which will usually be troubled by late frosts. Wherever possible, grow apples in the open and pears against a warm, sunny wall where they will do well in the espalier form and may be grown to a height of 40 feet.

Rootstocks

Though rootstocks do play a part in the habit and cropping of pears, the choice is not nearly so wide as for apples. This is due partly to the fact that pears respond well to the already existing rootstocks, also to the fact that because this fruit is considered (in Britain at any rate) less important than the apple, nothing like as much interest has been taken in the pursuit of experiments on other rootstocks, which might possibly prove more satisfactory.

As long ago as 1667, Merlet, the French horticulturist, recommended working pears on the quince stock, as producing far better fruit than when worked on the then commonly used hawthorn. At the same time, Le Gendre made reference to this in detail in his *Manual of the Cultivation of Fruit Trees,* noting that the 'graft swells is eqally fast with the stock, with none of the others do'. The quince stock is still used, Quince A and B may be compared with Type I and II in apples, producing a large tree and taking longer to come into heavy bearing than the more dwarfing stocks. These two

stocks. These two stocks are usually employed for bush trees, for orchard or large garden planting, and, in good pear growing districts, should be planted 15-18 feet apart.

Quince C is that most frequently used, this being similar to Type IX for apples. It makes a dwarf tree and comes quickly into bearing, the weight of fruit, when in full bearing, almost bringing tree growth to a halt. This is the stock used for pyramids and for the cordon and espalier form. Pears which are normally slow to come into bearing, such as 'Doyenne du Comice' and 'Buerré Hardy', should always be worked on this stock.

Where a large standard tree is required, pears are worked on the pear stock and this stock is also used for those of weak habit.

With several varieties it has been found that they will not 'take' to the quince stock and need to be what is termed by the nurseryman 'double-worked'. This means that a variety known to 'take' well on quince, such as 'Beurré d'Amanlis' or 'Beurré Hardy', must first be used to intermediary, the incompatible variety then being grafted on to this, when the result will be completely satisfactory. 'William's Bon Chrétien', 'Dr Jules Guyot', 'Packham's Triumph', and 'Bristol Cross' require 'double-working'.

Pear trees on quince stock must be planted with the graft at least three inches above soil level, so that scion rooting does not occur. This would give additional vigour at the expense of cropping. Again, it should be remembered that pears on quince require a richer and more humus-laden soil than those on pear stock, which will tolerate and may even crop better where the soil is neither so deep nor so rich.

Pollination

As with apples, some pears are triploid varieties, and not only require a diploid pollinating variety flowering at the same time, but also a second diploid variety so that each can pollinate the other.

The following are triploids:

Beurré d'Amanlis	(E)
Catillac	(L)
Jargonelle	(E)
Pitmaston Duchess	(L)

From this it is seen that two are early flowering and two bloom late. With either then, it will be necessary to plant two early or late flowering diploids.

These pears bloom early:

Beurré Easter	(S.S)
Beurré Superfin	(S.F)
Conference	(S.F)
Doyenne D'Eté	(S.F)
Durondeau	(S.F)
Louise Bonne	(S.F)
Marguerite Marillat	(S.F)
Seckle	(S.S)

These pears bloom mid-season:

Beurré Bedford	(S.F)
Emile d'Heyst	(S.S)
Glou Morceau	(S.S)
Josephine Malines	(S.S)
Merton Pride	(S.F)
Packham's Triumph	(S.F)
Thompson's	(S.S)
William's Bon Chrétien	(S.F)

These pears bloom late:

Clapp's Favourite	(S.S)
Doyenne du Comice	(S.S)
Dr Jules Guyot	(S.F)
Fertility	(S.S)
Gorham	(S.F)
Hessle	(S.F)
Laxton's Superb	(S.F)
Marie Louise	(S.F)
Winter Nelis	(S.S)

Strangely with pears, several varieties are unable to pollinate each other though both may be in

RIGHT Pear 'Conference'

LEFT Pear 'Gorham' espalier trained

Grape 'Pirovano 14' growing out of doors

bloom together. The very fertile diploid, 'Conference', is unable to pollinate the triploid 'Beurré d'Amanlis', though both are in bloom at the same time. So do not plant them without another early flowering pollinator, such as 'Marguerite Marillat' or 'Durondeau', and expect to obtain a heavy crop as is so often done. Neither will 'Seckle' pollinate 'Louise Bonne', though both are partially self-fertile and in bloom together, early to mid-season; nor will 'Fondante D'Automne' pollinate 'Seckle', 'William's' or 'Louise Bonne'. So consider carefully before ordering your pear trees.

A number of varieties are self-fertile, and able to set their own pollen, but they will bear a much heavier crop if planted with other varieties in bloom at the same period.

Early and mid-season flowering varieties, and mid-season and late flowering may be planted together, and may be relied upon to pollinate satisfactorily.

Pruning

Everything that has been said about apple trees is much the same for pears, but here again we discover the name of each tree, and learn something of its habits before taking up the pruners.

Pears are divided into two sections, those with a vigorous upright habit, and those of a weaker and semi-weeping habit. In the former group are 'Comice' and 'Durondeau' and 'Clapp's Favourite'; of those with slender habit are 'Louise Bonne' and 'Beurré d'Amanlis'. The important thing in pruning is for the upright growers to have their buds facing outwards, while the slender, weeping growers should be pruned so that the buds, as far as possible, face in an upward direction. Most of the weepers are tip bearers and should be pruned but little, for they make only a few fruiting buds, but those of vigorous habit may need to have their spurs reduced to obtain fruit of size and quality. The same remarks about the tip bearers in pears also apply to the tip bearers of apples, e.g. 'Worcester Pearmain', 'St Edmund's Russet', 'Grenadier', and 'Discovery'. These trees will require but little pruning though every variety should be treated on its merits. Do not over-prune any tree; first try light pruning, then wait for the results. Never prune for pruning's sake, and a little at a time is far better, especially with established trees, than being too drastic, though 'Mr. Barker's Comice' pears are likely to disprove the old adage! First look at the trees, then try to imagine them in fruit, and remember that the aim is a healthy, well-balanced tree, one able to bear the maximum amount of the best quality fruit over as long a period of years as possible.

It should be noticed that each shoot or lateral will form both fruiting and wood foliage buds, the former being easily distinguished by their habit of appearing on short, woody stems, while the wood-making buds lie flat along the stem, are smaller, and of a pointed nature.

Harvesting and Storing

Pears must be given greater care in their picking than apples, for not only do they bruise more easily, but they will rapidly deteriorate on the tree if allowed to become over-ripe, or if subjected to adverse weather, such as a period of moisture or night frosts.

Generally a pear will be ready to gather when, upon lifting with the palm of the hand and exerting no pressure on the fruit, it readily parts from the spur. This is a better method than following the text book as to the correct ripening periods of the different varieties, for so much depends upon the season and upon the situation of the tree in the garden. Given a particularly warm summer with periods of prolonged sunshine, then pears will come to maturity before their usual time. But if the fruit does not readily part from the spur when lifted it means that it is still drawing nourishment from the tree. Yet equally important with the pear is not to allow it to become over-ripe, for not only will its

A 'Conference' pear, before and after summer pruning

keeping qualities badly deteriorate, but it will have lost much of its fragrance and flavour. The lifting test is more reliable than the colouring of the skin, for this depends so much on the soil, and if you wait for the fruits to attain a certain colouring they may have passed their best. In this respect, the best of all early pears, 'Laxton's Superb', must be gathered and eaten while still pale green, when it will part from the spurs upon lifting. To allow it to become a buttercup yellow colour, which it soon will if left on the tree, will result in its losing its flavour. Similarly 'William's Bon Chrétien', the canner's 'Bartlett Pear', will become dry and of a disagreeable flavour if allowed to hang too long.

All pears, whether to be eaten at once or to be stored, must be removed in the palm of the hand,

and carefully placed on a wooden tray which has been lined with cotton wool. Always gather the fruit when quite dry and store in a slightly warmer place than for apples. At all times pears like warmth, a temperature of 45°F suiting them best; an airy attic room, if dark, and a cupboard or drawer is better than a cellar or shed which will be colder. If placed in a cold room, pears will sweat badly and quickly lose quality. So that the fruits will not lose their bloom, the best method is to place them upright on a layer of cotton wool so that they are not quite touching. As with all stored fruit, keep each variety to itself.

Varieties

Though John Scott in his *Orchardist*, published in

1860, tells us that he then grew over eighteen hundred varieties of the pear at his fruit farm in Somerset, only a few are now planted commercially in England. It is felt, however, that because the commercial grower of pears is compelled to plant only those that produce the most outstanding fruit for size and flavour—to enable him to compete with importations from the Mediterranean countries where the climate is much more suitable for the pear—we have come to regard these one or two varieties as the only pears worth growing. This is far from being the case. There are numerous varieties much better suited to the amateur's garden than the temperamental 'Doyenne du Comice' and 'Seckle' and they will crop more readily, prove hardier, and be more resistant to disease. It is of course necessary to give detailed consideration to pollination, and in the past this has not been done, with disappointing results. As we have seen, those two magnificent pears, 'Laxton's Superb' and 'William's Bon Chrétien', so often planted together, are incompatible. But where one's garden receives its fair share of sunshine, there is no fruit to equal the pear, grown where it can be thoroughly ripened, but always it must be given a position where it may receive some sunshine, or else it is better not planted at all.

To Ripen July and August

DOYENNE D'ETÉ The first to ripen, late in July, its small yellow fruits being sweet and juicy, but it makes only a small weakly tree unless soil conditions suit it.

JARGONELLE It is of straggling habit, and is a triploid variety, hence the need for pollinators, but it is extremely hardy, is highly resistant to scab, and bears a heavy crop of long tapering fruit, with its own musky flavour. Excellent pollinators are 'Durondeau' and 'William's Bon Chrétien', the former ripening in October, the latter in September. Plant with them 'Laxton's Superb', and the huge 'Roosevelt' for Christmas, and you will have a succession of fruit.

LAXTON'S EARLY MARKET Though a new variety, this has already established itself as the best pear for late July, and, like all early apples and pears, should be eaten from the tree. The medium-sized fruit, with its yellow skin, flushed with scarlet, possesses a delicious perfume. It blooms early and in an exposed garden may be troubled by late frosts.

LAXTON'S SUPERB This is one of the best pears ever introduced, and makes superb eating if gathered mid-to-late August and allowed to stand 48 hours in a warm room before being eaten. But it must be harvested just as the green skin takes on a yellow tinge; if left later, the quality will have deteriorated badly. The great value of this pear is that though ripening early it blooms late; good in the bush form in a small garden, for it is of upright habit.

A 'Bon Chretien' pear tree, in full blossom. Grown as a fan on a cottage wall

To Ripen Early-Mid September

BEURRÉ D'AMANLIS Valuable for its hardiness. It makes a tree of vigorous, straggling habit, requiring plenty of room, and bears a medium-sized russeted fruit of rich perfume. Raised at Amanlis in France about 1795, it is a triploid, and should, be planted with 'Beurré Superfin' and 'Beurré Bedford'.

DR JULES GUYOT A valuable pear for less favourable gardens, for it blooms late yet crops heavily and acts as a good pollinator for most varieties. It bears a large fruit with yellow skin dotted with black, and should be eaten from the tree.

GORHAM A new American pear, very fertile, which makes a neat, upright tree. It is similar in size and colour to 'William's Bon Chrétien', the fruit retaining its pure white colour when bottled. Highly resistant to scab.

TRIOMPHE DE VIENNE This is one of those

hardy, reliable pears, now quite neglected. The fruit is not large but is of brilliant colouring and flavour. The tree is of dwarf habit and bears a large crop season after season. An excellent variety where those of more temperamental habit prove a failure.

WILLIAM'S BON CHRÉTIEN Possibly the best all-round pear ever introduced. It makes a strong growing yet compact tree, and bears a heavy, but not regular crop. Introduced into America about 1820 by Enoch Bartlett (hence its canning name), the pure white flesh is of a melting, buttery texture.

To Ripen Late September to Mid-October

BEURRÉ BEDFORD Making a neat, upright tree, ideal as a pyramid and bearing heavy crops of glossy primrose-yellow fruits, it is a self-fertile variety, and ideal for a small garden.

BEURRÉ HARDY Making a vigorous, upright tree, especially suited for orchard planting, this is a hardy variety, and a most reliable cropper. The fruit is unique in that the flesh is rose-tinted and also carries a delicate rose perfume.

BEURRÉ SUPERFIN This should be grown where 'Doyenne du Comice' proves difficult, for its golden fruit possesses almost the same quality and flavour. It is quite hardy, but blooms early and may suffer from frost.

BRISTOL CROSS This has quickly become a favourite. The fruit, with its bright yellow skin covered with russet, is juicy and sweet, while it crops heavily just before 'Conference'.

FONDANTE D'AUTOMNE It is hardy and crops regularly, remaining pale green when ripe, and is sweet and juicy with pronounced flavour.

LAXTON'S FOREMOST A magnificent pear for late September, and a fine exhibition variety, with its clear primrose-yellow skin. It is an upright grower and crops freely, the fruit having buttery flesh, in no way gritty. Ideal for the small garden, and crops well on a west wall.

MARGUERITE MARILLAT Probably the finest pear in its season. It is hardy and fertile, making a compact, upright tree. Its enormous golden fruits are flushed with scarlet and are sweet and juicy. A pear for every warm garden. Its foliage turns deep crimson in autumn.

MERTON PRIDE It has 'Williams' and 'Glou Morceau' for parents and is a tree of vigorous, upright habit. Its fruits attain good size and ripen green.

To Ripen Late October—End November

CONFERENCE Most valuable as a pollinator (except with 'Beurré d'Amanlis'), for all mid-season flowering pears, and bearing one of the most delicious of all fruits, its dark green skin being extremely russeted. It is reasonably hardy and no pear crops more regularly.

DOYENNE DU COMICE With its deliciously melting, cinnamon-flavoured flesh, this is the outstanding variety of all pears, but difficult to crop. It makes a spreading tree and must be given a warm position and a soil well enriched with humus. It likes its feet in moisture, its head in sunshine. Pollinated by 'Bristol Cross', 'Beurré Bedford' and 'Laxton's Superb'.

DURONDEAU Raised in 1811 by a Belgian bearing the same name, this makes a compact tree, and is extremely hardy. It likes plenty of moisture. If gathered at the end of September, the handsome golden fruit with its crimson cheek will keep until the end of November.

EMILE D'HEYST Extremely hardy but should be grown in bush form, on account of its spreading, weeping form. The 'Lane's Prince Albert' of the pear world. The richly flavoured fruit with its strong rose perfume should be eaten from the tree late in October, as it does not store well.

LAXTON'S RECORD One of the best November pears, which should be grown where some of the

An espalier-trained 'Merton Pride' pear

others prove difficult. The medium-sized fruit has a yellow skin, flushed with crimson and russet. The flesh is juicy and melting, with a powerful aromatic perfume.

LAXTON'S SATISFACTION A high quality pear with same parents as Superb. It is fertile, crops heavily, and bears a very large fruit of rich flavour. It makes a tree of vigorous but extremely upright habit.

LOUISE BONNE This pear is a strong grower, making a large well formed tree, and is a heavy cropper in the warmer districts. The green fruit, with its crimson flush, is of outstanding flavour. Grown at least 300 years ago.

PITMASTON DUCHESS The large golden-russeted fruit is exceptional flavour and a favourite for exhibition, but it is a shy bearer and too vigorous a grower for a small garden, and takes longer to come into bearing than most pears. It is also a triploid variety.

Ripe in December to January

GLOU MORCEAU To ripen correctly it must be given a warm, sunny position. It acts as a good companion and pollinator for 'Comice'. The fruit is extremely juicy, and free from grit, and should be eaten early December.

PACKHAM'S TRIUMPH A New Zealand introduction which has already proved itself on a commercial scale in Britain, the fruit keeping in perfect condition from mid-October until late in December. It is a vigorous grower and a free bearer, the fruit being similar in both appearance and flavour to 'Comice', and without that pear's difficulties in culture.

ROOSEVELT This is the largest of all pears, and a most handsome fruit in cultivation, the smooth golden-yellow skin being tinted with salmon pink. It is a vigorous but erect grower and free bearer, the fruit being at its best in December.

SANTA CLAUS For eating in the New Year, this is one of the best pears. The fruits are almost as large as 'Roosevelt', of delicious flavour, and with an attractive, dull crimson russeted skin. The tree is of vigorous but upright habit, and is a free bearer, proving, with its resistance to scab, extremely useful in districts of moist climate.

WINTER NELIS Exactly the same remarks may be used for this variety as for 'Glou Morceau', as to its culture. It makes only a small fruit, but is flavour is outstanding, rich and melting, having the perfume of the rose, and will store until February.

Ripe February to April

BERGAMOTTE D'ESPEREN This variety should be given the warmth of a wall to ripen and mature its fruit, which with its pale yellow skin is rich and sweet until March.

BEURRÉ EASTER The richly musk-scented fruit will store in perfect condition until Easter. It is hardy and a heavy cropper, but requires careful culture throughout.

CATILLAC A late bloomer, vigorous grower, and extremely hardy, cropping heavily and requiring plenty of room. The huge crimson-brown fruit should not be harvested until November. Carefully stored, it will keep until May. It is used chiefly for stewing, but will make pleasant eating during spring. It is a triploid, and should be planted with 'Beurré Hardy' and 'Dr Jules Guyot' for pollination. At least 300 years old.

JOSEPHINE DE MALINES It bears a heavy crop of small though deliciously flavoured fruits, at their best during February. It is a hardy variety, but prefers the warmth of a south or west wall if planted in the north. It is a regular bearer, but is of rather weeping habit, not always easy to manage. Raised in Belgium by Major Esperen.

OLIVIER DE SERRES Raised at Rouen a century ago, this little-known pear possesses fine keeping qalities. The fruit is deep olive coloured, covered with patches of fawn, the flesh being sugary and juicy with 'a savoury perfume', to quote Scott. It makes a small tree.

Hardy varieties in order of ripening:

Laxton's Superb	Beurré Hardy
Jargonelle	Durondeau
Dr Jules Guyot	Emile d'Heyst
William's Bon Chrétien	Catillac
Beurré d'Amanlis	Josephine de Malines

Pears of spreading or weeping habit:

Beurré d'Amanlis	Emile d'Heyst
Catillac	Josephine de Malines

Varieties of dwarf habit:

Beurré Bedford	Laxton's Superb
Beurré Superfin	Olivier de Serres
Dr Jules Guyot	William's Bon Chrétien
Laxton's Foremost	

Varieties requiring warm conditions:

Bergamotte d'Esperen	Olivier de Serres
Doyenne du Comice	Thompson's
Glou Morceau	Winter Nelis
Marie Louise	

QUINCE

The quince is properly *Cydonia oblonga,* and to be successful it requires a moist, heavy soil when it will bear large elongated fruits and will live to a great age, growing twisted and gnarled to a height of only 12-15 feet and needing little attention. But the fruit will ripen successfully only in a really warm garden.

The quince is self-fertile and begins cropping when four to five years of age. It is propagated by stools or suckers which are removed from around the plant with a sharp spade and grown on as standards, being planted about 18 feet apart in a sunny position. Apart from the removal of dead wood, it will require little pruning over the years but will appreciate a yearly mulch of decayed manure and humus such as clearings from ditches.

The highly flavoured fruit is gathered at the end of October when quite dry and stored on a layer of cotton wool in a dry, frost-free room until fully ripened, the flesh then being deep golden-yellow. If carefully stored, it will keep until Christmas.

With its white flowers and dark green foliage, felted on the underside, the quince is a most ornamental tree and is most suitable for planting in a corner of the lawn, for it remains compact with the minimum of attention. It will also do well on the bank of a stream or pond. Its fruit makes delicious jam.

Varieties

CHAMPION An old variety coming quickly into bearing and bearing large apple-shaped fruits which ripen to a deep golden colour.

MEECH'S PROLIFIC An American variety, noted for its earliness and regular cropping; the smooth-skinned fruit ripens to pale yellow and is of delicious flavour.

PORTUGAL The best for all purposes, bearing heavily, the large oblong fruits ripening early to deep orange while the flavour is outstanding.

3 Stone Fruits

PLUMS AND GAGES

No fruit is quite so rich and delicious as the plum, expecially those possessing Greengage blood. They have a juicy, almost treacle-like sweetness, and a long period of maturity from late July until November, when several varieties will still be hanging in the trees. Others may be stored until that time and possibly longer.

For a garden likely to be troubled by frosts it will be wiser to plant late flowering apples, damsons, and the very latest of the plums to bloom, for as a general rule the plum is the first of all fruits to open its bloom at the beginning of April. For this reason, plums planted commercially are always the most unreliable of all fruits, for they either escape frosts, and crop so abundantly that the price of fresh fruit is uneconomical to the grower or they may be badly damaged by frosts, when there is little fruit available. Where frosts prove troublesome, such as where the land is low lying, or perhaps close to a river, then all but the very latest flowering plums should be avoided, and these should be given the shelter and protection of a warm, sunny wall.

Plums do not require such a large amount of sunshine as pears, and provided they can be given frost protection they will ripen well on a west or east wall, so leaving the southerly positions for the pears, with the apples being planted in the more open and exposed parts of the garden.

Growing Against a Wall

Plums do better as bush trees than as standards, and in the fan-shaped form rather than the horizontal form which suits the pear best. Where planted in a small garden, apples should be planted as cordons, pears as espaliers, and plums as fan-shaped trees against a wall. This is not only the most reliable method, but also the most economical, for a wall plum, well supplied with moisture and nitrogen, will soon cover an area ten feet high and a similar distance in width.

Suitable varieties will depend upon the aspect and district, the plums being more hardy than the gages, while there are also plums more hardy than others, and the selection should be made accordingly, planting the late flowering plums and gages in a more open situation, with the more tender and choice dessert varieties against a wall. So many walls are clothed in uninteresting ivy when they might be growing delicious fruit, but with wall trees it must be remembered that they must never lack moisture. Lack of humus and moisture at the roots is the cause of so many giving disappointing crops. A wall, especially where it receives some sun, will bring out the flavour to its maximum, but if the trees are not supplied with abundant summer moisture the fruit will remain small, the flesh dry.

The plum will come quickly into bearing in the fan-form, and is in no way troubled by biennial bearing as are many apples, neither does it require

Plums 'Cambridge Gage'. Gages are not grown as often as they used to be but are regaining popularity

the same attention to pruning as either the apple or pear. It bears the bulk of its fruit on the new wood, and, apart from the removal of any dead wood, the pruners are better left in the garden shed. Excessive pruning, for pruning's sake, and especially in the dormant period, will cause untold harm by 'bleeding'. This is something from which all stone fruits suffer.

All dead and decayed wood should be removed and burnt by mid-July each year, and this, together with any shortening of unduly long shoots, should be done early in spring, just when the trees are coming into life after their winter rest. At this time any cuts will quickly heal over.

Pollination

As with apples, the most richly flavoured plums and gages usually require a pollinator, especially where the connoisseur's plum, 'Coe's Golden Drop', has been used as a parent, for its blossoms are sterile and will not pollinate each other. About half the most popular plums possess self-sterile blossom and require a pollinator, while the rest are self-fertile and will, unlike apples and pears, bear a crop entirely without any pollinator. Some of these, however, are only partly self-fertile, and will set heavier crops with a pollinator flowering at the same time. Again, plum pollination is less complicated, in that the blossom period of the entire range of plums covers only about 18–19 days, and except for the very latest to bloom, such as 'Marjorie's Seedling' and 'Pond's Seedling', most will overlap, and so the flowering periods may be classed as Early and Late for pollinating purposes. It may be said that the early flowering self-fertile varieties will pollinate the early flowering sterile varieties, and the same with those which bloom late. It is therefore a more simple matter than when considering apples, pears and cherries, where many varieties do not prove suitable pollinators, though in bloom at the same time. Of all plums, only the following in no way overlap, or only by a day or so, and those of group (a) should not be relied upon to pollinate those of (b) and vice versa:

Early (a)	*Late (b)*
Bryanston Gage	Belle de Louvain
Count Althann's Gage	Czar
Jefferson	Late Transparent Gage
Monarch	Marjorie's Seedling
President	Oullin's Gage
Warwickshire Drooper	Pershore

All plums and gages remain in bloom, unless damaged by frost, for exactly ten days, a shorter period than any other fruit, and those of group (a), the first to bloom, will have almost finished when those of group (b), the last to bloom, commence to flower.

It should be said that President is incompatible as a pollinator to 'Cambridge Gage', though both are in bloom at the same time.

Unfortunately many gardeners, after giving careful consideration to the selection of suitable varieties for various soils and climates, do not take the pollinator factor into consideration; it is pure luck if the self-fertile varieties are planted, and where self-sterile varieties fail to set their fruit, this is blamed on the soil, climate, or even upon the nurseryman. With plums, pollination may be divided into two sections, those that bloom early to mid-season, and those in bloom mid-season to late:

S.S=*Self-Sterile* S.F=*Self-Fertile*

Early Flowering

Black Prince (S.S)
Blue Tit (S.F)
Coe's Golden Drop (S.S)
Early Laxton (S.S)
Early Prolific (P.S.F)
Jefferson (S.S)
Monarch (S.F)
President (S.S)
Thames Cross (S.F)
Victoria (S.F)
Warwickshire Drooper (S.F)

Late Flowering

Angelina Burdett (S.F)	Marjorie's Seedling (S.F)
Belle de Louvain (S.F)	Pershore (S.F)
Czar (S.F)	Pond's Seedling (S.S)
Giant Prune (S.F)	Severn Cross (P.S.F)
Kirke's Blue (S.S)	White Magnum Bonum (S.F)
Laxton's Delicious (S.S)	

Though the self-fertile varieties will set fruit with their own pollen, they will set much heavier crops when planted with varieties in bloom at the same period.

Soil Conditions

Whereas a far greater number of dessert apples and pears have been planted in Britain this century as against those for culinary use, the opposite is the case with plums, the greater percentage such as 'Czar', 'Yellow Pershore', and 'Belle de Louvain', having been planted for the canning and jam industries. The result is that if we wish to enjoy those richer-flavoured plums and gages, we must grow them ourselves on suitably prepared soil.

Plums like a heavy loam, and John Scott in his *Orchardist* says 'plums succeed best in strong, clay soils, mixed with a proportion of loam. On such soils the plum reaches the highest perfection in the shortest possible time'. A soil retentive of moisture is the secret of success with plums—one continually enriched with nitrogen preferably of an organic nature.

Light soils should have large quantities of shoddy or strawy farmyard manure incorporated at planting time and especially when planting wall trees. A liberal mulch of an organic manure, rich in nitrogen, should always be given in April each year. Where this is unobtainable, give one ounce of sulphate of ammonia to each tree at the same time, and immediately after any pruning has been done.

Especially with wall trees and with recently planted trees in the open, artificial watering should be done whenever necessary during a dry summer.

Though several varieties, such as 'Pond's Seedling' and the old greengage, will crop well and remain healthy on a chalk laden soil, most other varieties soon show, like pears, signs of chlorosis and never bear well. When there is a reasonable depth to the soil, this may be largely overcome by working in plenty of humus-forming manure. Under opposite conditions, where there is almost a complete absence of lime in the soil, the two most tolerant varieties are 'Czar' and 'Victoria', for as long as the soil is heavy and not waterlogged they will bear well. Shoddy and composted straw should be added where the soil proves excessively heavy and sticky. 'Czar', possibly the most accommodating of all fruit trees, will also bear abundantly in a light, sandy soil that contains a very small percentage of loam.

One may ask: what weight of fruit is to be expected from a 20-year bush tree, growing in an average soil, and being constantly mulched with organic nitrogenous manures? Taking good years with bad, and a wide selection, the average should be about 40 lb per tree, with 'Victoria', 'Czar' and 'Pershore' as high as 50-60 lb, and with 'Coe's Golden Drop' and 'Kirke's Blue' as low as 8-10 lb per tree but still worth growing for their delicious fruit. However, where given favourable conditions, when for instance, they are planted against a sunny wall in a southern garden, with their roots well supplied with moisture and nitrogen the shy bearers will crop more heavily, but there may not be a marked difference with the others.

Propagation and Rootstocks

The choice of rootstock is not large, and generally bush and fan-trained trees are grown on what is known as the common plum and Brompton stock, and standard trees for large gardens or orchards on the Myrobolan stock. The latter is generally used for the heavy cropping varieties, such as 'Czar' and 'Monarch'.

Owing to the incidence of gumming and the chances of introducing disease, plums are budded rather than grafted. Budding is done in July, for plums and cherries, the bud being removed with a strip of bark, cut out with the pruning knife. This is then fixed against the wood of the selected stock, into which a cut in the bark has been made six inches from the base. The bark on both sides of the cut is carefully lifted from the cambium layer, and into this the bud is fixed. It is held in position by tying with raffia, leaving only the actual bud exposed. In from four to five weeks the union should have taken place, when the raffia is removed. The following March the stock is cut back to within one inch of the bud, which will grow away to form the tree.

The gages and plums in the artificial forms are mostly budded on to the common plum or Brompton stocks. The varieties 'President', 'Czar' and 'Marjorie's Seedling' however, are incompatible with the common plum stock and so are usually budded on to the Myrobolan. The common plum makes a robust tree, resistant to silver leaf, and so always used for 'Victoria' and 'Pond's Seedling', while it is generally used for the less vigorous varieties such as 'Coe's Golden Drop'.

For a small garden the Brompton stock is probably the best, for the trees grow steadily but come quickly into bearing; they send up few suckers, which is an important consideration for the amateur, and require little attention apart from the occasional removal in spring of any dead wood.

At one time the Common Mussel stock was widely used, but the trees on this stock require copious amounts of water and tend to sucker badly. With this stock the trees come more quickly into bearing than on any other, but like Type MIX with apples, they bear abundantly for a time and then lose vigour.

Several of the gages, in particular 'Oullin's Golden' and 'Count Althann's', are incompatible with the Myrobolan stock; several others, such as 'Yellow Pershore', crop well and are generally planted on their own roots, but being slow to form suckers they cannot be used for propagating other plums on a commercial scale.

Pruning

Spring is the best time to carry out any pruning of plums, just when the buds are beginning to burst, for it is at this time that the wounds quickly heal over and almost no 'bleeding' occurs, which not only reduces the vigour of the tree but provides an entrance for the dreaded Silver Leaf disease, the fungus deriving its nourishment from the cells of the tree, thereby greatly affecting its constitution. Early autumn pruning, which may be carried out on early fruiting varieties when the crop has been cleared, is permissible, but all cutting should be done between the end of April and mid-September, for during the winter the cuts will remain 'open' for dangerously long periods.

In any case, plums require very little pruning; the trees will form their fruit buds throughout the whole length of the younger branches, especially with the standard trees which are established; thinning of overcrowded growth either in May or September, depending upon lateness of crop, will be all that is required. A well-grown plum tree will be able to carry a much larger proportion of wood than will any other fruit tree; as with apples and to a lesser extent, pears drastic reduction, even of neglected trees, must never be performed.

When renovating a neglected tree, it may be advisable to cut away with the pruning saw one or two large and partially-decayed branches. If so, this should be done during May, a time when the large cut will heal rapidly and the energies of the tree may be directed to the remaining wood. With plums it is even more important to cut out any wood close to the stem from which it is being removed so that the wound will heal rapidly and completely. But before making any cuts, see if the tree can be renewed in vigour by removing some of the small, thin wood which plums make in quantity. Possibly root pruning will be more satisfactory than the cutting back of any large branches.

Removal of Suckers

One of the greatest troubles with plums is the continued formation of suckers at the roots. If left, they will utilize much of the nourishment needed for the proper functioning of the tree. These should be removed whenever the roots of the tree are pruned, and must be cut away right from their source, otherwise they will continue to grow again. It is first necessary to remove the soil from around the tree to expose the roots. It will be found that the suckers generally arise from a point in the roots just below the point where the scion has been grafted on to the rootstock. This calls for the utmost care in removing the soil right up to the scion, and then in cutting out the sucker shoot with a sharp knife. For bush or standard trees it is advisable to ring round half the tree one year and to complete the removal of suckers and vigorous roots the following year. It is essential to pack the soil well round the roots when the work has been done or there will be the chance of the tree becoming uprooted by strong winds.

Treatment of Fan-Trained Trees

In renovating fan-trained trees, in which form the plum crops abundantly, more pruning will be necessary. This should take the form of pinching back shoots in mid-summer and in removing completely all unwanted new wood. A number of young growths may be pinched back between mid-June and mid-July to form a new spur system; these will need to be cut further back, in the same way as described for apples and pears. Plant early in September rather than in winter. Then by degrees the old spurs may be drastically reduced to make way for the new ones. In conjunction with the shoot thinning of wall trees, root pruning should be given every three or four years. This will prevent excessive wood growth.

The formation of a bush and standard form of plum tree takes the same lines as described for apples and pears. Planted in the maiden form they may be formed as required, the yearly pruning consisting of pinching back the new wood to form fruiting buds.

Forming the Fan-Trained Tree

Both plums and cherries crop abundantly in this form, all varieties proving suitable, though naturally some are more vigorous than others and will require more frequent pruning at the roots. The method of forming the fan is to cut back the maiden to an upward bud. This should leave on the lower portion of the stem two buds, which will break and form arms. Unsuitably placed buds should be removed, and any not breaking must be nicked or notched as previously described for the formation of espaliers.

After the previous season's growth they are pruned back to 18 inches and the leader or central shoot is cut back to two buds. It is from these buds that the fan-shaped tree is formed.

Canes are used for tying in the shoots so that they may be trained to the required shape. As growth continues, each shoot may be cut back the following spring to two more buds which will complete the shape of the tree, though canes will be needed until the shoots have taken on the required form.

Cultural treatment will henceforth consist of cutting back a third of the new wood formed by the branches each May, and the pinching back of all side growths. The shoots will continue to break and, where there is room, a number may be tied in to continue the fan-like shape.

The lack of a really dwarfing rootstock for producing plums and gages, so as to make them suitable for planting in the small garden, has perhaps contributed more than any other factor to the

A fan-trained 'Early Laxton' plum

amateur gardener's lack of interest in this fruit in recent years.

The summer-pruned pyramid, budded on to the semi-dwarfing St Julien A rootstock, would appear to be the most suitable for small garden planting. One-year-old trees are planted ten feet apart in November. This will allow them to become well anchored by the time pruning commences about April 1st, when the trees are cut back to about four feet six inches above ground level and the laterals or side shoots are pinched back to nine inches from the main stem. Then about mid-July, the trees are again pruned, the laterals being shortened to six inches and the main branch shoots to about nine inches, making the cut to an outward pointing bud to encourage the tree to form horizontal branches so that the top and centre remain more open. In April of its second year the leader shoot is shortened to about one-third, and this is repeated each year until the tree reaches the required height. In early July the laterals are again pruned back, and in this way the tree is able to concentrate on fruit production rather than make excessive wood. It will have formed the minimum amount of wood necessary to support a heavy crop.

Where the garden is very small, only those plums should be grown which will naturally make only a small tree. 'Early Laxton' is one, and it is the first to fruit. This is followed by 'Goldfinch' and 'Utility', both Laxton introductions; then 'Jefferson' (which the others will pollinate) and lastly 'Count Althann's Gage' which ripens about October 1st. In general, most of the gages make more compact growth than the plums and are especially suited to the modern small garden.

Varieties

Plums

Ripe Late July and Early August

BLACK PRINCE Ripe before the last days of July, it makes a small tree, yet is a huge cropper, the small black velvety fruit having a true damson flavour, delicious for tarts and for bottling. It is extremely resistant to silver leaf disease.

BLUE TIT It bears a blue fruit with the true greengage flavour and is one of the best early plums for dessert. Makes a small, compact tree and is very fertile.

CZAR Makes a fine orchard tree with its vigorous habit, yet it is compact and a most reliable cropper. Its blossom appears late; it is very resistant to frost and so it bears heavily in cold gardens, and especially in heavy soils. The fruit is of a bright shade of purple, of medium size, and is useful both for cooking and for dessert. Ready for use at the beginning of August.

EARLY LAXTON The first plum to ripen, towards the end of July. The small, golden-yellow fruit carries a rosy-red flush, and is sweet and juicy. It blooms early and is pollinated by 'River's Early Prolific' or 'Laxton's Cropper'. It makes a small tree and is valuable for a small garden.

RIVER'S EARLY PROLIFIC Making a small but spreading tree, this is a good companion to 'Early Laxton', for it is grown chiefly for cooking, the small purple fruit possessing a rich damson-like flavour. Pollinated by the early flowering gage, 'Denniston's Superb', Hogg says, 'rarely ever misses a crop'.

Ripe Mid-August to Month End

GOLDFINCH To ripen mid-August, this is possibly the best of all plums. It has 'Early Transparent Gage' blood, and is eqally delicious, the golden-yellow fruit being sweet and juicy. It makes a compact tree and bears consistently heavy crops.

LAXTON'S BEAUTIFUL Has 'Victoria' as a parent and bears a similar fruit, but not quite as good a flavour. It bottles better than any early plum, and should also be used for jam rather than for dessert. It makes a large, vigorous tree and bears enormous crops.

PERSHORE (YELLOW) Used almost entirely for canning, bottling and jam. It makes a bright yellow fruit with firm flesh. It is valuable for a frosty garden, for it is very late flowering.

UTILITY One of the most handsome plums and a fine all-round variety. It bears a large exhibition plum of bright purple-red. Early flowering, it may be pollinated by most of the early blooming plums, especially 'Denniston's Superb'. Matures between 'Goldfinch' and 'Victoria'.

VICTORIA The most widely grown plum of all. Extremely vigorous, it is the most self-fertile of all plums; it is frost resistant, crops well in all forms, and is used for every purpose. Its only weak point is that it is often troubled by silver leaf disease. Ripe at the end of August. Like 'Czar', it crops well in clay soils.

Ripe Early to Mid-September

ANGELINA BURDETT Known to early eighteenth-century gardeners and much too good to become extinct, yet little propagated. The large fruit is of deep purple, speckled with brown. It is ripe at the very beginning of September, but will hang for a fortnight when, as Hogg says, 'it forms a perfect sweetmeat'. It will also keep for a fortnight after removing, and is extremely hardy and a regular bearer.

BELLE DE LOUVAIN Of Belgian origin, it makes a large tree and is slow to come into bearing, but for bottling and cooking it is most valuable.

EDWARDS A new American variety, it makes a large, spreading tree and crops regularly. The fruit is blue-black, the flesh creamy-yellow, like an improved 'Belle de Louvain' and sweeter. In bloom with 'Czar'.

GIANT PRUNE Raised from 'Pond's Seedling', to which it is similar in size, colour and flavour. It blooms late.

JEFFERSON Almost like a gage in its flavour and rich dessert quality, the pale green flesh being sweet asd juicy. Raised in the USA, it blooms early and requires an early flowering pollinator such as 'Denniston's Superb'. It makes a compact, upright tree, ideal for a small garden, but should be planted in the more favourable districts. The fruit is pale green, flushed with pink.

KIRKE'S BLUE To follow immediately after 'Jefferson', this is an equally delicous plum for dessert, its large violet fruits being sweet and juicy. 'Czar' and 'Marjorie's Seedling' are the two best pollinators.

LAXTON'S CROPPER This is an excellent all-purpose plum for September, the large black fruit hanging for several weeks when ripe. It is a strong grower and bears a heavy crop in all districts. Will store well.

POND'S SEEDLING It makes a large tree and is valuable for cold gardens, in that it blooms late. The rose-crimson fruit is large and handsome, and if not of the very best dessert qualities, it is good. Crops well in a chalk-laden soil.

THAMES CROSS A new plum bearing large pure golden-yellow fruit. Has 'Coe's Golden Drop' as a parent, and the flavour is similar.

WARWICKSHIRE DROOPER Making a large, vigorous tree with drooping branches, this is an excellent all-purpose plum, where room is available. May be described as a later and improved Pershore. The yellow fruit is shaded with scarlet and grey.

WHITE MAGNUM BONUM Hogg describes it as a 'culinary variety highly esteemed for preserving'. It blooms very late and is valuable in this respect, while the pale yellow fruit is borne in abundance. It makes a huge, spreading tree and does well in a heavy soil.

Ripe Late September and Early October

COE'S GOLDEN DROP It blooms very early and should be given the protection of a warm wall. It also likes a soil containing plenty of nitrogenous humus. It bears a large fruit of quite exceptional flavour, pale yellow, speckled with crimson. At its best about the beginning of October, the fruit will keep until the month end. With its rich apricot flavour and almost treacle sweetness, it is the most delicious of all plums. It makes a spreading tree, requires an early flowering pollinator, and is a shy bearer. This is the 'Cox's Orange' or 'Comice' of the plum world. 'Denniston's Superb' is the best pollinator.

LAXTON'S DELICIOUS This is one of the finest of dessert plums, the deep yellow fruit, flushed with red, being juicy and deliciously sweet. It has 'Coe's Golden Drop' as a parent, but is a much better cropper, especially as a wall tree. Like its parent, the fruit may be kept several weeks if harvested about the third week in September. A vigorous grower, it blooms late. 'Oullin's Golden Gage' or 'Marjorie's Seedling' are suitable pollinators.

LAXTON'S OLYMPIA Making a large, spreading tree, it blooms late and ripens its fruit in early October. The coal-black fruit is of medium size, is sweet, and possesses a flavour all its own, similar to preserved plums from the Mediterranean. It bears a very heavy crop.

MARJORIE'S SEEDLING Extremely fertile and of vigorous upright habit, it makes a large tree. It is the last to come into bloom, and the latest to ripen its large crimson-purple fruit. Ready for gathering at the end of September, the fruit will hang until the end of October, when it may be used for all purposes.

MONARCH Similar in all respects to 'Marjorie's Seedling', the tree habit, quality and colour of the fruit being the same. But it must be considered inferior to 'Marjorie's Seedling' in that it blooms very early and is frequently damaged by frost; neither does the fruit hang so well.

PRESIDENT An excellent dessert plum, being large, rich purple, with deep yellow flesh, juicy and sweet. Makes a large, spreading tree. It blooms very early and requires a pollinator.

SEVERN CROSS This is the latest of all dessert plums, for it hangs well into October, and is valuable where a succession of fruit is required. It makes a tall, vigorous tree, the fruit being golden-yellow, flushed and spotted with pink, extremely juicy and of good flavour.

Extremely hardy plants:	*Long hanging plums:*
Angelina Burdett	Angelina Burdett
Czar	Laxton's Delicious
Early Prolific	Marjorie's Seedling
Laxton's Delicious	Pond's Seedling
Pershore	Severn Cross
Pond's Seedling	
Victoria	

Plums of vigorous, spreading habit:

Coe's Golden Drop	Pond's Seedling
Czar	President
Laxton's Bountiful	Warwickshire Drooper
Laxton's Olympia	White Magnum Bonum

Plums of dwarf, compact habit:

Black Prince	Jefferson
Early Laxton	Kirke's Blue
Goldfinch	

Varieties

Gages

To Ripen Early Mid-August

DENNISTON'S SUPERB Really a gage-plum hybrid, but possesses the true gage flavour and is extremely hardy and fertile. Like 'James Grieve' among apples, this plum acts as a pollinator for more plums than any other variety. It was raised in New York in 1835, it blooms early mid-season, and can set heavy crops without a pollinator. It is of vigorous habit in all soils, and ripens its green fruit, flushed with crimson, by mid-August. One of the best of all plums or gages.

EARLY GAGE This is the first of the gages to ripen, at the beginning of August. The tree is vigorous and healthy, and when pollinated ('Denniston's Superb') bears heavily, the amber-yellow fruit possessing a rich but delicate flavour.

EARLY TRANSPARENT It makes a dwarf tree and is able to set a heavy crop with its own pollen. It blooms early and ripens its fruit during mid-August, when the pale apricot skin is so thin as to show the stone. The richly flavoured fruit possesses a distinct fragrance when ripe.
OULLIN'S GOLDEN GAGE 'Ripe mid-August and a remarkably fine dessert variety', wrote Dr Hogg. Like 'Denniston's Superb', this seems to be a hybrid raised in France a century ago. It is valuable in that it is one of the latest gages to bloom, and though good for dessert it is one of the best for bottling and jam.

Ripe Late August to Early September
CAMBRIDGE GAGE It bears a fruit similar to the true 'Greengage', but is hardier and is a heavier cropper. Flowers late.
LATE TRANSPARENT Making a small, dwarf tree, and setting a heavy crop with its own pollen, it possesses similar characteristics to 'Early Transparent', though it blooms later. 'Laxton's Gage' is a pollinator. The bright yellow fruit is speckled with red, the flavour being rich, almost peach-like.
LAXTON'S GAGE The result of 'Greengage' × 'Victoria', it makes a large, spreading tree and blooms quite late. The yellowish-green fruit, which possesses a rich flavour, is ripe at the end of August. It is a heavy bearer in most soils.

Ripe Mid-September to Early October
BRYANSTON The fruit is ripe mid-September, pale green, speckled with crimson, and with a russeting nearest the sun. It makes a large, spreading tree, is early flowering and, with 'Victoria' as a pollinator, which is essential, it crops profusely.
COUNT ALTHANN'S GAGE One of the most richly flavoured of all the gages it makes a large but compact tree, blooms late and ripens its fruit towards the end of September. Introduced from Belgium a century ago, the fruit is unusual for a gage in that it is dark crimson, speckled with brown. Should be eaten as soon as ripe. Must have a pollinator, when it will crop heavily.
GOLDEN TRANSPARENT Like all the 'Transparents', it makes a dwarf tree, is self-fertile and blooms late. The fruit ripens early October, the last of the gages to mature.
GREENGAGE At its best during September, depending upon the locality, when its greenish-yellow fruit is rich and melting, and faintly aromatic. Known to early eighteenth-century gardeners, it is a shy bearer unless pollinated with 'Victoria'. Should be grown in a sheltered garden.
REINE CLAUDE DE BAVAY Hogg describes it as a 'first class plum of exquisite flavour'. It is ripe about early October and will hang for several weeks. It makes a neat, compact tree and is self-fertile, blooming very late. The richly flavoured fruit is large and of almost orange colour, speckled with white. The best gage for a small garden.

Early Flowering:

Bryanston (S.S)	Early Transparent (S.F)
Denniston's Superb (S.F)	Greengage (S.S)
Early Gage (S.S)	

Late Flowering:

Cambridge Gage (S.S)	Laxton's Gage (S.F)
Count Althann's Gage (S.S)	Oullin's Golden Gage (S.F)
Golden Transparent (S.F)	Reine Claude de Bavay (S.F)
Late Transparent (S.F)	

Very late flowering gages and plums, to miss late frost:

Belle de Louvain	Marjorie's Seedling
Czar	Oullin's Golden Gage
Late Transparent Gage	Pond's Seedling

Gages of dwarf, compact habit:

Early Transparent	Late Transparent
Golden Transparent	Oullin's Golden Gage
Greengage	Reine Claude de Bavay

CHERRY PLUM

The Myrobalan or cherry plum, so called on account of its small fruit, is used as a rootstock for certain plums and is a valuable tree (like the damson) to act as a hedge or windbreak. It grows into a wide, round head with plenty of rich green foliage which it retains well into winter. The flowers appear early, are quite immune to frost and are self-fertile. The fruits are either red or yellow, depending upon variety, and though small, are pleasantly sweet and juicy when stewed and used in tarts and flans or bottled, retaining their shape and being more like cherries than plums. Uncooked, they are sour and tasteless.

The new hybrid 'Trailblazer' has purplish-brown foliage and bears, in August, juicy crimson fruits of good size. It is the result of a cross between the Japanese and cherry plum and has hybrid vigour in that it grows 15 feet tall.

Plant the cherry plums six to eight feet apart as a windbreak. They usually do better in a well-drained limestone soil. They are worthy of growing if only for their blossom and hardiness, but, as with crab apples, their fruit is an added bonus.

DAMSON AND BULLACE

The damson, a native of the country around Damascus, hence its name, remains comparatively neglected. Yet it is so hardy that it could well be used much more for providing a shelter or windbreak for fruit trees in an exposed district. Or for that matter, these hardy fruits may be planted as a substitute for the earlier flowering plums. As to soil, damsons will crop abundantly in a thin soil, and they flourish in abundant moisture, as do plums. They should also be given a nitrogenous dressing each year, preferably in spring. Damsons bloom later than plums, and neither frosts nor the strongest of cold winds trouble them. Retaining their foliage right through autumn, they provide valuable protection for other fruit trees.

Possessing a flavour and fragrance all their own, delicious when used for tarts and pies and for making jam, also bottling to perfection and retaining their flavour for several years, the damsons are one of the most valuable fruits.

With the exception of 'Farleigh Prolific', all will set fruit with their own pollen, but as with most fruits, where two or more varieties, possibly for succession, are planted together, heavier crops result.

These hardy fruits may be planted about the garden where others would not grow well, or they may be planted in a hedge-row, or as a shelter belt, their silver-grey blossom being most ornamental, and their fruit most attractive throughout autumn.

DAMSONS

BRADLEY'S KING It is extremely hardy, blooms late and is a heavy bearer, besides making a vigorous tree, the wood not being brittle. It bears its fruit mid-September and is almost as large and richly flavoured as the 'Shropshire Prune', being of an attractive dark crimson colour, while the foliage takes on the autumnal tints usually associated with the pear.

FARLEIGH PROLIFIC This is the most prolific bearer of all, if given a pollinator, e.g. 'Bradley's King'. Known also as 'Crittenden's' or the cluster damson, its fruit hanging in huge clusters, it is the first of the autumn damsons to mature, ready for use early September. Its small, coal-black tapering fruits make superb jam. It forms a small compact tree.

MERRYWEATHER With its large, round blue-black fruit, it may easily be mistaken for a plum, yet it possesses the rich flavour and fragrance of a true damson. It makes a large spreading tree and blooms quite early, so should be planted where late frosts are not troublesome. Yet it is extremely hardy and bears a heavy crop, which will hang through October.

RIVER'S EARLY This is the only summer-fruiting damson, ready for use early August. It blooms very early and should not be planted where frosts prove troublesome. In more favourable gardens it sets a heavy crop and makes a compact tree.

SHROPSHIRE PRUNE Though for flavour its fruit is the most outstanding of all, it makes but a small, slender tree, and crops only lightly unless planted in a heavy loam, well supplied with nitrogen. At the end of September it bears a large, oval fruit which is suitable to use as dessert when fully ripe. Also known as the Westmorland damson.

BULLACES

LANGLEY BULLACE Making a compact, upright tree, it ripens its fruit later than the damson, as do all the bullaces. It is a wild species of the prunus family, which make tough, thorny wood, ideal for hedgerow planting. This is a more recent introduction and possesses the true damson flavour, unlike the others. It is extremely hardy and ripens its fruit in early November but will hang until almost the month end.

NEW BLACK BULLACE This is an improvement on the old Black variety, well known to Tudor gardeners. It makes a neat, upright tree, is hardy and bears a tremendous crop of juicy, but acid fruit, best used for jam.

SHEPHERD'S BULLACE Valuable for a cold garden, in that it blooms late and bears a heavy crop at the beginning of October, the fruit being grass-green when ripe, tart, but juicy.

For succession:

Cherry Plum	Early August
River's Early Damson	Early August
Farleigh Prolific	Early September
Bradley's King	Mid-September
Shropshire Prune	End-September
Shepherd's Bullace	Early October
Merryweather Damson	Mid-October
New Black Bullace	Mid-October
Langley's Bullace	Early November

QUETSCHE

The Carlsbad plum of Austria, it makes a vigorous tree but its growth is neat and upright. It flowers and fruits late, the long black oval fruits hanging until November when they make delicious eating after stewing, in tarts and flans.

CHERRY

The cherry, unless planted for its blossom, as well it might be, is rarely grown in the amateur's garden. For one thing, it succeeds only as a standard, or half-standard, and in this form will take almost ten years to come into reasonable bearing. None of the sweet cherries is able to set any fruit with its own pollen, but it is not enough to plant together several varieties which bloom at the same time, in the expectation that they will pollinate one another, for only certain varieties are capable of doing this. Again, a cherry in the standard form makes such a large tree that it tends to crowd out other fruit trees growing near. Then again, the question of birds is a constant worry, for even if the trees do set a good crop, quite half the fruit might be taken by birds. By all means plant a cherry, or a number, where space permits, for they remain in bloom longer than any other fruit and provide a charming display during the spring. By planting a wide selection of fruits, beginning with the first of the plums and ending with the latest flowering apples such as 'Crawley Beauty' and 'Edward VII', a display of blossom may be enjoyed from the end of March until early June.

But if cherries in the standard form prove too unproductive for the ground they occupy, then the small grower might have room for two or three trees in the fan-shape form, planting them against a wall. It is not suggested that they should be grown instead of pears or plums in this way, though, where several out-buildings are available for wall planting, then sweet cherries, the earliest fruit to mature, may be enjoyed in addition to the other fruits. For a fan-shaped tree a 16 ft wide framework of horizontally fixed wires will be necessary. Fasten the wires to nails so that it is one inch from the wall to allow for tying in.

Soil Requirements

Cherries like exactly the opposite conditions to plums, though both are stone fruits. Whereas the plum depends upon a heavy moist soil, copious quantities of nitrogen to crop well, and requires almost no potash and very little lime, the cherry likes a dry soil, preferably a light loam over chalk, a dry, sunny climate, and plenty of potash. Nitrogen it does not require in more than average amount. In cold districts and in a warm but moist climate, cherries do not crop well, and a too rich soil will also cause excessive gumming.

Lime and potash are the primary needs of the cherry, so when planting in a soil deficient in lime, incorporate plenty of lime rubble at planting time. The planting of both plums and cherries is best done during November. When planting, take great care to ensure that the bark of the tree is in no way damaged, otherwise it will permit bacterial canker or silver leaf disease to enter the wound, plums and cherries being highly susceptible to both diseases. No manure should be given at planting time; nitrogenous manure would only encourage an excess of lush growth, but one ounce per tree of sulphate of potash should be given in early April each year. Rake it into a circle around the base of the stem. Wood ash, rich in potash, may be incorporated at planting time. If planting standard trees, allow them between 20-25 feet.

Pruning

As to pruning, the same remarks apply to the sweet cherry as to the plum. In the first year, reduce the leader shoots by half; during late spring cut out any dead wood and leave it at that.

Morello cherries, which may be grown in colder gardens than sweet cherries, require rather more attention. Cut back the main shoots by a third in spring each year, after shortening the leader by half in the first year.

In the case of the fan-trained tree, it is only the side growth which should be removed. Pinch back to about six leaves late in June, and then further pinch back to four buds early in September. If it is noticed that the main leaders are making excessive growth, do not cut them and so cause further stimulation; they will respond better if the shoots are bent down for a period of twelve months; bring them forward from the wall and tie the tips against the main stem. This will weaken growth and they may be pruned and tied back in their normal position in 12-18 months. Root pruning as described will do much to keep the cherry in check.

The Morello or acid cherry requires a different treatment. Acid or sour cherries bear their fruit on the previous season's wood, and so the aim must be to encourage a continual supply of new wood. For this, the laterals should be cut back halfway each autumn, then in spring all side growths should be cut or pinched back to two inches of growth. The previous season's shoots should now be bearing both new wood and blossom buds, and it is upon these that the present year's fruit is borne. At the base will be found several buds which should be removed to leave but a single bud which will continue to make new growth through the summer for fruiting next season.

Like the sweet cherries and plums, the Morellos can be allowed to carry plenty of wood without fear of reducing the amount of fruit, so thinning is not so necessary and should be done only when need arises. Root pruning will help to keep wall trees in check. As the acid cherries are prone to brown rot disease, all diseased wood when observed must be carefully removed.

Rootstocks

For centuries cherries have always been grown on the wild cherry stock, propagated by layering. A form, specially selected by the East Malling Research Station, to give greater uniformity of performance, is now being used by nurserymen. Propagation is by budding as described for the plum.

The genetic dwarfing of seedling rootstocks on to which 'Merton Glory' has been used as the scion variety, has resulted in a series of cherries which have been greatly reduced in vigour, yet which produce reliable crops of top-quality fruit which ripens several days earlier than on comparable trees which have not been subjected to dwarfing.

The dwarfing which has so far given the best results is with a hybrid obtained from a crossing of *Prunus avium,* the native bird cherry, with *P. cerasus.* The time may shortly be on hand when it will be possible to plant cherries on a dwarfing rootstock, like apples on MIX, in the smallest garden. This should result in greater ease in picking and spraying, and the bearing of heavy crops from only a limited area of ground.

Pollination

As mentioned, the correct pollination of cherries is a complicated business. Only certain groups are able to cross-pollinate one another, and the research done in recent years to determine the most suitable pollinators would have revolutionized cherry growing if other conditions were also in favour of their being more widely grown.

It has been carefully noted that each variety has a flowering period of 18 days, almost twice that of the plum, while the time from the first to bloom, 'Notberry Black', until the latest has finished flowering, 'Bradbourne Black', is 24 days, again almost twice the flowering period of the plum. Except for the very earliest and latest to bloom, all the cherries overlap with their flowering times on account of their long period of bloom. Yet contrary to expectations, this plays little or no part in their pollination. The sweet cherries will not pollinate the acid or Morellos, and only certain varieties will pollinate one another:

Variety	*Pollinators*
Amber Heat	Bigarreau Napoleon, Governor Wood, Roundel Heart
Bigarreau De Schreken	Bradbourne Black, Florence, Gaucher, Roundel Heart
Bigarreau Napoleon	Bradbourne Black, Florence, Roundel Heart
Bradbourne Black	Bigarreau Napoleon, Gaucher, Roundel Heart
Early Rivers	Bigarreau de Schreken, Emperor Francis 'A', Governor Wood, Noir de Guben, Waterloo
Emperor Francis 'A'	Bigarreau de Schreken, Early Rivers, Frogmore, Waterloo
Florence	Bigarreau Napoleon
Governor Wood	Early Rivers, Emperor Francis 'A'
Knight's Early Black	Bigarreau de Schreken, Waterloo
Roundel Heart	Amber Heart, Bigarreau Napoleon, Bradbourne Black, Governor Wood, Waterloo
Waterloo	Amber Heart, Bigarreau Napoleon

Flowering Times: V.E=*Very Early* V.L=*Very Late*

Early:

Early Rivers	Merton Premier
Emperor Francis (V.E)	Notberry Black (V.E)
Merton Bigarreau	Waterloo

Mid-season:

Elton Heart	Knight's Early Black
Frogmore	Merton Heart
Governor Wood	Roundel Heart

Late:

Amber Heart	Florence Heart (V.L)
Bigarreau Napoleon	Gaucher
Bradbourne Black (V.L)	Noble (V.L)

These are the most reliable pollinators:

Bigarreau Napoleon	Waterloo
Roundel Heart	Early Rivers
Governor Wood	Emperor Francis

At the John Innes Institute at Merton, work has continued over many years in the breeding of new cultivars (varieties) which might prove self-fertile and so reduce the need for pollinators. These self-fertile seedlings were isolated in 1954 by Messrs Lewis and Crowe; in Canada, Lapins has made use of them to obtain other self-fertile cultivars from which 'Stella' was selected for release in 1973. It was twenty years earlier that the discovery, at the John Innes Institute, that pollen of 'Napoleon' treated with X-rays and used on 'Emperor Francis' produced self-fertile mutations, resulted in the seedlings 2420 and 2434, which were used by Lapins. 'Stella' was the result of using pollen of the variety 'Lambert' to the seedling 2420, and this may be the forerunner of a new series of self-fertile varieties. But it must be remembered that 'Napoleon' is a shy bearer and may have transmitted this characteristic to its progeny. It will take many years before the appearance of self-fertile varieties which are proven croppers of reliability.

Varieties

The most popular sweet cherries are:

AMBER HEART Also pollinated by 'Waterloo' and ready mid-July. This is the best all-round cherry in cultivation, being hardy, a consistent cropper, and doing well as a standard or fan-trained tree. Widely used by the canners. The attractive yellow fruits are flueshed red. This is also the popular 'White Heart' sold by the barrow boys. To grow cherries commercially, 'Waterloo' and 'Amber Heart' would be a suitable choice.

BIGARREAU NAPOLEON Pollinated by 'Waterloo' and 'Roundel Heart', this is a delicious cherry for dessert, large, very sweet and vivid red in colour. Ready end of July.

BRADBOURNE BLACK Plant in a large garden or orchard, for it makes a large, spreading tree. It is a heavy cropper, the huge cromson-black fruit being of delicious flavour. Excellent for a frosty garden planted with 'Napoleon' and 'Roundel Heart', for they pollinate each other and all bloom late.

EARLY RIVERS This is the earliest variety to fruit, ready mid-June and bears huge jet black fruit in profusion. It is a hardy variety, nd the tree has enormous vigour.

EMPEROR FRANCIS Grown with 'Early Rivers' (or 'Waterloo') this variety would ensure a crop in June and another ('Emperor Francis') in late August. It is a fine all-round variety, the large, dark crimson fruits being of excellent flavour. The first cherry to flower and the last dessert cherry to fruit.

FLORENCE Another bright red cherry which does well when planted with 'Napoleon', cropping about ten days later. A heavy cropper as either a standard or fan-trained tree.

FROGMORE Useful for a small garden in that it makes a compact, upright tree. It bears heavily and comes into bearing earlier than most cherries, bearing large yellow and red fruit.

GOVERNOR WOOD It makes a large, spreading tree; when pollinated with 'Emperor Francis' or

'Early Rivers' it bears a huge crop of yellow cherries, flushed pink, exceptionally rich and sweet.
KNIGHT'S EARLY BLACK Of compact habit and useful for a small garden, it bears a heavy crop of large, jet-black fruit of excellent flavour.
MERTON HEART This new cherry is now being widely planted to follow 'Early Rivers' and 'Waterloo'. It is a heavy and consistent cropper, and bears a large deep-crimson fruit of rich flavour. Should be grown with 'Emperor Francis' or 'Early Rivers'.
NOTBERRY BLACK The earliest to bloom and fruit, ready early July when the large round fruits are crimson-black, sweet and juicy.
ROUNDEL HEART This variety may also be planted with 'Waterloo', as they pollinate each other. It produces very large deep purple fruit which is ready for picking early July.
STELLA The first-named, self-fertile sweet cherry, it makes an upright tree and comes early into fruit. It is a late variety, the large heart-shaped fruit ripening to almost black.
WATERLOO Early to mid-season flowering, and a suitable pollinator for 'Early Rivers', 'Emperor Francis', etc. It makes a compact tree but bears less regularly than most cherries, though its fruit, deep crimson coloured, is sweet and juicy.
Cherries in order of ripening their fruit:

Early Rivers	Mid-June
Governor Wood	Late June
Knight's Early Black	Early July
Frogmore	Early July
Notberry Black	Early July
Roundel Heart	Early July
Merton Heart	Mid-July
Waterloo	Late July
Amber Heart	Late July
Bigarreau Napoleon	Early August
Florence	Mid-August
Bradbourne Black	Mid-August
Emperor Francis	Late August

To protect the fruit from birds, close fish-mesh netting should be hung over the trees as soon as the fruit has set; this may also be used for covering the heads of young standard trees until they become too large. Some protection for the fruit may then be given by fastening tobacco tin lids together and suspending them among the trees, to clatter in the wind.

Acid or Culinary Cherries

The acid cherries, 'Flemish Red', 'Kentish Red', and the Morello cherry, are all self-fertile and will set their fruit without the aid of a pollinator. They are more hardy than the sweet cherries, their blossoms being less susceptible to frost. For a cold garden they are a valuable fruit, beautiful when in bloom, and their leaves take on the autumnal tints of the pear. Both the 'Flemish' and 'Kentish Red' bear their fruit very early, at the end of June, when they are valuable for jam and for tarts; the Morello's fruit is ripe in August. Trees of the 'Flemish Red' are more upright and less drooping than those of the 'Kentish Red'; the Morello makes a densely branched tree. Each may be planted against a cold north wall as a fan tree, or they may be used, with damsons, for a windbreak, or for those cold corners to which other fruit will not take kindly.

The fruit of the Morello is large and takes on a rich crimson-black appearance when fully ripe, but always maintains its acid-bitterness.

4 Cane Fruits

The most widely neglected of all fruits, the cane fruits are likely to become more widely planted in future, now that the deep-freeze unit is considered an essential part of the kitchen. The cane fruits retain their quality after freezing better than any other fruits.

Between the two world wars the raspberry, most important of the cane fruits, almost passed out of commercial cultivation. Until the introduction of New Zealand clones, free from virus, after the Second World War, the weight of crop continued to deteriorate year by year. There was also little choice of variety, and so the whole of the raspberry crop came within a period of two to three weeks when heavy rainfall, often experienced in July, caused the complete failure of the crop.

Now all this has changed with the introduction in the early 1950s of virus free stocks and new varieties for succession. It has culminated with the arrival of the revolutionary 'Glen Clova', which when grown well, will give almost double the weight of fruit expected from the older raspberries. This is because it frequently produces two laterals from a single node and, with the droplets of the fruits closer together than with others, the berries when frozen, retain their firmness, if transported, better than any other variety. Moreover, the discovery of a gene in 'Malling Jewel', which controls the size of fruit, producing almost 50 per cent more droplets, must enable varieties to be raised in future which are capable of producing almost double the size of fruit obtained from pre-war varieties. Modern cultivars are capable of maturing more rapidly than all other soft fruits. The raspberry will soon rival the strawberry in commercial popularity; it has the advantage of being greatly superior to the strawberry for freezing. Raspberry planting is now continuing on a greater scale than in previous years, and before long there should be at least 10,000 acres under cultivation. The raspberry is once more a profitable crop.

Of the other cane fruits, 'Oregon Thornless' blackberry, raised in America, is giving large crops of big juicy berries, the druplets being large and fleshy with the seeds small. The thornless characteristic of the canes, derived from *Rubus canadensis* which is endowed with the gene for thornlessness, is contributing to the popularity of this fruit. Like all blackberries, however, it relies upon a warm autumn to ripen satisfactory crops, for the blackberry (with the exception of 'Bedford Giant') takes twice as long as the raspberry (70 days instead of 35) to bear fruit from flowering time.

The thornless loganberry, too, which makes picking so much easier, is now being more widely planted than previously. Like the raspberry, its fruit retains its firmness after freezing and is excellent for tarts and flans, served with whipped cream.

To cover a new fence, the blackberry and loganberry quickly send out their shoots to a length of six to eight feet, and their foliage is light and airy and most decorative. They may also be grown against a trellis or screen made of stout posts and galvanized wire, used to divide one part of the garden from another; or, planted against a garage wall, they will prove effective as a screen and will give heavy crops of valuable fruits.

BLACKBERRY

Only 1,000 acres are under commercial cultivation in Britain and few gardens grow them, yet blackberries may be grown in unwanted ground where, provided they are supplied with humus and kept free of dead wood, they will continue to bear fruit for many years. In much the same way the plants of the more vigorous varieties such as 'Himalaya Giant' may be planted as a hedge. Loganberries are not suited to this purpose, for their wood is brittle and liable to be cut back by cold winds. Planted eight to ten feet apart and trained along stout galvanized wires, blackberries will form a most valuable windbreak, at the same time yielding large crops.

Where used in this way, the plants will be grown in rows; this method is also to be recommended for field and garden culture where growing as a specialized crop. Or the plants may be grown up stout poles like rambler roses. Where growing up poles, planting may be closer, allowing about six feet apart; they may also be planted at the back of a border or about the vegetable garden, taking up little space in this way.

Soil Requirements

Blackberries require an abundance of humus to encourage them to bear a large, juicy berry, and as nitrogen is continually required to make new growth, large quantities of shoddy or farmyard manure should be incorporated into the soil. Lawn mowings, seaweed and peat all have value in supplying humus, and this should be augmented with farmyard manure, old mushroom-bed compost, hop manure or shoddy. A heavy loam suits the hybrid berries best, for it is more retentive of moisture. Where a sandy soil is to be made suitable, additional humus must be provided. In a starved soil the berries will be small, seedy and lacking in juice. The plant will also make little new growth, becoming a mass of dead wood and by degrees the plants will die back. With blackberries, the formation of new wood is important to maintain the health of the plant, but with loganberries the production of new wood is vital for a heavy crop the following year.

In April, each plant should be given $\frac{1}{2}$ ounce of sulphate of potash, raked into the soil around the stems, followed by a mulch with strawy manure in early May. This is necessary to control the moisture, for it must be remembered that the fruits swell during the driest period of the year. A heavy mulch of decayed manure will add several pounds of fruit per plant. Like all soft fruits, blackberries and the hybrids make an abundance of active surface roots which supply the greater part of the moisture and nourishment required.

Planting and Propagation

Neither blackberries nor the hybrid berries should be planted too deeply. Almost any time during the winter months will be suitable, but with a heavy soil it is preferable to plant in November, or in March when moisture conditions permit. The stakes and wires should be in position before the plants are set out, the stakes having been creosoted well in advance so that the fumes have dispersed before planting. Immediately after planting, the shoots are cut back before being tied to the wires, and spaced evenly to prevent overcrowding.

Alternatively, rooted 'tips' may be planted. These are obtained from canes which have been

Cultivated blackberries produce bigger, better trusses of fruit than the wild form

bent over and the tips planted beneath soil level and made secure. If this is done during July and early August, using the new season's canes, rooting will have taken place by early November. The rooted 'tips' are then severed from the parent but left in position until March, when they are used either to make fresh plantings or to replace decayed plants in the fruiting rows. A special bed can be made where every new shoot is tip-rooted and used for making additional plantings for fruit production. This will ensure that every cane formed is used only for fruiting.

Pruning of blackberries is done by cutting out any dead wood and excess growth that will interfere with ripening and picking.

Covering Wall

Almost every house has a bare wall somewhere, which, if covered, would greatly enhance the property. But rather than plant ivy or Virginia creeper, which tend to damage the property if neglected, why not let these bare walls produce some fruit? One of the best plants is the Japanese wineberry. It is one of the most handsome of all wall plants, for its canes quickly make considerable growth, attaining ten feet or more in a season. Not only do they remain a rich crimson through winter, but also the berries (which make delicious jam) are long-lasting and of a vivid amber colour. There is no better plant for covering a trellis. With the possible exception of the loganberry, most of the hybrid berries are so hardy that they will prove suitable for a cold, northerly wall.

Rather than being fastened to the wall by nails into the mortar, the canes should be trained against wire fixed permanently to the wall. In this way the old fruiting canes may easily be removed and the new canes fastened to the wires.

Varieties

Early-Fruiting

ASHTON CROSS Though a hardy, vigorous variety, this has never become popular. It is strongly resistant to virus and could therefore be grown with advantage in virus-troubled areas. It is an early mid-season variety, bearing a large, round berry, jet-black in colour but only of moderate flavour.

BEDFORD GIANT This, together with 'Himalaya Giant', is considered the best for canning and freezing. It is the earliest variety, ripening towards the end of July and in only half the time taken by other blackberries. The fruit is large, juicy and sweet, but it is not such a generally reliable cropper as 'Himalaya Giant'. Probably raised from a raspberry cross, its canes grow to ten feet in length.

MERTON EARLY A variety from the John Innes Institute, it ripens its fruit towards the end of July and bears a heavy crop. The fruit is large, of exceptional flavour, and contains few seeds. It is the only variety propagated from seed, sown in a cold frame in March. The seedlings are transferred to nursery beds, planted six inches apart, in July. They are moved to their fruiting quarters the following April. This variety resembles a loganberry in that the fruit cane dies after fruiting, next season's crop being grown on the new canes. It is of dwarf, compact habit and should be planted six feet part in the rows. It is an ideal variety for a small garden.

Mid-Season Fruiting

HIMALAYA GIANT Raised in Germany from seed brought from the Himalayas and introduced to Britain in 1900. One of the most popular varieties with the canner, it is widely planted commercially owing to its hardiness and ability to bear fruit on the old wood as well as the new, thus giving an immense crop. It is a wonderful variety for providing a windbreak or hedge, but is so vigorous that when grown in a small garden it must be kept under strict control.

KING'S ACRE BERRY A hybrid blackberry, this early mid-season variety should be in every garden. It is a strong grower though not so rampant as most blackberries. It bears delicious fruit which parts from the core like a raspberry, making it exceptionally suitable for dessert and culinary purposes.

MERTON THORNLESS Introduced in 1938, it is neither a strong grower nor a heavy cropper, but when given good cultivation it has become popular for canning. The canes are entirely thornless, so the plant is popular with pickers and with amateur gardeners. It is now being replaced by 'Oregon Thornless'.

OREGON THORNLESS Raised in Oregon, it is proving to be the best all-round blackberry in cultivation, both in Britain and in America where it is now widely used for canning and deep freeze. It has finely divided foliage, like the parsley-leaf blackberry. Its canes grow up to eight feet in length and are entirely free of thorns. It begins to ripen its heavy clusters of large berries early in September and continues until early November, a single plant being capable of yielding up to 14 pounds of large, round jet-black berries.

PARSLEY-LEAVED Found growing as a chance seedling, this is a variety with attractively serrated leaves which turn to the most arresting colours in autumn. An arch of the parsley-leaved blackberry makes an imposing sight and also bears a heavy crop of aromatic fruits which are large, oval and cromson in colour.

Late Fruiting

JOHN INNES Raised from the thornless *Rubus rusticanus var. inermis,* and introduced in 1923. Cane growth is vigorous. Like 'Himalaya Giant', it fruits well on the old canes. But it crops abundantly only in warm districts where it may be used as a windbreak, but in cold districts fruiting is generally so late as to be almost useless.

LOWBERRY A hybrid of American origin, it is a magnificent berry, being a cross between a loganberry and blackberry and combining the better qualities of both parents. It bears true loganberry shaped fruit, quite two inches long, but of a shining, jet-black colour with the sweet flavour and delicious aroma of the blackberry.

LOGANBERRY

Like the raspberry and other cane fruits, it is only gaining in popularity with the advent of the deep freeze unit for its fruits, which retain the plug after picking, remain firm and keep their quality. It is a hybrid berry, a chance cross between a wild blackberry and a raspberry which took place in California in 1881 when it was found in the garden of Judge Logan at Santa Cruz. The learned man, after testing the fruit and considering it delicious, named it after himself and within a short time it was being grown commercially for canning and jam throughout the States of California and Oregon. But, as with most cane fruits, after 50 years the canes developed virus diseases and crops diminished until the virus-free LY 59 strain was developed; this gave the fruit a new lease of life. It has great vigour and will send out new canes to a height of eight feet and more; hence the trellis or screen against which the plants will grow must be made eight feet high and made secure against winds, because when the plant is fully grown the supports must carry a great weight of fruit and foliage.

The loganberry crops heavily in most soils and is almost immune to frost, though it does not like cold winds. The fruit grows up to two inches long and is dull wine-red coloured. When fully ripe it has the taste of red wine. In appearance, the large firm fruits are a cross between those of its parents.

There is a thornless form which, though not quite such a heavy cropper as LY 59, makes picking and tying a pleasure rather than a trial. It bears its fruit during August, bridging the gap between the main raspberry crop and the main blackberry crop.

Pruning

Loganberries possess a rather different habit from

blackberries. The canes are brittle and grow more like raspberry canes. They should be trained in fan shape rather than along wires, as with the more pliable blackberry cane. And whereas blackberries should be spaced from ten feet apart, depending upon individual vigour, loganberries will not require more than eight feet between each plant.

To prune, treat as raspberries. Each year after fruiting, cut back the old canes to three inches of ground level and tie the new season's canes to the wires for fruiting the following season. Hence the reason for the loganberry and the hybrid berries requiring even more nitrogen than the blackberry, for they have to bear new canes at the same time as fruit.

The more nitrogenous manures that can be given, the more vigorous will be new cane growth. As for blackcurrants, pig or poultry manure composted with straw will prove valuable and in April the plants will appreciate a one-ounce-per-square-yard dressing of sulphate of ammonia, or one cwt per acre, applied during a rainy period. With loganberries, as with blackcurrants, it is rarely possible to provide an excess of nitrogen. For this reason the two should be grown together. They also enjoy the same climate and situation—full sun and a sheltered position.

Perhaps the fact that one cannot expect to enjoy fruit the first season after planting has detracted from the popularity of the plant. Against this, it makes up by continuing to bear large crops over many years.

After planting in November, cut back the canes to about three to four inches of ground level when a number of new canes will arise early in summer. These are tied to the trellis or wire frame at intervals of about 15 inches, spacing out the canes as evenly as possible when, by the end of summer, the screen will be clothed in canes and foliage, a handsome sight; next August the plants will be laden with bunches of large crimson berries. Should the tips of the canes have been caught by frost, it is advisable to remove them in spring to prevent disease from entering the plant at this point. But, normally, the loganberry possesses the disease-resistant qualities of the blackberry.

Propagation

The loganberry is best propagated by layering the tips of those canes which are most readily bent to ground level without breaking them. Place the tips about three inches into the soil and hold in place by a wire layering pin as used for border carnations. Keep comfortably moist when, after several weeks, new growth will be seen above the layered tip. Rooting will then have taken place; the plant is cut away from the cane which can then be tied to the frame, and the newly rooted tip is planted in its fruiting quarters.

RASPBERRY

Though the raspberry may be said to have a shorter season than the strawberry, recent introductions are capable of extending the season from early July until the end of autumn. For the amount of ground it occupies, no fruit crops more heavily than the new variety, 'Glen Clova'.

The raspberry enjoys a soil capable of retaining moisture in summer while forming and ripening its fruits. Unlike the strawberry, which will crop well on light land provided it is not lacking in potash, the raspberry prefers a heavy loam and the plants will produce little new cane and a poor, seedy sample of fruit in a too-dry soil. Ample supplies of moisture in summer are of paramount importance in raspberry growing, for the plants have to make cane growth, foliage, and bear a heavy crop within the same period of time.

Preparation of the Soil

Before planting (which should be done during November and December, before the soil becomes too wet or frost bound) as much decayed compost

Blackberry *Rubus fruticosus*

Medlar *Mespilus germanica* ripe fruits

as obtainable should be worked into the soil. Pig, poultry and farmyard manures are ideal, and these can be augmented by a quantity of decayed straw or garden refuse. Bracken treated with an activator, to which has been added poultry or pig manure, will make an ideal compost. Work in as much humus as possible, for it must be remembered that the plants have to produce not only a heavy crop of fruit, but also an abundance of new cane to provide for next season's crop. This calls for a soil rich in nitrogenous humus. Care must be taken to select a frost free position, especially for those varieties which tend to suffer in this way. 'Malling Promise' is a variety that seems prone to frost attack, whereas 'Newburgh' is resistant. Indeed, the raspberry may quite easily be grown in a frosty area where strawberries are known to suffer badly, provided that the later flowering (and fruiting) varieties are grown. Here, 'Norfolk Giant', 'Newburgh', 'Glen Clova' and 'Malling Jewel' are suitable. Raspberries will benefit from a light application of sulphate of potash after planting, but they do not require such concentrated amounts as the strawberry or gooseberry; bonfire ashes, stored dry, and raked into the prepared bed should be sufficient for most soils.

Planting

Plant when the soil is in a friable condition. If sticky, heel in the canes and protect with straw until conditions improve. Always purchase clean stock that has been certified as being free from the 'mosaic' virus disease. The raspberry will produce a profitable crop indefinitely if clean stock is obtained and soil conditions are to its liking. 'Norfolk Giant' and 'Newburgh', both highly-resistant to frost damage, are equally immune to virus attacks.

The canes should be planted about 18 inches apart in the rows, depending on the vigour of the variety. 'Malling Promise', which is particularly vigorous, should be allowed an extra six inches, and as much as five feet should be allowed between the rows, with an extra foot for the vigorous varieties.

Plant neither too shallow nor too deep. The latter is a common failure when planting raspberries, for many rely on deep planting to support the cane. Two inches below the surface of the soil is the required depth. Deeper than three inches may mean that new growth is never seen; the old gardeners certainly know what they were talking about in this matter. The same rules apply to blackberries too.

When the canes have been planted and made firm, they should be cut back to 12 inches from soil level. This is to encourage vigorous new shoots to appear during the first season. Those who believe they can obtain a fruit crop the first summer and still build up a strong plant will be disappointed.

Where the soil is particularly heavy and the land not well drained, planting is best done in March. Cane growth will be stimulated by giving the rows a one-ounce-per-square-yard dressing of sulphate of ammonia in March each year.

Staking and Tying

Staking need not be done until the new shoots are appearing and have reached 18 inches in height, which will be about June, following autumn planting. Possibly the best time for the work would be April, so as to relieve the busy picking and hoeing season of May to August. There are numerous methods of staking raspberries:

(a) The canes may be planted and supported in tent fashion, planting one cane to each of three strong canes or laths, inserted into the soil 18 inches apart and tied together at the top in tent fashion. The stakes should be seven feet in length to allow almost six feet above ground.

(b) The canes are fastened to a series of wires attached to six to seven feet long posts placed at intervals of about eight to nine feet. Against the wires, the new canes are tied in.

(c) The wires may be run down either side of the

Raspberry 'Malling Jewel' in autumn, after thinning, showing the young canes properly trained and spaced canes to form a 'box'. This method is very common, but unless particularly well made, with very stout wire, the canes will come out of the 'box'. Again, at least six to seven feet long posts will be needed, with the wire taken down the rows at 12-inch intervals almost to the top of the stakes. Where shorter stakes are used and the wire is not taken right to the top, many of the taller canes may be broken during a spell of windy weather.

(d) There is also the rope method. Here the canes are fastened together in arches, held in position by strong stakes. By this method it is not necessary to fasten the individual canes to the wires, and there is less fear of breakage by wind. It has been found that bending the canes partially checks the flow of sap to their tops, and thus ensures even ripening and swelling of the fruit right down the canes.

Where canes are being planted against a wall or interwoven fencing, they may be held in place by wires fastened at intervals. Correct staking and tying are most important in raspberry culture; badly staked rows mean not only broken canes but make cultivation and picking difficult.

Mulching

During the summer the canes will benefit from a monthly mulch, first given in early June. This will keep the roots cool and will help the soil to retain the moisture content necessary for the production of a large, juicy berry, and the formation of the necessary new growth. Raspberries detest a light dry soil, and although liberal amounts of compost will greatly help in this respect, it is only half the battle. A regular summer mulch will complete operations. Lawn mowings are ideal and a quantity of granulated peat placed down the rows in late May will prove greatly beneficial. Where there are no grass mowings, partially composted straw or well rotted farmyard manure will be equally good. Provided that plenty of manure has been used in the preparation of the soil, peat and grass mowings are most useful, as they can more easily be worked into the soil in autumn.

Pruning

In October, after fruiting has eneded, the old wood which has borne a crop of fruit the past summer should be cut back to three inches above ground level. If too much of the old wood is allowed to remain it will only tend to harbour disease. The new season's shoots should be carefully tied to the wire, if this has not already been done, and all weak growth cut out, leaving about six to eight new canes to each 'stool' or root, depending upon the vigour of the variety. Weeds should be removed from the rows and the summer mulches forked in, taking care not to fork too near the stools. A dressing of well rotted manure round the base of the canes will complete the work. All wood cut out must be burnt immediately.

The season of fruiting will also play its part in pruning operations. Where autumn fruit is desired, the canes should be cut back to within six inches of the ground in early March, as autumn fruiting varieties bear their fruit on the new summer's growth and not on the canes formed during the previous year. They will need liberal applications of farmyard manure to form the fruit by autumn. Commencing with the early 'Malling Promise', and ending with the extremely late 'November Abundance', it is possible to obtain a succession of fruit over a period of five months.

Propagation of Canes

For those wishing to increase their stock for the home garden on only a small scale, it will be possible to obtain the necessary canes from the fruiting plantation by lifting the stools where they are thick in the row. The canes are divided by pulling them apart from the 'stool'. Only canes of healthy appearance should be used; any canes showing blight, wilt or virus must be burnt. Nor should new plantations be made where old canes have previously been fruiting for several years—this applies to all soft fruits, especially strawberries and raspberries.

Where canes are required for sale, a different method of propagation is used, for it is impossible to grow both for fruit and for canes, except where growing on a considerable scale. Where a profusion of canes is required, stool beds are planted. No staking is done and the canes are set out 12 inches apart, in rows three feet apart. To encourage an abundance of new growth the canes are cut back frequently. They should be mulched in the normal way throughout the summer. When being dispatched for sale, they must on no account be allowed to suffer from drying winds; they must be taken under cover as soon as lifted, counted, and tied up in sacking at the earliest possible moment.

Varieties

Early

GLEN CLOVA One of the finest of all raspberries, it usually ripens just after 'Malling Exploit' and 'Jewel'. Forming two laterals from each node, it crops heavily, the medium-sized fruit of pale red being round and firm and rather more acid than other earlies, but it freezes and travels well.

LLOYD GEORGE When first introduced it was the best of all raspberries, as important to the raspberry-grower as 'Royal Sovereign' was to the strawberry-grower. But, like that grand variety, it suffered from every conceivable disease, until it became necessary in Britain to introduce New Zealand stock. This stock–free of virus and extremely vigorous–has again allowed it, if not now standing supreme, to produce a heavy crop of top-class fruit. Though the flavour of the fruit is not equal to that of 'Malling Exploit', it is good, even size, firm and of a bright red colour. It freezes well.

MALLING EXPLOIT An outstanding variety for the garden, and popular for jam making and freezing. Early fruiting, it produces plenty of cane, and in gardens is best grown against a wall. It has proved in some instances a heavier yielder than 'Malling Jewel', and its flavour is first rate; equally important, the fruits remain vivid scarlet for a considerable time after picking, and do not become soft. They are also large, and suitable for growers of dessert raspberries for sale in punnets.

MALLING JEWEL This must be first choice for early fruiting in a frosty district, because the blooms open later than those of the other earlies. It makes a tall, smooth, upright cane which turns an attractive purple in late August. The large, conical fruits, abundantly produced, are rich crimson and pleasantly sweet, but without aromatic flavour. Besides being a heavy bearer, it is excellent for freezing and canning. It is, in fact, the best early raspberry ever raised, and none crops better in a hot, dry soil.

MALLING PROMISE This was the first of the many excellent varieties from East Malling. It has 'Newburgh' for a parent and is, with 'Royal Scot', the first to ripen its fruit. It bears a heavy crop of huge, conical berries which tend to become soft, especially in a rainy season, so they are used for dessert rather than for processing. This variety is popular in Scotland, although the canes are apt to suffer slight damage during late frosts.

RED CROSS This drought resisting variety is extremely resistant to disease, and is a vigorous and heavy cropper of large, juicy fruit. One of the best varieties yet raised, but it is now difficult to obtain completely virus-free stocks.

ROYAL SCOT One of the best of all raspberries, introduced from Scotland, and having strong cane growth. The first raspberry of all to ripen, it carries its berries evenly along the small branches, so they are easy to pick. They 'plug' well and remain firm on the canes for some time, even in wet weather. The fruit is large, deep salmon red when ripe, and has a delicious flavour. For the garden this variety is outstanding, but the commercial grower prefers one which, like 'Malling Notable', will ripen all its fruit together and can be cleared from a plantation in three pickings; 'Royal Scot' requires six pickings, and is thus ideal for the amateur's garden.

Mid-Season

MALLING ENTERPRISE Sister to 'Malling Jewel' and a valuable variety, although it will not make new cane growth unless it is grown in a heavy loam containing plenty of moisture-holding humus. On heavy land and in frosty areas it is the best of all varieties. The canes are smooth and turn a rich crimson in early autumn; the berries are large, firm and sweet.

MALLING NOTABLE Extending its fruiting into mid-season 'Malling Notable' follows closely on the heels of 'Malling Jewel', but is not so good. Cane growth is not strong, and the canes have a habit of bending over. The fruit is large, juicy, of a dull crimson colour, and 'plugs' easily. It is not such a heavy cropper as 'Malling Jewel', although the fruit is outstanding in quality. Not entirely suitable for the amateur's garden, because all its fruit is ready at once.

MALLING ORION Of vigorous habit, the canes growing six to seven feet tall and with the fruiting laterals erect, making for ease in picking. It bears heavily, in some areas more so than 'Malling Jewel', its round dark red fruit plugging easily and being sweet and juicy. It is excellent for freezing but not so good for jam.

MILTON A top-class, mid-season raspberry for the amateur. It crops well during a wet season. It bears a large berry which ripens to a deep pink and hangs well; it does not become soft and sticky in wet weather, or when fully ripe. It produces plenty of cane and an abundance of sweetly aromatic fruit; it is a lovely berry for eating from the cane.

NEWBURGH An American introduction. In some places its vigour has been reduced by cane midge; but where this is not prevalent and clean stocks can be obtained it is an outstanding variety, favoured by exhibitors on account of its huge fruits which 'plug' easily and remain dry for some time; indeed, it is apt to be rather too dry and tends to crumble.

PHYLLIS KING Resembling 'Malling Jewel' in its freedom of cropping and erect laterals, it makes a strong tall cane and bears a very large conical fruit of sealing-wax red but may be somewhat affected in a period of prolonged rain.

PYNE'S ROYAL This variety has withstood the test of time and must be the oldest still in commerce. It bears a magnificent crop, and is a grand sight; the fruit is sweet, large and juicy, and makes wonderful jam. A fine exhibition raspberry, as with the new Malling introductions and 'Newburgh'. If it has a fault, it is its shyness at producing new cane growth.

ST WALFRIED A Dutch introduction, and a good one. It is an August fruiting variety, bearing quite unique, long-shaped fruit of vivid red colour, and very juicy. It 'plugs' well, remains firm when picked, and is now a recognized commercial raspberry in Europe.

TAYLOR Well suited to a heavy loam and, like 'Newburgh', of American origin. The canes grow tall, are light brown in colour, and are completely free of prickles, so the fruit is easily picked and the canes can be fastened to the wires without trouble. The fruits are large, pleasantly aromatic and not too sweet. Like American 'Red Rich' autumn strawberry, the fresh acid flavour is a pleasant change from that of the sweet varieties.

Late

MALLING ADMIRAL This fruits rather later than 'Norfolk Giant', the berries being the largest of all varieties, somewhat conical in shape but with a tendency to crumble after plugging, while the dark red fruits tend to be rather acid. For flavour and in all other respects, 'Norfolk Giant' remains the best of the late summer varieties.

MALLING LANDMARK This is the latest summer variety, fruiting later than 'Norfolk Giant', and although useful in this respect the vigour of the plant and the quality of the fruit are nothing like so outstanding as the earlier fruiting Malling varieties. The fruit is soft and difficult to plug, but is of good flavour.

NORFOLK GIANT Not only is this long established variety valuable for its immunity from disease, but also it opens its flowers late and so escapes damage in the most frosty areas. Fruiting late, it is also useful for carrying on until the autumn varieties are ready. It is the best raspberry for bottling, canning and quick freezing, and although, as a dessert fruit for garden cultivation, it leaves much to be desired, its other useful qualities will ensure its value for many years.

Yellow Varieties

There are a number of yellow fruiting varieties which should be grown on a small scale in the garden for providing fruits for the house. The three best varieties given here are good for bottling, make delicious jam, and possess a delicate flavour for dessert.

AMBER QUEEN This delightful raspberry is most distinctive. The canes are strong and abundantly produced; the fruit is large, juicy and of a most attractive shade of orange-yellow, tinted red. Now rare in gardens.

GOLDEN EVEREST The best of the 'yellow' varieties which are renowned for their delicious apricot-like flavour. It fruits over a long period and bears as heavily as the best of the newer red varieties.

YELLOW ANTWERP The large berries of rich, golden yellow are sweet and juicy. It is a heavy and reliable cropper.

Autumn Fruiting

These are a most useful group, producing fruit on the new season's cane, which should be cut down early in spring. The varieties follow the late summer fruiting raspberries, and in favourable districts will bear until the frosts.

HAILSHAM An old favourite, hardy, vigorous and free cropping. The rich crimson fruit is deliciously flavoured and ready for eating in October.

LORD LAMBOURNE The berries are of a rich golden-apricot colour, borne in great profusion, and the foliage of the canes is bottle-green, making a most wonderful sight in late October.

SEPTEMBER This new American raspberry is the most reliable of autumn fruiting varieties, bearing from early September until the frosts. But it fruits late. The entire plant should be cut back to just above soil level in December after fruiting, when it will fruit on the new season's canes. This is the best variety to plant in a dry, gravelly soil or one over chalk or limestone.

NOVEMBER ABUNDANCE The latest of raspberries, often cropping until early December. It is one of the few to hold an Award of Merit, and bears rich red fruit of excellent flavour but it is now rarely to be found.

ZEVA A Swiss introduction, it crops late summer until November. It makes such sufficiently sturdy cane growth that it may be grown without support. It bears heavily, making a large berry one inch long, dark red in colour and of delicious flavour.

Black Raspberry

This is a hybrid raspberry and is a fruit of great interest. The canes grow in clusters from the rootstock, like a blackcurrant, but the habit is compact, making it an ideal fruit for a small garden. It may be planted against a low wall or in the border. The plant should be treated as a raspberry: cut back the canes to six inches of ground level after planting in November: each year eliminate the old canes after fruiting.

The fruit is similar to a raspberry in appearance but is more like a mulberry when fully ripe and possesses much of the mulberry flavour. The fruit, like that of the blackberry is borne on long, arching sprays which ripen from late in July until early October. It is delicious for tarts and jam making.

WINEBERRY

Native of the Caucasus and extending across Central Asia to Japan, it is now known as the Japanese Wineberry and is a most handsome plant in every way. Its canes are thornless but are covered in crimson hairs which make for a brilliant splash of colour during winter. Though it produces new cane annually, the old canes should not be cut out until early March. Leave them to brighten the winter garden. They are especially handsome against a grey stone wall.

The raspberry-like canes grow six feet long and should be trained against wall wires in the same way as loganberries. Culture is also similar, the plants requiring ample supplies of nitrogenous manure. Throughout summer they should never lack moisture.

The round amber-coloured fruits are quite small but have a sweet, refreshing flavour all their own, rather like the yellow raspberries. They are ready late July and throughout August, and when fully ripe make excellent tarts and jam.

YOUNG'S DEWBERRY

In Britain it is known as the youngberry. It was raised in America by crossing the dewberry with the loganberry, itself a hybrid berry. It requires similar treatment to the loganberry, for its canes are brittle and it does not like cold winds. Plant in November against a trellis, and cut back the canes to four inches above ground. The new canes will grow six to seven feet long and should be tied fan-wise to strong wires stretched between stakes.

The fruits being to ripen late July and are round and wine-red, ripening to almost black. They are of good flavour but the large numbers of thorns on the canes make them difficult to pick.

By crossing back the youngberry to its logan-berry parentage, the boysenberry was raised in America in 1926. It requires the same culture as for the youngberry. While it bears mulberry-coloured fruits of delicious flavour, it bears well only in the warmest gardens. It is not nearly so valuable as the loganberry and 'Oregon Thornless' blackberry.

5 Soft Fruits

These are by far the most popular of all fruits. They include the strawberry, rhubarb and gooseberry, which are required in large numbers by the canners and for jam making.

BLACKCURRANT

About 10,000 acres are in commercial cultivation, yielding about 20,000 tons of fruit. The blackcurrant is much in demand for making fruit drinks, jams and flans, and with the extended cropping season of new varieties and greater control of disease, the fruit is now becoming more widely planted. Several varieties, bearing large berries, are now being grown as dessert. The blackcurrant is a valuable source of vitamin C. 'Baldwin' and 'Westwick Choice' are especially reliable.

Soil Requirements

Of all soft fruits, blackcurrants favour a heavy soil, one enriched with nitrogenous humus and capable of retaining an abundance of moisture throughout summer. Only one variety, 'Baldwin', does well on a light soil; in general, a shallow soil is quite incapable of producing a heavy crop. The plants have a vigorous rooting system which not only penetrates to a great depth but also forms masses of fibrous roots just beneath the surface of the soil. Thus, while a deeply worked soil is important, a mulch each year will greatly increase the amount of new wood produced, and it is on both the new and the old wood that the fruit is borne. As much new wood as possible should therefore be encouraged; indeed, a profitable plantation will depend upon the amount of new wood produced, for the fruit buds are borne along the whole length of the branches. These branches appear from buds which are below the surface of the soil: it is important to guard against damage to these buds, and to the surface roots, by avoiding cultivations too close to the plants. Hence the importance of planting into clean ground, while a yearly mulch of strawy farmyard manure will suppress annual weeds.

Because the formation of new wood is of primary importance and the plants will, where possible, be growing in a heavy soil, nitrogen is of greater importance than potash. Blackcurrants like a heavy soil and a warm climate; gooseberries prefer a light soil, plenty of potash and cool conditions. Their likes and dislikes are completely opposite; whereas gooseberries will crop well, given the partial shade of orchard trees, blackcurrants must have full sun. They do, however, require a position protected from strong winds, for these not only cause bud dropping but also lead to unsatisfactory pollination by insects. Of all fruits, blackcurrants require ample pollination if a good crop is to be ensured. Though an open, sunny position is preferred, protection must be given from prevailing winds by erecting wattle-hurdles, or by planting a hedge of blackberries. The plants, especially 'Wellington XXX' and 'Boskoop Giant', also suffer from frost, and those which bloom early should, especially, be planted away from low lying, frost troubled ground. Where late frosts persist, pieces of muslin should be placed over the bushes at nightfall. And while this fruit does best in a heavy soil, this does not mean a badly drained soil which will encourage disease. A well drained heavy loam is ideal for the blackcurrant, and before planting you should incorporate as much farmyard manure or other nitrogenous humus materials as possible. Shoddy is excellent for this fruit, and hop manure, peat, and leaf-mould—as well as straw which has been composted with an activator—will all prove of value for the amateur.

An ideal compost may be made by composting straw and poultry manure which has been kept dry and is rich in nitrogen. Heavy crops of blackcurrants may always be expected where there are poultry; indeed, this is the best of all fruits for the poultry farmer to grow. The amateur should give each plant a handful of bone meal, slow to release its nitrogen, at planting time.

Those who live near the coast will find fish waste, fish manure and chopped seaweed all suitable for supplying the necessary nitrogen over a long period. As much as twenty tons of farmyard manure or composted straw to the acre is not excessive, but of shoddy five tons will be sufficient, as it has a higher nitrogen content than farmyard manure. Feathers, and hoof and bone meal, both of which release their nitrogen slowly, are also of value. But while nitrogen is so essential for this fruit, a satisfactory crop will not be obtained where nitrogenous artificials are used, and where humus in quantity is not present in the soil, for it is vital to provide the plants with moisture.

A soil that dries out quickly is of no use to the blackcurrant. A light soil may be made more retentive of moisture by incorporating additional quantities of humus and by giving an extra heavy mulch in summer, preferably of strawy farmyard manure or of composted straw. This may be given towards the end of May at the same time as for gooseberries and for strawberries, when a straw mulch is used instead of peat. The mulch is then dug into the ground in autumn when the crop has been cleared. In addition to this, established plantations will benefit from a two-ounce-per-square-yard dressing of sulphate of ammonia or nitro-chalk applied in April, given during a rainy day. But to obtain the maximum benefit from artificials, humus must be present in the soil. An additional application of nitro-chalk, given at the rate of two cwt per acre, or one ounce per plant, during early autumn, will give a greatly increased crop the following season, and this is now widely practised by growers.

Planting

Planting distances will depend upon the vigour of the variety. Those making a more compact plant—for example, 'Amos Black' and 'Westwick Choice' – may be planted five feet apart each way, without fear of overcrowding. Both are suitable varieties for a small garden. Those of more vigorous yet of upright habit, such as 'Westwick Triumph', should be allowed six feet, while those of vigorous, spreading habit – for example, 'Wellington XXX' – are best allowed an extra foot between the plants.

A method of planting that is now followed is to allow an extra two feet between the rows, and to plant closer together in the rows. The advantage is that cultivation can be done between the rows more easily with a mechanical implement and with less risk of harming the roots, although with closer planting there is less risk of damage either by frost or from cold winds. This method may be followed when planting in exposed ground, and is most suited to those varieties having a less vigorous and more upright habit. Those with a spreading habit may require the removal of alternate plants when five to six years old. Blackcurrants do not grow on a leg, like gooseberries or redcurrants. A two-year-old plant is the most satisfactory.

As with all soft fruit, plants infected by disease will never prove profitable. With blackcurrants it is important to obtain stock guaranteed free from 'reversion' or 'big bud', caused by the Gall Mite. Where present, the flower buds fail to open and little fruit is obtained. The specialist growers and well-known suppliers of fruit trees supply guaranteed plants at no extra cost.

Planting may take place at any time between early November and the end of March; but where possible, and where the ground is well drained, early winter planting is the best. However, as the shoots should be cut back to about three inches of the base upon planting and, like the raspberry, will produce no crop the first season, it matters little when planting is done, the state of the ground being the governing factor. If the ground is prepared during October, planting is done in November. The shoots are untouched until mid-March, when they are cut back to stimulate the formation of plenty of new growth, no mulching being done during the first summer. Firm planting is essential; the plants should be re-firmed when they are pruned back after winter frosts. If two or more varieties are planted together, a much better fruit set will result.

Pruning

Pruning consists of the removal of the older shoots as the plants make excessive growth, but little pruning will be necessary for the first two to three years. Overcrowded shoots should be cut back right to the base during October, when the shoots are removed for propagation. Also, several shoots which have made excessive growth could, with advantage, be cut back to a 'break' and the younger shoot grown on. This will keep the plant free from too much old wood. Varieties with a spreading habit should be kept in shape to facilitate picking and cultivation.

Propagation

Blackcurrants are the easiest of all soft fruits to propagate, for they make plenty of wood and root with few losses; hence the reasonable price of the plants. Provided that the plants remain free from disease, they may be readily increased by removing, in early October, the shoots formed during the previous season. These shoots are shortened to about 12 inches long but, as no 'leg' is required, all the buds are allowed to form shoots.

The severed shoots are inserted in trenches of peat and coarse sand, three inches apart, with the rows nine inches apart. They are made quite firm by careful treading, and will require no further attention until the following summer, by which time they will have rooted.

During summer the rows should be mulched, either with peat or strawy manure, and the plants kept moist. They are then carefully lifted in early October twelve months after being inserted, and are planted out, cutting back as described. The following season they will come into fruit and will continue to bear for as long as twenty years or more, if carefully pruned and mulched. This is important in stimulating a constant flow of fresh wood.

Varieties

Early-Fruiting

BOSKOOP GIANT Raised in Holland and introduced to England in 1895. It makes a bush of vigorous, spreading habit, the fruit truss being long, the berries large and sweet. It is, however, intolerant of cold winds, and though self-fertile is highly susceptible to frost damage. At the 1948 trials at the East Malling Research Station, in a year of late frost, this variety set the lowest proportion of fruit of any variety, 23 per cent, compared with 51 per cent by 'Seabrook's Black' and 'Mendip Cross'.

A healthy crop of blackcurrants like these can only be obtained by careful pruning and cultivation

LAXTON'S GIANT Rarely has any currant created such enthusiasm as 'Laxton's Giant', for it heralds quite a new break in this fruit. It is a genuine dessert variety. Bearing fruit the size of a black 'Early Rivers' cherry (and even larger in gardens where it enjoys a cool, heavy, loamy soil) it may be eaten like a dessert gooseberry, being both sweet and juicy. It bottles well and is delicious in a tart or flan. It makes a large bush, bears a heavy crop, and in some districts reaches maturity as early as the end of June. It is both frost and disease resistant, and is able to hold its ripened fruit on the bush for at least a month. For the exhibitor's table it is unrivalled.

MENDIP CROSS The result of a 'Baldwin/Boskoop' cross, it possesses all the good qualities of the latter and none of its defects. It is of more compact habit, is extremely frost resistant and bears a heavy crop, the fruit being sweet, juicy and of medium size. The best early currant for an exposed garden.

WELLINGTON XXX With 'Mendip Cross' this is possibly the best all round blackcurrant, for it crops heavily in all districts. It also has 'Boskoop' and 'Baldwin' for parents, and was introduced at East Malling in 1913, yet is only now being widely planted. It is of vigorous, spreading habit and bears a heavy crop of large, thick-skinned fruit, which matures after the earlies and before the mid-season varieties. The fruit travels well and is valuable for freezing, but it should not be planted in a garden where late frosts are troublesome.

Mid-season-Fruiting

BLACKSMITH Introduced in 1916. It is such a heavy and reliable cropper that, but for a tendency to reversion, it would be much more widely grown. Bud burst is late, which makes it suitable for frost areas. The fruit is large and borne in long double trusses. With 'Baldwin' it is one of the few blackcurrants to crop well in light soils. It is noted for its high vitamin C content.

MATCHLESS Its neat upright habit commends it to the small garden, though not for a frosty district, as bud burst is early. It bears a heavy crop, the berries being sweet and thin-skinned.

SEABROOK'S BLACK This is an excellent variety for the amateur's garden, for it makes a compact bush of upright habit. Though it bursts its buds early they are very resistant to frost. The trusses are borne in twos and threes, the berries being large and rather acid but in great demand for canning and jam making. It is very resistant to 'big bud'.

WESTWICK TRIUMPH To follow 'Wellington XXX', this would be a suitable choice, especially for a small garden, for it makes a compact bush of upright habit. Though a mid-season variety, bud burst is so late as to make it immune to frost damage. The fruit is large and borne in long trusses whilst it has a high vitamin C content. It is sulphur-shy.

Late-Fruiting

AMOS BLACK Raised at East Malling from a 'Baldwin' cross, the plant possesses the same compact habit as the parent. The shoots are slender and upright, making it an ideal small garden variety and allowing closer-than-usual planting where it is grown commercially. It blooms later than any variety and matures its fruit in September. The medium-sized berry possesses a tough skin, which makes it a good traveller.

BALDWIN An old favourite, the 'Hilltop Strain' being the best. Like 'Leveller' gooseberry, it is exacting as to soils and climate, requiring large quantities of nitrogen and warm conditions. Its value to the large fruit grower lies in its ability to hold its fruit after becoming fully ripe, while for the amateur it is a compact grower. The favourite of the juice extractors, it is richest in vitamin C.

COTSWOLD CROSS A new variety, having the same parentage as 'Amos Black' and the same good qualities. It has proved a heavy cropper. The berries are large and borne in short clusters.

DANIELS' SEPTEMBER This makes a large, spreading bush and, with bud burst being early, it does best in a warm district where frosts are not troublesome and where there is ample pollination. The berries are large, thick-skinned and suitable for canning.
LALEHAM BEAUTY This is the latest of all varieties; it holds it berries until early October, thus prolonging the season considerably. The berries are thick-skinned, sweet and juicy.
MALVERN CROSS May be classed as a late mid-season variety. It makes a neat bush with upright growth. Bud burst is late, the berries being large, thick-skinned and juicy.
WESTWICK CHOICE Following 'Blacksmith', it may be described as a late mid-season variety. Like that variety, it is much in demand, together with 'Baldwin', for the fruit trade. Bud burst is much earlier than with 'Blacksmith', and so cultivation should be restricted to favourable districts. Like 'Wellington XXX'. this variety can bear especially heavy crops. The fruit is large and juicy, and has a high vitamin C content.

BLUEBERRY

The cultivated blueberry is a form of the bilberry or wortleberry. It forms low bushes about twelve inches high. Because of lack of suitable strains and growing conditions, these bear only lightly, and therefore, except for home use and a limited local sale, are uneconomic to grow with a view to large-scale marketing.

It was Dr. Colville of the U.S. Department of Agriculture who pioneered the cultivation of a selected form of the bilberry, *Vaccinium corymbosum,* which would appear to have cranberry 'blood' in it and is known as the blueberry. The most vigorous varieties are 'Bluecrop', 'Rubel' and 'Jersey', which laid the foundations of the industry in America and have also proved successful in Britain.

Soil Conditions

The species *V. corymbosum* has for long been cultivated in private gardens, not for its fruit but for its white heather-like flowers and its foliage which takes on tintings of crimson, bronze and yellow in autumn. It requires the same soil conditions as the rhododendron and azalea–an acid soil of a peaty nature with a pH value of about 4.5. Here in partial shade, and in a soil in which no other fruits would grow, *V. corymbosum* will make a bush almost five feet tall, possibly more than six feet in a mild, damp climate. Protected from cold winds, which the blueberry does not enjoy any more than the black-currant, it will bear a heavy crop of large, juicy, richly-flavoured fruits, which are very much easier to pick at this height than from the low bushes of the wild species. It is an ideal plant for the country to provide cover for game, or for providing colour and fruit from land which normally would give neither. It is also valuable for planting in wet, not too well drained land, for the blueberry responds best to a moist climate and a soil which retains summer moisture.

If the soil is of a sandy nature, then work in quantities of a cheap grade, acid peat to retain the requisite moisture, or the berries will remain small and lack juice. They also respond well to a mulching of decayed, strawy manure given during early summer. The nitrogen in the manure will encourage the formation of new growth, which is apt to be slow in a district of low rainfall.

With manuring, much still remains to be done before the most suitable soil conditions are known. The American growers provide a balanced fertilizer of chiefly potash and phosphates each April, and in certain districts some growers have obtained up to 20 pounds of choice fruit per plant from plantations as large as 50 acres in area, though the average yield is about 14 pounds per plant from the age of four years. In Britain, where planted on a small scale commercially, the yield has been about seven pounds per established plant.

Planting

The plants are expensive to purchase, but they will bear fruit for thirty or more years. They are set out three to four feet apart, with the rows eight feet apart where planting commercially, in the style of the 'hedge' system for blackcurrants. Where planting for game cover, or about the shrubbery, allow six feet between the plants. To give shelter from cold winds, especially if the position is at all exposed, the plants should be set out slightly closer, but it must be remembered that they make thick, round, bushy plants; too close planting will deprive them of sunlight and air, and the resultant brittle, twiggy wood will decay and die back.

Plant deeper than is usual for fruit bushes, for this will encourage the formation of sucker-like shoots (like blackcurrants) below soil level and build up a large plant as quickly as possible. The use of nitrogenous manures greatly increases such production of new shoots.

March is the best time to plant, although as with all deciduous shrubs, there is no reason why planting in well-drained ground should not be done any time from November until early April.

The plants come into flower early in May, bearing sprays of bell shaped, bluish white flowers, like lily of the valley. They remain several weeks in bloom, and the first fruit ripens early in August, continuing until late October. The fruits are borne in tens on short sprays. To ensure pollination, two varieties should be grown together such as 'Early Blue' and 'Jersey' (which is later).

Cultivation

Apart from providing a mulch in early summer, it is essential to keep the plants free from the weeds which tend to choke young plants and rob mature ones of the soil moisture needed to swell the fruit. This is borne in profusion on the slender sprays which remain in an upright position, simplifying picking.

Where growing on a small scale, there may be some loss of fruit through birds, although, because the plant is black, on nothing like so large a scale as with redcurrants. Where planting a few bushes for home use or in an ordinary soil, large amounts of cheap grade peat should be placed round the roots at planting time. It is advisable to place netting, removed from the redcurrants or strawberries, over the plants early in August.

Propagation

The plants may be increased in several ways, hence it is difficult to understand why they remain expensive. Seed may be sown in shallow drills as soon as ripe in early October. Germination will take place the following spring, and the young plants may be moved to special beds for growing on in early autumn. At no time should the seedlings be allowed to suffer from lack of moisture.

Alternatively, the plants may be increased by layering shoots in autumn, bending them down until they reach the soil, then partially splitting the stem. This is inserted in the ground and held in position by a layering pin, in the same way as when layering carnations. Rooting will have taken place by early the following summer, when the rooted portion is severed from the parent and transplanted. Again, suckers may be removed and grown on; or shoots of the new season's wood, six inches long, are removed early in August and inserted into a peat and sand mixture under a glass bell jar or cloche. Rooting will have taken place by the winter, and the plants are moved to beds the following spring for growing on.

Varieties

EARLY BLUE An early variety, best for a cold, northerly garden, it bears heavily, in short sprays, the fruits being sweet and juicy.

JERSEY The best late maturing variety, it should be grown in warm gardens for it to reach its best, when it will produce a heavy crop of large round blue-black fruits.

PEMBERTON It follows 'Early Bird' and is a most reliable cropper in colder districts, its thin-skinned fruits being large and juicy.

GOOSEBERRY

The gooseberry is at its best in a cool climate where the fruit can mature slowly, thus bringing out the maximum flavour. It was about one hundred years ago that the dessert gooseberry reached the zenith of its popularity in England. There the friendly rivalry of the gooseberry shows, held in many villages, created an interest in this delicious fruit which make it the most popular of all.

Climate and Situation

Indifferent to cold conditions and adverse weather, the gooseberry may be classed as the fruit grower's last line of defence. It never makes the money strawberries do, but never fails when other soft fruits may. For this reason, and because the fruit will hang on the bushes until there is labour available for picking, at least a small area should be planted with gooseberries on every fruit farm and in every garden. On high wind-swept ground or where excessive rain prevents the profitable fruiting of any other soft fruit, the gooseberry may be grown as a specialist crop.

Soil Requirements

Gooseberries are tolerant of frost and cold winds, and for this reason may be planted as a windbreak. But soil requirement plays a larger part in the production of a profitable crop than with any other fruit. Gooseberries prefer a light, well drained soil containing some humus. This is essential where growing dessert fruit, for without ample moisture throughout the early summer months the fruit will not swell. A cool soil is also essential, and for this reason the plants never crop well in shallow, chalky soils which become hot in summer. But an excess of nitrogen should not be given, for this will only encourage mildew. Gooseberries should be grown 'hard' so that the wood ripens well, and since the fruit is borne on the old and new wood, as with red-currants, it is more important to maintain a balance between old and new wood than to strive for the formation of an excess of new fruiting wood. This means providing both potash and nitrogen.

Where growing large fruits for exhibition, the plants should regularly receive an application of manure water, which should be given from the time the fruits begin to set. To delay feeding, especially if the weather is warm and dry and the plants are lacking moisture, will cause the skins to burst in the same way as tomatoes.

Pruning and Propagation

Where exhibition fruit is required, the shoots should be cut back each winter to about two-thirds of their length, or to about three inches of the new wood, for this will direct the energies of the plant to the fruit rather than to the formation of an extension to the shoots. Where growing in cordon form, the shoots are pruned back in March to within three inches of their base.

The commercial grower will give the same treatment where growing for high class dessert fruit, but for culinary and canning varieties little pruning is done. Only overcrowded wood is removed, although all dead and decayed wood should be cut away each winter.

Varieties of drooping habit, such as 'Green Ocean' or 'Whinham's Industry', should be cut back to an upward bud to counteract this tendency, and those varieties most prone to mildew, e.g. 'Howard's Lancer' and 'Keepsake', or those of vigorous, spreading habit, should be given only limited supplies of nitrogen. Those, such as 'London', which make little growth require larger quantities. Gooseberries of upright habit should be cut back to an outward bud to prevent overcrowding at the centre of the bush. To obtain the best results, the habit of each should be studied.

Where growing for show, where the heaviest berry in its particular colour class wins the prize, some thinning should be done in a season when there has been a heavy 'set' of fruit. Thinning should not be done until the berries have commenced to swell, however, for the birds may have already done the job. 'Woodpecker', 'London', 'Lord Derby', 'Princess Royal' and 'Surprise' are all varieties which respond to thinning and liberal feeding.

Gooseberries are always grown on a 'leg' to prevent, as far as possible, the formation of suckers. It must be said that the cuttings are never well disposed to take root and require every assistance. Only new wood should be used (easily detected as it is light in colour) and shoots about ten inches in length are ideal. Now comes a problem which perhaps accounts for much of the failure to root; this is the non-insertion of the cuttings while the sap is still in a fresh condition at the severed end. All too often the shoots are left lying about the potting shed while the ground is prepared, or they may be sent through the post without the necessary damp moss being wrapped round the stem to retain the moisture. To encourage a high rooting percentage it is vital to act quickly. The cuttings should be removed from the parent plants, prepared by having all but the top three or four buds removed so as to obtain a good 'leg', and inserted in the ground with the minimum delay.

The time to take and insert cuttings is September. First, a narrow trench is prepared in a sheltered position; behind a frame is ideal. This is made V-shape to a depth of nine inches, and three inches of sand mixed with a little peat is spread along the bottom. Into this the cutting is placed, first having been dipped into one of the hormone solutions or powders to encourage root formation. The soil is then pressed round the cuttings which are placed about three inches apart. There should be little need for artificial watering at this time of year, but the soil should always be kept moist. If cloches are available for placing over the trenches, then so much the better, for conditions can thus be controlled. Where cuttings are being raised for stock purposes, it is better to look over the bushes for the most suitable shoots before general pruning is carried out.

Besides the more usual bush form, gooseberries crop well as double and single cordons. For the small garden, where room is restricted, this is an excellent way of growing – either in rows exactly as for cordon apples, or against a wall. A cool, partially shaded position will suit them well.

The single cordon is trained by cutting back lateral growth to a single bud, the leader or extension shoot being grown on. Also, new growth formed during summer should be pinched back to within two inches of the base or main stem in late July, after fruiting.

The double cordon is made by cutting back the main stem to buds about nine inches from the ground, one in either direction, the shoots being trained first at an angle of 45°, then horizontally. These shoots are tied back to wires, then cut back to two buds on the upper part of the shoots, the others being rubbed out. Redcurrants are treated in the same way.

Planting

Gooseberries may be planted at any time during winter, but as they come into fruit early in summer in the most favourable districts, November planting is advocated. If the soil is heavy and not too well drained, March planting is advised. Planting distances will depend upon methods of cultivation and upon variety. As with blackcurrants, it is now popular to plant closer together in the rows and to allow a greater distance between the rows. This makes cultivation easier when the plants have become large. But gooseberries do not require protection against frost, nor are they susceptible to cold winds, being planted as a hedge or windbreak, so the more orthodox planting which facilitates picking may be

ABOVE Cob nuts *Corylus avellana*
LEFT Mulberry *Morus nigra*

Cherry 'White Heart' ripening

preferred. As the gooseberry tolerates and enjoys partial shade, it is a suitable crop to plant between young apple trees. The gooseberries are removed when about twenty years old to allow the orchard trees the maximum of room for cultivation.

After cuttings have been rooted they should be moved to a specially prepared nursery bed, preferably where there is partial shade, and planted three feet apart each way; or they may be planted into their permanent quarters the same distance apart and, after two years, alternate plants are removed and replanted six feet apart. For the spreading varieties, six to seven feet should be allowed, and for those of more compact, upright habit, four feet would be sufficient; closer planting is possible in the small garden where growth may be kept under control. Single cordons should be planted two feet apart and double cordons three feet.

Requiring similar amounts of potash and nitrogen, strawberries are a suitable crop for growing between the rows, while the plants are young, but care must be taken not to damage the roots. Alpine strawberries, liking shade, do well when planted between gooseberries. The gooseberries will also provide strawberries with protection against frost.

Red Varieties

BEDFORD RED An early variety, a neat upright grower which bears large round fruit in quantity. A fine variety for the small garden.

CROWN BOB This is a large, hairy red for mid-season. An easy grower and a heavy cropper. Makes a large spreading bush.

DAN'S MISTAKE A fine dessert red of spreading habit so named because it was a chance seedling. The berries are large, oval and of a pale red colour, mostly borne on the previous year's wood and at the ends of the shoots.

ECHO This is a very old variety of excellent flavour. The size of the fruit is large and the season very late. Makes a bush of perfect shape for the small garden.

LANCASHIRE LAD Raised in 1824, the berries are delicious when cooked green in June and most useful when ripe for dessert later in the month. Makes a large bush and large berry.

LONDON This is the heaviest gooseberry in cultivation, bearing a round smooth fruit in mid-season. The bush makes little wood and must be well fertilized.

LORD DERBY Ripens late – possibly the latest red. Bears large, oval fruit of excellent flavour. Grand for exhibition.

MAY DUKE Good for culinary purposes, picked green in May and delicious for dessert in June.

RIFLEMAN Bears a large, hairy berry late in the season. The flavour is delicious. The crop is always heavy, but the fruit is borne at the centre of the bush, making picking difficult. Late to mature.

WARRINGTON This is the jam-maker's favourite. The colour is vivid crimson, the fruit small, firm and very late.

White Varieties

CARELESS The most useful and widely grown gooseberry in cultivation; bottles and cans well, is a heavy cropper of greenish-white fruit, grows anywhere, and produces a handsome berry of good flavour. Most popular of all for canning.

KEEPSAKE A white, tinged with green, very early and an excellent market variety. It resembles an early 'Careless'. A very heavy cropper. Has proved excellent for canning.

LANGLEY GAGE One of the few gooseberries to receive an Award of Merit from the Royal Horticultural Society, but on tasting this is easily understood. Bears a small, silver, transparent berry of outstanding flavour – like nectar. Of neat, upright habit but the fruit, formed mostly at the centre of the bush, is difficult to pick.

PRINCESS ROYAL Always in the first three at gooseberry shows; bears a huge, smooth, creamy-white berry of exceptional flavour.

WHITE EAGLE Not so well known as 'Whitesmith'

and 'White Lion', but is at its best between the two and, like them, bears large, oblong-shaped berries of the sweetest flavour.

WHITE LION A superb variety, very late but almost equal to 'Leveller' in size and flavour. Extremely vigorous and hardy, it would always be the choice for a late gooseberry. Bears a heavy crop.

WHITESMITH The first of the 'white' trio to fruit. Bears a large, downy berry of delicious flavour the length of the stem, and is most prolific. Should be in all gardens for its early fruit and freedom of cropping.

WHITE TRANSPARENT Raised in 1871. It makes a large, but upright bush and bears a huge transparent berry, with smooth skin and a flavour both rich and sweet.

Yellow Varieties

BEDFORD YELLOW A most handsome berry, being of a rich golden yellow streaked with red. A mid-season variety and a heavy bearer; the fruit is large, hairy and of wonderful flavour.

BROOM GIRL A fine market yellow, very early with fruit of medium size. The dark yellow colour, shaded olive green, gives it a most attractive appearance, while its flavour is outstanding.

COUSEN'S SEEDLING A good bearer of attractive, firm, medium-sized fruit.

EARLY SULPHUR Very early. Bears fruit of excellent flavour and of an attractive primrose-yellow colour. Makes a large, vigorous bush.

GOLDEN GEM A handsome, deep yellow berry, mid-season to late and of wonderful flavour. A very heavy cropper. A 'Whitesmith' cross introduced in 1897.

HIGH SHERIFF A little-known variety, early, and bears fruit of a rich orange-yellow colour of good flavour and oblong in shape.

LEVELLER The favourite modern dessert gooseberry, but is only a huge cropper when fertilized with potash and manure and then only on certain soils. The 'Cox's Orange Pippin' of the gooseberry world.

During the winter pruning of standard gooseberries shorten all side shoots back to three buds

Green Varieties

DRILL Late but not so late as 'Lancer' and a useful gooseberry for a successional supply. The colour is deep green, large and of good flavour. Makes a neat, compact bush and crops heavily.

GREEN GEM A variety introduced in 1922. A good, all-round green, heavy cropping and useful – picked early for bottling and later for dessert.

GREEN OVERALL A delicious gooseberry which should be better known, for besides its unique flavour, the fruit is covered with attractive greyish down. Will form a huge berry in any soil.

GREEN WALNUT Very dark green, of medium size and first-class flavour. Makes a small, neat bush and is excellent for town gardens.

GUNNER Although introduced in 1820, this variety is only now coming to the front. It is of the valuable late mid-season group which closes the gaps. The sweet olive-green berries are large and hairy and of most striking appearance.

HOWARD'S LANCER If it were not susceptible to mildew it would be just about the best gooseberry ever introduced. It is a strong grower and regular cropper, and can be used for bottling, cooking and dessert, for which it is the latest of all to mature.

SHINER This could be described as a white variety, shaded green. It makes a vigorous bush and a large, unique, almost square berry of great sweetness.

THATCHER Makes a huge, oblong berry, dotted with red, very rich and sweet. The habit of spreading, vigorous and rather drooping.

REDCURRANT (and WHITECURRANT)

The most satisfactory way of growing this crop is

in double cordon formation, planted against a wall where the fruit can be protected by netting draped from hooks. The plants will remain in bearing for twenty years or so, and will be little troubled by pest or disease, although birds remain a constant worry to the large grower; often as much as half the crop may be taken as the berries are reaching maturity. Small pieces of tinfoil fastened to canes and placed at regular intervals about the bushes will be of help in scaring off the birds, and fish netting should be used for covering wherever possible. It is also advisable to pick the fruit the moment that it is ripe. To delay a single day will be to lose a large amount to birds. The redcurrant has not so long a season as the blackcurrant, nor can it hold its fruit as well. Adverse weather when the crop is ready for picking may also cause considerable losses.

Pruning and Propagation

Little pruning is required, for the fruit is borne on the old as well as on the new wood but; as with gooseberries, unduly old and all decayed wood must be cut away to prevent the bush from becoming overcrowded and to maintain its health. Upon planting, all shoots must be cut back to a bud about three inches from their base, and this will form the main stem. This should be done during early April, and the following year the new shoots should also be cut back to a bud within three inches of the point at which the shoots were formed. Such action will build up a shapely plant and encourage the formation of a good head. Afterwards, the occasional shortening back of an unduly vigorous shoot or the removal of old or overcrowded wood is all that is necessary.

The cordon is formed by growing on the main stem or shoot and cutting back all side shoots, while the double cordon is formed by cutting back the main stem to a bud about eight inches above soil level. Two buds, one on either side of the stem, are trained in an outward direction as described for gooseberry cordons. Cordons against a wall, or alongside a path, should be planted two feet apart and securely fastened to strong wires, while double cordons are allowed about three feet six inches.

To increase the stock, 15-inch shoots of the new season's wood should be removed early in October and, as the plants are grown on a leg, all except the upper four buds should be removed. The shoots are then inserted three inches deep and six inches apart into a trench of peat and sand, and made quite firm to encourage rapid rooting. Like gooseberries, redcurrants are slower to root than blackcurrants, and they should be given assistance by inserting the rooting end of the cuttings in hormone powder. The shoot is allowed to remain in the row for either one or two years, after which it is planted in its permanent quarters and the head formed as described.

Soil Requirements

Both red and white currants enjoy the same manurial conditions as the gooseberry, and they should always be planted near each other if both crops are required. The plants must be given a deeply dug soil which preferably should be of a light nature. It must be free from perennial weeds and should contain some humus. This need not be of such a heavy nitrogenous nature as for blackcurrants, for an excess of nitrogen will encourage an excess of plant growth to the detriment of fruit.

A balance between fruit production and plant growth should be maintained. Like gooseberries, these currants enjoy plenty of potash in the soil, given in the form of wood ash which has been stored dry. This is raked into the top soil after planting, and again each spring. Where growing commercially, give each plant a two-ounce dressing of sulphate of potash in April and harrow or rake it into the soil. To supply humus, incorporate

Redcurrants 'Laxton's Number One'

seaweed, hop manure, decayed leaves and garden compost, or peat, possibly augmented with some shoddy or farmyard manure. Both red and white currants like humus; where this is lacking the fruit will remain small, seedy and devoid of juice, and the plants will not make much new growth. It is vital to provide the plants with plenty of humus where growing against a wall, in which position a shortage of moisture often causes failure to crop well. Like all soft fruits, red and white currants appreciate an early summer mulch of strawy manure, seaweed or peat which will help to maintain moisture in the soil.

Planting

Planting may take place at any time during the winter months, but preferably between October and December, which will allow the plants time to settle down before frosts. Being of compact habit, with the possible exception of 'Laxton's No. 1', the plants may be set out three to four feet apart each way, allowing five feet for 'Laxton's'. Before planting, any roots which may have formed on the leg should be removed, otherwise these are liable to form suckers, which must be removed with a sharp knife.

With red and white currants it is important to select a sheltered position, for they detest cold winds almost as much as blackcurrants. Not only will a strong wind cause bud dropping, but it will also damage the plants by breaking off the brittle wood. For this reason these currants always crop better in warmer districts or in a walled garden. Where the garden or ground is exposed, then grow gooseberries instead, or the hardier 'Fay's Prolific' or 'Red Lake'.

Where growing only a few plants, a weekly application of liquid manure, as for dessert gooseberries, will make a great difference in the fruit, almost doubling the size. But as with gooseberries, commence this feeding as soon as the fruit begins to set, otherwise, if left until the berries are swelling, the additional moisture may cause the skin to burst.

Used as fresh fruit, red and white currants in combination make a pleasing decoration, and with their rich fragrance and rather tart flavour they will greatly improve a dish of raspberries, in the same way as the acid 'Red Rich' strawberry improves the particularly sweet varieties.

Varieties

Early-Fruiting

EARLIEST OF FOURLANDS Bud burst is early, so it should be confined to a sheltered garden. It makes a large bush, but the habit is upright and compact. It bears a long truss and large scarlet fruit.

FAY'S PROLIFIC An American variety, raised in New York State in 1865. It comes late into bloom but early into fruit. It also makes a small, compact bush and fruits freely.

LAXTON'S NO. 1 Has the reputation of being the outstanding redcurrant for commercial purposes, and indeed for all purposes. It is a strong grower, a reliable cropper in all districts, and is the first redcurrant on the market. The berries are firm and of a good rich colour, although not so large as those of 'Red Lake'.

Mid-season-Fruiting

HOUGHTON CASTLE Bud burst is late. It makes a large, spreading bush and crops heavily, the big, deep-crimson fruit being richly flavoured.

LAXTON'S PERFECTION Only in a moist climate and in a sheltered garden does this variety give of its best. It makes a tall, upright bush, the fruit trusses being long and heavily laden with bright red berries of exhibition quality. It may be described as a late mid-season variety, as it retains its fruit well into August.

RED LAKE Introduced into Britain from the Minnesota Experimental Station, it has gained an Award of Merit. It makes a neat, compact bush of upright habit, and may be classed as an early mid-season variety. The fruit is borne in long trusses, the berries being of dessert quality, large, bright scarlet and juicy, with a glossy, tough skin. The fruit stands up to adverse weather and will transport long distances. If only one variety is to be grown, this should be it.

WHITE DUTCH It is the only white variety worth growing, cropping heavily. The ivory-coloured fruits are large and of good flavour.

Late-Fruiting

RABY CASTLE It blooms late. It makes a small, neat bush and bears a heavy crop, but the fruit is small unless grown well.

WILSON'S LONG BUNCH The latest of all, hence its value in prolonging the season, but a good, late redcurrant is badly needed. It forms a bush of very spreading habit, but is late into bloom and misses all frosts. The pale, cerise-pink berries are borne in long trusses, hence its name.

RHUBARB

It has the ability to produce a large quantity of fruit over a long period and from only a very small space. The roots may be lifted and forced in a greenhouse or cellar to provide an early New Year crop, or covered and semi-forced for a spring crop, to be followed by fruit for early summer use pulled from naturally grown roots. Rhubarb will be indispensable for the first six months of the year, and for the maket grower there is always a ready sale for forced rhubarb sold locally.

Soil and Cultivation

Before the young roots are planted, the land must be well cultivated. A heavy loam, well drained and yet moist, is the ideal, although where considerable quantities of manure and compost are available, rhubarb may be grown on almost any soil. But a deeply cultivated, well manured soil will encourage a heavy crop of thick, succulent stems. Deep trenching, and at the same time working in as much farmyard manure or home-made compost as possible, will provide the required humus. Old mushroom-bed manure is also ideal, as it is for all other soft fruit crops.

Peat is also useful for working into the soil, but this should be supplemented with manure or shoddy. Remember that the larger the leaf the more vigorous will be the crown the following season, so everything must be done to encourage as much leaf growth as possible – and this means heavy nitrogenous manuring.

Rhubarb also loves bone meal, and four ounces per square yard applied when the land is made ready will be greatly beneficial. Should the land be heavy, the same quantity of basic slag should be substituted for the bone meal, and a one-ounce-per-square-yard dressing of sulphate of potash every other spring will not be found excessive. Very early varieties, which are to be covered in the open, will respond to a two-ounce-per-square-yard application of sodium nitrate as soon as the new growth appears. Rhubarb will also appreciate four cwt of lime per acre, applied each winter.

All weeds must be removed before the roots are planted out, but the soil should first be allowed to settle down for several days. The earlier, less-vigorous varieties are planted out in rows three feet apart each way, and the later varieties should be allowed an extra six inches each way. This distance will allow the roots to reach a good size, and allow room for covering and pulling. For the first season, lettuce or strawberries may be planted between the rows, but where the strawberry is to be allowed to crop a second season, the rhubarb roots should be allowed an extra six inches between the rows.

The roots should be set out when the soil is friable. They must be firmly trodden in, and the soil should be brought up level with the crown bud.

Planting

The young crowns or eyes, or roots, as they are

variously called, are planted out during winter. November and early December is the best time, for this allows the roots to become established before the frosty weather, so that they will produce a number of stems during the first summer. If it is proposed to begin rhubarb growing in this way, the roots may be purchased as offsets containing a bud with a piece of root attached. If few or no stalks are removed during the first season, the roots will have made plenty of growth by the following summer, and will be sturdy enough to be semi-forced, or forced in heat the subsequent winter. Where growing for sale it will perhaps be better to concentrate on two varieties, an early and a mid-season, both of which may be forced to extend the season. When required for home use only, then a single root of several varieties may be grown.

Where it is intended to force the roots, no stems should be removed for two years. Provided applications of fertilizers, manure and peat mulches have been given each winter and spring to build up a sturdy root, the third season will show a good-sized clump, which may then be semi- or cold-forced in early spring, or forced in heat the following winter.

Methods of Forcing

Those without heat may grow rhubarb of the same quality as that grown in heat, and in view of the high costs of fuel, cold-forcing is more economical. One method is to force alternate rows in alternate years by removing the crowns in late February, dressing with a mulch of manure and covering each with an earthenware pot or even a small tea chest. Between the pots or chests, straw is heaped to help retain the sun's warmth. Wattle hurdles are erected to keep off cold winds, and as much brushwood as can be found is placed inside the hurdling for additional protection. The plantation is given no further attention apart from the removal of the straw as soon as new growth is observed, and a dressing of sodium nitrate is applied at the rate of half an ounce per square yard. The straw is then replaced and left until the stems are seen to be pushing up the chest and pot lids, when they will be found ready for pulling and bunching. This early rhubarb will be a rich, pink colour; although it is several weeks later than heat-forced rhubarb, it will be in equal demand by the housewife who is more rhubarb-minded in late spring and early summer than during the winter days, when boiled puddings tend to dominate the table.

Rhubarb may be cold-forced in a number of other ways. Where it is intended to use lights, the roots are planted in beds rather than in rows. This will mean planting them closer, and leaving a path between each bed. Turf may be placed around the beds to add warmth, and to raise the glass so that the stems are allowed to develop to their correct length. Old bricks or stones are suitable but are less warm. The lights are placed over the beds, which are given exactly the same treatment as previously described. To keep off bright light and to conserve as much warmth as possible, straw and sacks should be placed over the lights and held down by lengths of wood.

When it is intended to force the roots in a building, a cellar or stable is ideal. A quantity of hot, well-rotted compost must be available to stimulate growth. This may be prepared by rotting straw with an activator and additional heat can be gained by adding to the compost a small quantity of dry poultry manure, some oak and beech leaves, and any available farmyard manure. The whole is turned several times until it reaches a thoroughly decomposed condition and is generating a large amount of heat. The compost should be ready for taking indoors during early February.

Meanwhile the roots are lifted and left exposed to the elements for two or three weeks. The more

Under staging is an ideal place for forcing early rhubarb

severe the weather, the more will they benefit. Early in February the compost is spread out on the floor of the room to a depth of six inches, and several inches of soil placed on top. Over the whole the roots are placed close together, and a quantity of peat and fine soil is then tightly firmed around the clumps, filling in all cavities. The bed is given a thorough watering and all windows are darkened to encourage the stems to grow long and straight, and to be of a good colour. The same procedure is used when the roots are forced in heat, only in this case the manure bed is generally dispensed with, the roots being taken indoors in December. It must be remembered that those roots intended for forcing should not have been pulled the previous summer. All growth must be allowed to die down in the autumn before the dead leaves are cleared away, and the roots lifted early in December to weather.

Where growing for semi-forcing in the open, if the roots are pulled only moderately and the covers removed after three to four weeks' pulling, they can be gently forced the following spring. There must however be no pulling the preceding summer, and the roots must be manured in the autumn.

Those roots forced over a hotbed or in heat should be removed as soon as all pulling has ended, and replanted in beds which have been well replenished with manure and fertilizer. There they must be left for at least eighteen months, until they have recovered from their more severe forcing. No pulling should be done until such time as they have fully recovered. Ultimately they may be forced again, but only cool-forced in the nursery beds.

Propagation

Rhubarb is increased by division of the crowns or by seed-sowing; though a true stock may only be obtained by division.

The clumps are lifted in October and November, and the roots are cut into pieces, each containing an eye or bud. A three-year clump may be divided into as many as six or more offsets.

Dust the divisions with hydrated lime to keep them as clean as possible; many growers do this when making new plantations with their own roots. The divisions are made with a sharp spade or knife, and care must be taken to handle the roots as gently as possible. Provided that the bud is undamaged, even though there is virtually no root adjoining, the plant will grow in the spring, although it may take longer to build up into a sturdy forcing clump.

The raising of plants from seed will save money but they will take three years to come into bearing. The two most reliable varieties for the reproduction of seedling fruit are 'Myatt's Victoria' and 'Glaskin's Perpetual'. All varieties except, 'The Sutton', a seedless variety, bear seedpods late in summer. Unless it is desired to save the seed, these seed stems must be cut off at ground level as soon as they form, in order to direct the strength used in the formation of seeds to the roots. This is essential if forcing is contemplated.

If the seed (which must not be more than two years old) is sown in boxes in a heated greenhouse or frame in September, the seedlings can be moved to the open ground in late March; alternatively, sow seed direct into the frames in late March, or even into drills in the open ground. Provided that the seed is kept moist it will readily germinate, and the plants will be large enough to transplant by June. They should then be planted in beds one foot apart. The following spring every alternate plant is removed and planted elsewhere. The ground must be well manured and thoroughly cleaned before the seedlings are transplanted. No pulling must be done for the first two seasons, after which the roots will be ready to produce a crop, and be suitable for forcing, in their third year.

Varieties

Early

EARLY SUPERB This is an excellent variety which received a Highly Commended award at the 1949 Royal Horticultural Society's Rhubarb

Trials. It is a heavy cropper, and reaches maturity before 'Royal Albert'. It forces well in heat or under lights.
HAWKE'S CHAMPAGNE Another early variety, it bears stems of the brightest crimson and forces excellently.
PARAGON Where soil is of a clay nature, this should do well. It bears long sticks of bright scarlet colour which have a brisk flavour when cooked.
RED SUNSHINE A new Australian variety, early to mature and bearing huge sticks of a rich crimson colour, sweeter than most rhubarbs. It forces well.
ROSENHAGEN A new Dutch variety with deep crimson sticks; it matures early and forces well.
ROYAL ALBERT This must be just about the best rhubarb for cool-forcing in the garden, as it is very hardy, very early and produces a stem of the brightest scarlet.
TIMPERLEY EARLY A fine new early; it forces well and bears long, stout stems of an excellent colour when ripe.

Second Early
CANADA RED A Canadian introduction, excellent for cool forcing. The large stalks are of a brilliant crimson colour, freely produced over a long period.
DAWE'S CHALLENGE It follows 'Myatt's Linnaeus' and 'Stott's Monarch', and as an all-round variety is unrivalled under all conditions.
MYATT'S LINNAEUS This is a grand variety to follow the earlier rhubarb. It is an exceedingly strong grower and forces well, besides making large stems when grown in the open ground.
STOTT'S MONARCH This fine rhubarb matures at about the same time as 'Linnaeus'. It is a strong grower, a heavy cropper, and the stems–which mature green in colour–are deliciously sweet.
SUTTON'S RED A most handsome rhubarb which crops heavily and is perhaps the best variety for bottling and canning, retaining its colour over many months.

Late-Maturing
DAWE'S CHAMPION Another fine rhubarb which matures just before 'The Sutton' and 'Victoria', and closes the gap following 'Stott's Monarch' and 'Sutton's Red'. It is a heavy cropper, and does well in all districts, providing the most colourful stick of all the rhubarbs.
GLASKIN'S PERPETUAL As the name implies, this is a continuous cropper, producing green stems, shaded red. It is an excellent garden rhubarb.
MYATT'S VICTORIA This is the last of the rhubarbs to mature, and it must be the most popular variety for open ground pulling. It is excellent for canners, as it makes a strong stem and crops heavily.
THE SUTTON This is one of the few rhubarbs to receive an Award of Merit. It is not so late as 'Victoria'; it forces well and makes an immense stem of the most brilliant crimson. As it does not seed, it crops over a longer period than most varieties.

STRAWBERRY (Alpine)

These richly-flavoured strawberries should be in every amateur's garden. The fruit makes delicious jam and adds a special fragrance when mixed with the ordinary strawberries. Also, as they enjoy a certain amount of shade, the plants may be used for those more sunless corners about the garden where the ordinary varieties would not ripen well. Again, where space is strictly limited, for an edging to a border or for growing in pots or window boxes, the runnerless alpines (increased by division like a primrose) will prove suitable. They like a moist soil, thoroughly enriched with humus, so you should work in as much decayed manure, peat and leaf-mould as possible. The plants will then continue to fruit throughout late summer and autumn. The alpine strawberry, not to be confused with the autumn-fruiting perpetual, is *Fragaria vesca,* known to continental gardens at the beginning of the sixteenth century, and introduced into England two centuries later.

They were, then, at once acclaimed for the quality of their fruit, and today, although they are not widely grown commercially, they find a ready sale to top-class restaurants for mixing with the less-delicately-flavoured, late-summer strawberries. Although the fruit is small, the size may be enlarged by thinning and by liberal feeding. The main flush of fruit is obtained during July and August, but the plants continue to yield until the end of autumn.

Propagation is by division, or by runners where these are formed, but the most vigorous plants are obtained from seed. All the alpines grow readily in this way. The best method is to sow the seed in autumn in boxes containing the John Innes sowing compost. The boxes are placed in cold frames until the seedlings are planted out in early April, allowing 20 inches between the plants. They will bear well for two years, and should then be divided, or fresh plants should be raised from seed.

Varieties

BARON SOLEMACHER Forming no runners and easily raised from seed, the tall-growing plants bear most handsome, long red berries of rich flavour when ripe. If thinned and liberally fed, the fruits grow quite large.

BELLE DE MEAUX Raised in France about 1880, this alpine forms runners. The crimson fruit is wedge-shaped but quite small and of excellent flavour.

DELIGHT This is a creamy-white form of 'Baron Solemacher'. The fruits possess a distinct perfume as well as being very sweet. Served with the bright red 'Solemacher', they make a pleasing decoration and improve the flavour of fresh dessert fruit.

STRAWBERRY (Large Fruiting)

The most popular fruit, for it comes into bearing six to seven months after planting and no fruit crops more heavily. The fruits are rich in vitamin C and with 112 calories to the pound are right for those needing to diet. The fruit may also be used in many ways: to enjoy with cream, gathered straight from the plant, or to use for tarts and flans and also to make the finest quality jam which has no equal for use on scones with Devonshire cream.

Strawberry growing has been revolutionized in the immediate post-war years. In pre-war days there were three main commercial varieties: 'Madame Lefebvre', the earliest of the three to mature; 'Huxley Giant', a heavy cropper of rather coarse fruit; and 'Royal Sovereign', which had 'Noble' and 'King of the Earlies' for its parents. The latter contained the 'blood' of the celebrated 'Black Prince', a wonderful variety ripening to almost crimson-black and with a taste like that of old port. Of the three old favourites, 'Royal Sovereign' has for long been troubled by virus, but is as yet unsurpassed for the quality of its fruit, while 'Huxley' and 'Lefebvre' are grown chiefly for their hardiness and resistance to disease. But they all cropped at about the same time, which meant that there was an abundance of fruit for a period of only three to four weeks, and if frosts or wet weather ruined the crop, then the outlook for the strawberry grower was indeed bleak.

Now all this has changed, and by growing for succession, even where no glass protection is used, there will be fruit from early May until December. This ensures not only a long period of income for the commercial grower, but also that at least a part of the crop will avoid adverse weather conditions. For the amateur, the long fruiting period will also add interest to the garden. Even greater interest may be enjoyed if several of the alpine strawberries, and those varieties which will most satisfy the connoisseur of choice fruit, are also grown.

Preparing the Soil

Strawberries like a light, loamy soil, well supplied

Strawberry 'Cambridge Favourite'

with humus. Such a soil warms quickly with the early spring sunshine, and is generally well drained. Neither will it become too compact with constant treading during the picking season, as will a heavy soil, and so prevent oxygen reaching the roots. Plants growing in a heavy, badly drained soil may suffer considerable losses from red core root disease, especially when a wet winter is followed by a cold spring. Where the soil tends to be heavy, the best varieties to grow, being highly resistant to red core root rot, are the Cambridge introductions: 'Vigour', 'Sentry' and 'Rival' and also 'Red Gauntlet'. These crop heavily in a stiff loam, and are the most reliable varieties for rainy districts.

A clean and well manured soil is vital for a heavy crop. Planting into ground infested by perennial weeds, impossible to eradicate after planting, will never grow good crops. Preferably, strawberries should be planted into ground which has previously grown a crop of potatoes, for then the soil will be well pulverized and free from weeds. It is best to follow a rotational cropping system, allowing the land a rest for two years after every four-year (or two-year) crop.

First make the ground clean, then work in some humus. This may take the form of decayed farmyard manure, and be as much as twenty tons to the acre where the land is light and lacking in humus. The amateur will dig in what manures are available, material from the compost heap or straw decomposed by an activator, to which may be added either pig or pultry manure, decayed leaves, shoddy, spent hops or peat. These materials may also be used on a commercial scale. Seaweed is valuable, but everything depends upon situation; to minimize transport expenses, humus-forming materials should be obtained as near home as possible. In cases where shoddy is readily obtainable, it will be found many times richer in nitrogen than farmyard manure. Use it at the rate of two tons to the acre, and augment it by peat and a one-ounce-per-square yard dressing of potash.

Strawberries must have nitrogen, phosphorus, and potash, for they absorb these minerals from the soil in almost equal quantities. Fish meal and animal manures contain all three ingredients, and they should be used where possible. Remember that the lighter the soil, the more potash a plant will require. So, with a retentive loam, half the quantity may be given; and, in a sandy soil, half as much again. In place of sulphate of potash for the private garden, wood ash stored under cover has valuable potash content, but the ash will need to be used liberally. Potash should be raked or harrowed into the top soil just before planting is done, the other materials being worked into the soil when the ground is cleaned.

It is important, when preparing the ground, to incorporate plenty of humus-forming materials which will open up a clay soil and retain moisture in a light one. Strawberries must have an abundance of moisture during spring and summer to help to swell the fruit, yet the ground should be sufficiently well drained for excess moisture to seep away during winter. Strawberries crop best in a slightly acid soil. One with a pH value of 6.0–6.5 is desirable, and peat, also slightly acid, is the best form of humus. In peat, the plants will form masses of fibrous roots which enable them to obtain the maximum nourishment from the soil. Use peat in quantity, for it is cheap, whether you grow commercially or in the home garden. Strawberries should not be planted on newly-dug turf land, unless it has previously been treated for wireworm, for strawberry roots suffer more from this pest than any other fruit.

Apart from the use of sulphate of potash, strawberries do not take kindly to artificial manures. With their greater use of these during the past decade, the yield of commercial plantations has diminished. On the mainland of Europe today, and in Britain until 1940, strawberry ground received up to 50 tons of farmyard manure to the acre, or its equivalent in shoddy. On the Continent still, and in Britain until 1940, an acre of strawberries would yield between five and six tons of fruit, 'Royal Sovereign' being the most popular variety. Today in Britain the average yield is between two and three tons, but in County Wexford and County Mayo in Ireland, where the old manuring methods are still practised, the yield is more than double. Plenty of humus and organic manure is the secret of success with this crop. 'Cambridge Favourite' is perhaps the heaviest bearer; in its second year, in well manured ground, it will yield one pound per plant.

Planting

There is as much controversy today as there ever was over planting methods. Growers are divided between planting 18 inches apart in beds 5-6 feet wide, so that picking can be done from both sides, or planting in rows 3 feet apart and allowing 18 inches between the plants in the rows. Both methods will take about 10,000 plants to the acre, but whereas those growing in beds are allowed to form runners, which are left undisturbed to bear fruit, those planted in rows have the runners removed to form a separate plantation. Clean ground is vital to successful fruiting under the bed system, for perennial weeds could choke out the young plants. In a dry season, plants in beds crop more heavily than plants in rows, while the dense foliage provides protection from rains with little loss of fruit through splashing. So strawing or mulching is unnecessary for plants in the bed system.

If the soil is heavy or low-lying, it is advisable to plant either on raised beds or along the top of shallow furrows to guard against red core. There is, however, some risk of frost damage with plants growing on ridges and, where the land (or garden) is troubled by late frosts, it will be better to plant on raised beds. Here the plants, growing close together, provide mutual protection from frost and from cold winds. And, because there is a risk of mildew among plants on the bed system, only those varieties which are resistant should be grown in this way. Non-resistant varieties require a greater circulation of air.

Gardeners of old would plant in October and disbud during the first season, to build up a sturdy plant to fruit heavily in the following season. This meant that the plants occupied the ground almost eighteen months before fruiting. But, provided that they are given good cultural treatment, and are planted during August and September for early-fruiting varieties, and up to the end of October for those which fruit late in the season, the plants can be allowed to fruit during their first summer, although there may be some loss of stamina in the plants for future years.

A number of varieties produce better quality fruit in their first season from such a planting. It is, however, important to plant the earliest fruiting varieties before the end of August, and where it is not possible to do any planting until the beginning of the year, then all varieties except the autumn-fruiting perpetuals should be disbudded in their first season. Where the land is heavy it is advisable to plant early September, while the soil is still warm, and rooting will then be accomplished before winter. Plants set out later may be lifted from the soil by hard frosts, and may be damaged. In any case, it is advisable to tread all plants early in March, so that the roots may have full contact with the soil when they commence to grow.

As planting should never be done when the ground is wet and sticky, late-summer and early-autumn planting is to be preferred, though a light, sandy soil may be planted at any time.

Planting is done with a wide-nosed trowel, so that a good sized hole may be made, and the roots spread out. Roots placed into the soil bunched together will never perform their function, and the plants will remain stunted and bear only a light crop. Make the plants firm by treading.

Always plant 'runners', as strawberry plants are called, which have been removed from one-year-old parent plants. The most vigorous are those which have formed first, those nearest the parent, while runners from 'maiden' or one-year-old plants are more vigorous than from older plants.

It is advisable to try to obtain clean and virus-free stocks. Suppliers of runners usually concencentrate on producing either runner or fruit, never both, from the same plantation. The removal of runners, as soon as they appear, from the fruiting plants, enables these plants to concentrate their energies into the bearing of heavy crops, while exactly the reverse is the case with those plants grown for the production of runners. Here the plants are deblossomed rigorously, so that their energies are directed into the formation of sturdy runners. Where growing commercially, a plant cannot be expected to bear a heavy crop, in addition to producing large numbers of runners, without loss of stamina.

When planting, take care not to allow the roots to become dry, otherwise the plants may take a long time to recover and to form new fibrous roots. The best method is to place the plants either in boxes of damp peat, or in moss upon arrival, and they should be kept in this while being planted. With large-scale planting–and 10,000 plants will be required for one acre of ground–it is advisable to take delivery in two consignments, to allow time for planting the first lot before the second batch arrives. Planting should also be done quickly as possible, but adverse weather may hold up operations, and this should be allowed for when asking for delivery of the second batch. Always use a strong garden line for planting, taking care to space out the rows to sufficient width, to allow either a hand or mechanical hoe to be taken between the plants in early spring, to aerate the soil and to kill annual weeds.

Do not plant too deeply. Strawberries, like most soft fruits, are surface-rooting plants, hence the frequent necessity to top dress and mulch. It is also important to exercise care when hoeing, for it is not advisable to work too near the plants. The shallow-rooting quality of strawberries enables them to be grown in fairly shallow soils, provided that they are enriched with humus-forming manures to prevent drying out during a period of drought.

Early in April, especially following a long, cold winter, the plants should be given a light top dressing with sulphate of ammonia to stimulate them into growth. This should be applied during a period of rainy weather so that it is washed into the soil. The commercial grower should use one cwt per acre; the amateur gardener one ounce per yard, where growing in rows, or two ounces per square yard in beds.

If April is moist and warm, the plants will, by the month end, have commenced to form bloom and also runners. Where growing chiefly for fruit, the runners must be removed. The first fortnight of May is the most worrying period of the year for the strawberry grower, for a hard frost will, in a single night, blacken the blossom and spoil any chance of a good crop. This is why both amateur and commercial growers are advised to plant at least one of those varieties which come late into bloom; if only early varieties are grown, in one out of every three seasons the crop may be partially damaged. The grower is relieved when he knows the blossom has set its fruit without being damaged by the frost, for this goes far towards ensuring a heavy crop.

After the blossom has set fruit, the plants should be mulched. Peat, spread thickly between the plants and up to the crowns, will help the soil to retain its moisture while the fruit is maturing, and at the same time will suppress annual weeds. A peat mulch will also protect the fruit from soil splashing quite as well as the more popular straw, and wherever possible it should be used in preference. Straw is not so practical; it harbours slugs and mice, and tends to remove some of the nitrogen from the soil as it is trodden in. And, whereas the

Tucking straw beneath strawberry trusses

peat, after the crop has been picked, may be worked into the soil, the straw must be tediously gathered up and either burnt or composted.

Amateurs growing only a few plants could use thick layers of newspaper for keeping the fruits clean as an alternative to strawberry mats. The paper must be used thickly, and is placed between the rows, up the crown of the plants. Mats of bamboo or plastic are also economical and long lasting, but a combination of peat and newspaper – the former useful in so many ways about the garden and greenhouse – will prove satisfactory. But whatever material is chosen, it must be in position by the time that the fruits are beginning to swell and are still green, for when once they attain some size they will ripen quickly. Where only one or two plants of several varieties are being grown, maturing in succession, broken crocks or glass may be used to prevent splashing, and these will also conserve moisture. They will in addition hasten ripening by reflecting the rays of the sun on to the fruits.

Watering and Feeding

While the fruits are swelling, artificial watering will be necessary during a dry period. Strawberries must be given an abundance of moisture at this time, and the months of May and June, when the early mid-season crops are maturing, are usually the driest months of the year. Strawberries lacking sufficient moisture will bear only small, seedy fruit, lacking in flavour, and it may be necessary, where the soil is of a sandy nature or where the plants are growing in dry regions, to water until the completion of the crop. This, however, should be modified while picking is taking place because, of all soft fruits, strawberries and raspberries in particular should be marketed or picked for home use only when quite dry, otherwise the fruit will rapidly deteriorate.

Regular spraying of the beds will keep down red spider attacks, while watering with dilute liquid manure water, obtainable in concentrated form in bottles, and clean and easy to use, will help form exhibition-sized fruit of good flavour. Liquid manure will also help to build up a plant which will bear a heavy crop during the next year or so. An excellent method of irrigation is by the use of rotational sprinklers, placed at intervals about the plantation and fed from a hose.

As soon as the fruits become swollen they will colour rapidly, and the plants should be looked over daily, possibly twice daily if the weather is warm and sunny. After fruiting, the ground should be cleared of straw, if this has been used, and the rows or beds given a dressing of a mixture of peat and decayed manure.

What to do with the foliage, as it begins to die back in early autumn, is also a matter of controversy. Some burn it off together with the straw, a drastic method, while others take a grass cutter along the rows and in this way remove the top foliage; this is a more satisfactory method, especially as it may then be dug into the soil for humus.

The first runners will be ready for removal from the beginning of July. Maiden or one-year plants produce the best runners. The amateur should remove those required to make a new bed and destroy any others throughout summer. How long to allow a bed to remain in bearing must be determined by condition of the land, the health and vigour of the plants, and their cropping powers during the previous season. Some growers plant in August and plough in the plants as soon as they have fruited the following summer, but plants grown in a well cultivated soil will bear for two, three and even four seasons without deterioration of the fruit. Runners removed from maidens are used to form a second plantation, and, in turn, these plants yield runners. So, while bed (ii) is in its first year of cropping, bed (i) is in its second season and ready for removal. In this way, there is always a bed fruiting in its first year and another cropping for a second year, no runners being removed from second season plants.

For a second year plantation, a two-ounce-per-square-yard dressing with sulphate of potash should be given in early March, followed by one-ounce-per-square-yard of sulphate of ammonia in early April. Future beds will be healthier if the ground is rested from strawberries after every four years.

Strawberries Under Glass

With the high cost of heating, few can afford the luxury of a crop of strawberries grown in a heated greenhouse. But today there are several varieties which will naturally fruit under glass without heat, at much the same time as those grown in heat did in pre-war days. So, unless they are intended for a special purpose, such as an exhibition or banquet, strawberries are now rarely grown in heat. Excellent profits, however, may be obtained from open ground plants given glass protection, and there are two forms of glass for forcing, Dutch lights and cloches.

The commercial grower generally uses lights, the amateur uses cloches, but each is efficient. Under glass the fruit will be clean and no splash protection need be given, but unless correctly ventilated the plants may suffer from mildew and the fruits from botrytis, a disease which causes them to rot away before ripening. To ripen fruit under glass in a satisfactory condition calls for skill, and many go wrong by covering the plants too soon. When winter comes, the strawberry plant, like the grower himself (who has has six strenuous months, often picking from daybreak until dusk), is ready for a break, and it should be given a period of cold and rest to become revitalized. However early a crop is desired, no plants should be covered before mid-February, preferably towards the end of the month, after having first been given a dressing with potash. It is not only necessary to plant mildew-resistant varieties under glass culture, but also those varieties which do not make an excess of leaf. Strawberries are hardy plants, and demand the maximum of ventilation, and, in this respect, the less foliage the plants make the better will be the crop produced.

It will be necessary to decide upon the type of glass to be used before planting, for it is essential to be able to cover the maximum number of plants to make the glass economical. Dutch or ordinary garden lights may be supported on nine-inch boards, or on old railway sleepers. Under lights, set out the plants 15 inches apart each way. By this method it may be possible to plant four rows of a compact variety.

As the plants need as long a period of growth as possible if they are to bear fruit early in May, the beds should be made up in August. The soil must be deeply worked and enriched, and only top quality plants should be used. Where barn-type cloches are used, make a double row nine inches apart allowing 18 inches in the rows. A single row with the plants 15 inches apart may be covered with the ordinary tent cloche. It is more economical if used again in autumn and early winter to cover the perpetuals. It may also be used to protect the ripening fruit of a late variety, such as 'Cambridge Rearguard', during an unexpected periods of adverse weather.

Suitable varieties
for under glass culture are:

Cambridge Favourite	Cambridge Vigour
Cambridge Regent	Gorella
Cambridge Rival	Royal Sovereign

Additional varieties
for the connoisseur are:

Aurora	Reine des Précoces
Regina	Wadenswill 4

All these varieties are early maturing, resistant to mildew, of compact habit and ideal for cloching. The rows should be made from north to south to make for even ripening of the fruit.

Covering the Fruit

Before the plants are covered they should have had a thorough soaking, especially following a period of hard frost, which leaves the soil dry and powdery. Also dust the plants with flowers of sulphur to guard against mildew. This treatment should be repeated at fortnightly intervals. By mid-March the sun's rays will be warmer, and on suitable occasions ventilation should be given during the day-time. If a cold wind is blowing, allow the glass to remain over the plants, otherwise in a few minutes it will undo all the previous good work of protection. In an exposed position take care to ensure that the lights are prevented from being blown about and broken. They are best held in position by strong telephone wire extended over the glass.

At the time when ventilation is given, the plants will often require a soaking, though on the mild, moist days often experienced during late March the coverings may be left off for several hours to obtain moisture naturally. When possible, all moisture should be given before noon to enable the surplus to dry off the flower trusses before nightfall. Until mid-March it is advisable to withhold water, otherwise hard frosts may damage the plants as they make new foliage.

By early April the plants will be coming into bloom; to help with fertilization, remove the glass on suitable occasions; this will ensure that the plants receive all the ventilation necessary. Unless a cold wind is blowing, the glass protection should be removed entirely during the day, up to the time when the fruit begins to ripen. At this stage the glass should be kept in place to give protection and hasten ripening. The glass should be used, not for forcing purposes, but rather to guard the fruit against adverse weather and frosts, so that picking may begin early in May. There is little demand for the fruit until then, and it is during the last three weeks of May, when the weather becomes more summer-like, and until the first of the outdoor fruit is ripe, that protected strawberries make the highest prices.

Both first- and second-year plants may be covered but, to build up a vigorous growth for second year cloching, they must be heavily mulched as soon as fruiting has ended, and fed with dilute manure water throughout summer. After covering for two years it is advisable to destroy the plants.

Growing in Tubs

Where space is limited, fresh strawberries may be grown in tubs or barrels, into which holes one inch in diameter and 18 inches apart have been drilled to take the plants. The tubs should be filled with a suitable compost, and a small courtyard or verandah could possibly accommodate several tubs or barrels, and succession of fruit enjoyed. Tubs are preferable, for if planted in the usual way all the plants may be given abundant moisture. This is essential if the plants around the sides are to fruit well.

The half-barrel or tub should also be drilled with drainage holes, over which are placed first large crocks then a layer of turf. The tub is then filled to within one inch of the rim with turf loam which has been enriched with some decayed manure, some peat, a small amount of coarse sand and a handful of bone meal to each tub. They should be mixed well together and allowed to settle down before planting takes place in autumn, or in March for the perpetuals. If placed in a position protected from cold winds, an early June crop may be enjoyed. The compost must never be allowed to lack moisture. If May is a dry month, which it often is, give the compost a thorough soaking twice each week, so that the moisture will percolate to those plants situated at the base of the tub. It should not, however, run out at the bottom. Liquid manure water will also help large, richly flavoured fruits to form.

Strawberries may also be grown in large pots. They require the same compost as in tubs, but additional moisture, for compost in pots dries out rapidly during early summer and watering may be necessary twice daily. Pot-grown plants may be purchased early in March; they will be more expensive than runners, but will bear fruit the same season and may also be retained in their pots to fruit the following year.

Varieties

The strawberry grower today has a wide range of varieties suitable for all districts and soils and for spreading the season over a period. Experiments have proved that several varieties are suitable for freezing and canning and so, for whatever trade the grower is catering, he has a wide choice. Not all those described here are suitable for the commercial grower, but as the connoisseur of fruit must be satisfied, amateur varieties are also given. By following the choice of the professional grower exclusively we miss much that appeals to the highest tastes, and many old varieties are described in order of fruiting, the descriptions being as detailed as several years' experience of their cultivation allows.

Early

AURORA An excellent French variety for cloching, but its large crimson fruit ripens so quickly that the plants should be picked over twice a day, and the fruit marketed locally if possible. Very like 'Reine des Précoces', in that its glossy, deep-green leaves and large crimson berries are of handsome appearance, the fruits being of delicious flavour. Crops well in all soils.

CAMBRIDGE BRILLIANT A variety which crops well in lime-laden soils and bears large, brilliant scarlet fruit of similar shape to 'Royal Sovereign'. Good either for cloching or for open-air culture, it makes a compact plant and forms short, heavily laden fruit trusses.

CAMBRIDGE EARLY PINE One of the earliest of the Cambridge varieties, too leafy for cloches, but resistant to mildew. The medium-sized fruit is round, of a bright scarlet colour and with a smooth, glossy skin from which moisture quickly drains. In a wet season, or in an area of excess moisture, this is of great value. Although not one of the heaviest croppers, it is extremely consistent in light soils, and the blossom is very resistant to frost.

CAMBRIDGE PREMIER Resistant to mildew and red core root disease, it crops heavily and may be said to bridge the earliest varieties with the second earlies. If forces well. It is valuable for cloching, making a compact plant, while it crops well on all soils. The large, bright-orange, wedge-shaped fruit is firm and travels well, although the amateur may find a variety of richer flavour. Not as frost-resistant as 'Cambridge Regent', and where not given protection it should be grown for an early crop. If this variety has a fault, it is that the top of the berry sometimes remains green when the rest has fully ripened.

CAMBRIDGE PRIZEWINNER One of the best-flavoured of early strawberries, the fruit travels well and retains its colour. It is a consistent cropper and bears heavily in most soils. An exhibition variety, the fruit is round and even in shape.

CAMBRIDGE REGENT A prolific cropper, with blossom that is highly resistant to frost. The fruits mature 10-14 days before 'Royal Sovereign' and although it bears heavy crops in a light, sandy soil, it is at its best in a stiff loam. It is such a heavy cropper that it must be grown well. The large, orange-scarlet, wedge-shaped fruits, possess good texture and quality. It is not suitable for cloching, as it is susceptible to mildew.

DEUTSCH EVERN A German variety generally used for cloching. It bears heavily, with fruit of good texture but of small size, like 'Perle de Prague'. 'Cambridge Brilliant' or 'Regent' would seem to be better commercial varieties.

GORELLA Though somewhat susceptible to botrytis, it is such a heavy cropper and comes so early into fruit that it should be grown in every garden. A strong grower in all soils, the large uneven fruit is of glossy crimson.

HÂTIVE DE CAEN A very hardy, frost-resistant variety which crops well. It makes a large, leafy plant and matures very early, the deep pink fruit possessing a rich perfume and exceptional flavour.
MADAME LEFEBVRE This variety has now been replaced by a number of the Cambridge and continental introductions. It makes a large, bushy plant and bears a cerise-pink berry of rather soft texture.
PRÉCOCE MUSQUÉE The earliest strawberry par excellence for the connoisseur. With its rich perfume and delicate musky flavour, it is very similar to the old 'Black Prince' and should be grown in every garden. The fruit is large and does not travel well.
REGINA A favourite with the Germans and Russians for their early crops. The fruits are large, deep crimson and of exceptional flavour. The blossom is frost-resistant, and in soils containing plenty of humus it bears a heavy crop over a long period.
REINE DES PRÉCOCES Excellent under cloches, but where grown in the open it should be confined to a sheltered garden. Very resistant to mildew and botrytis, it bears a heavy crop of scarlet fruits. With its glossy, bottle-green foliage, this is a handsome variety in the garden.
SURPRISE DES HALLES Almost as hardy as 'Hâtive de Caen', the blossom being untroubled by light frost even though the trusses are held above the foliage. It bears a huge crop of deep crimson berries which should be marketed before fully ripe.
WADENSWILL Where the fruit can be placed on ice for an hour to bring out its unique fragrance, it has no peer among soft fruits. The berries are small, almost round, and are deliciously sweet. Raised in Switzerland, this is, as one would expect, a hardy, frost-resistant variety.

Second Early

CAMBRIDGE EARLY Introduced in 1937, when it found favour owing to its resistance to red core root disease and its reliable cropping in a heavy soil. Its round, medium-sized fruit ripens a few days before 'Royal Sovereign', and travels well. Does not crop well on a light soil.
CAMBRIDGE FAVOURITE Well named, for this variety is a favourite with commercial growers. The large, light-red fruit keeps and travels well, while it remains in bearing longer than any summer strawberry. It is a strawberry which has put money into growers' pockets, being in no way troubled by frost, mildew, botrytis or drought. It is the best of all strawberries for a light, sandy soil.
CAMBRIDGE RIVAL Year by year the good qualities of this variety have earned it increasing popularity. Like 'Regent', it prefers a heavy loam in which it crops heavily, the fruit trusses being held well off the ground – which makes for easy picking and ensures clean fruit. The berries are of conical shape and of a bright crimson with glossy skin, like 'Early Pine', and while making a large plant it does well under cloches. An extremely heavy cropper, the fruit possesses outstanding flavour. A panel selected from 120 members of the Royal Horticultural Society Fruit Committee selected it as being the most delicious strawberry, superior even to 'Royal Sovereign'.
CAMBRIDGE VIGOUR At trials of the East Malling Research Station, this proved the heaviest cropper, bearing almost double the crop of 'Royal Sovereign'. It is possibly the best strawberry yet introduced, for it it is a strong grower, is highly resistant to red core, and crops well even in a lime-laden soil. The medium-sized fruit is deep glossy crimson, very like that of 'Early Pine', but it is a heavier cropper and the fruit travels well. Early autumn-planted maidens crop well in the first season, while the plants also bear well up to four years old, though the fruits mature later than on maidens.

Mid-Season

BLACK PRINCE The small, glossy, crimson berries are like old port wine, almost treacle sweet. This variety forces well and crops well under cloches, the fruit making the most delicious of all strawberry jam, but it ripens quickly and does not freeze well.

CAMBRIDGE ARISTOCRAT One of the most delicious of strawberries, the fruit having crimson flesh of a sweetness and flavour comparable to the alpines. The plants are resistant to red core and mildew, and bear heavily, the fruit being ready a few days after 'Sovereign'. For jam, it is the equal of the older and less robust 'Little Scarlet', while for the essence market this is the favourite.

CAMBRIDGE SENTRY An excellent variety, cropping well in a heavy soil and valuable for its resistance to mildew and botrytis in a moist district. The fruit trusses are held erect above the foliage, making it unnecessary to protect it against splashing. The fruit, which is wedge-shaped, remains dry under the wettest conditions, and retains its bright crimson colour after canning and freezing. It is equally good for bottling and jam making.

GRANDEE Raised at Stuttgart, it bears the largest fruits of all, some weighing up to three ounces while two ounce fruits are common. The fruit is bright red, firm and glossy, so that it travels well. For flavour it is outstanding.

HAUTBOIS This is only for the amateur or connoisseur, for the fruits are too small for commercial use. It is the *Fragaria elatior* from which the modern strawberry was evolved, and it holds its fruit high above the foliage. Plants are obtainable in Ireland and bear large leaves and small, deep crimson-purple berries, which are particularly sweet and carry a delicious musky flavour.

HUXLEY GIANT Of robust constitution, this variety, introduced in 1912, crops heavily in all soils, is not troubled by red core or frost, and travels well. Its round, crimson fruit is the most irregular both in shape and in ripening of all strawberries, yet it is of such vigour that the plants crop well for several years.

PERLE DE PRAGUE May be said to be early mid-season. Is resistant to red core and bears a tremendous crop of good flavoured fruit, but of so small a size that it rarely commands top prices. Its texture is soft, and where possible it should be marketed locally.

ROYAL SOVEREIGN Introduced in 1892, it has never been surpassed for quality and appearance. The brilliant scarlet, wedge-shaped fruit always commands a ready sale, even during gluts. It prefers a light soil, but one enriched with humus, and the virus-free Malling 48 strain be grown. But like the choicest of fruits, 'Sovereign' suffers more from virus, mildew and botrytis than any strawberry, so is best grown in isolation. The original 'Laxton' strain possesses much more flavour than the East Malling strain.

RED GAUNTLET A valuable strawberry, being resistant to red core and a heavy cropper, the large scarlet fruits possessing excellent flavour. It is a compact but upright grower with small foliage, and its trusses are held well above the ground.

SILETZ An American variety, highly resistant to red core and verticillium wilt. Is excellent for bottling and canning. The medium-sized round fruits are borne in profusion and ripen to glossy crimson with crimson flesh.

SOUVENIR DE CHARLES MACHIROUX Grown in France for dessert in preference to others. Although its fruit is in no way handsome, when ripe it turns crimson with something of the flavour of the old 'Black Prince'.

Late Mid-Season

CAROLINA An old variety, grown in the days when 'Black Prince' was the best strawberry. The foliage is deep green, the fruits of brightest scarlet, wedge-shaped and carrying a distinct and delicious pine flavour.

DOMANIL A new Belgian introduction raised at Gembloux, it makes a large, vigorous plant with plenty of foliage, which tends to hide the fruit, thus making for late ripening. The large pointed berries are orange-scarlet with a sharp, acid taste.

FENLAND WONDER An interesting variety, for it was found fruiting in the wild state on a church wall and was thought to be such a fine strawberry that it has now become widely planted in some (now no longer grown) it would appear to be the answer to the 'Climax' grower's prayer, for the fruit is equally large and, while retaining its colour, travels better than any variety. It is one of the sweetest and best flavoured of strawberries and crops heavily over a long period.

MARMION A new variety raised at the Scottish Research Institute at Auchincruive. It has shown high resistance to red core in its trials. It makes a low, spreading plant with its fruit trusses low down, the large, round berries being bright orange with pale orange flesh.

MERTON DAWN Raised at the John Innes Institute, it has 'Cambridge Favourite' for one parent and, though rather later, shows all its good qualities. The large orange fruits are conical and the flesh firm so that it travels well.

MONTROSE It crops heavily and makes a vigorous, spreading plant though holding its fruit well above the foliage. The large, round conical fruits are orange-red with a good but slightly acid flavour.

SPANGSBJERG YDUN A Danish variety, it has cropped heavily in that country. It is immune to frost and bears well and over a long period in a dry climate.

SURPRISE The most important virtue of this vigorous variety is its resistance to red core, and although bred from the same parents as 'Climax', with a similar fruiting season, has shown none of its troubles. It crops heavily, the fruit being round, very sweet and of a bright scarlet colour. It also 'plugs' well.

TALISMAN It crops heavily, and its long, conical-shaped fruit is of good texture. Highly resistant to red core, it is excellent for canning, freezing and for jam, and commands top prices.

TEMPLAR A variety bearing large conical fruits of pale red, turning to dark red when ripe. It is resistant to red core and is a heavy bearer with its trusses held upright above the foliage.

Very Late-Fruiting

CAMBRIDGE LATE PINE Those who prefer a sugar-sweet fruit with a slight pine flavour will prefer this variety to Rearguard, but both should be marketed locally. 'Late Pine' bears large, round, bright-crimson fruit similar to the older 'Waterloo'. It bottles and cans well.

CAMBRIDGE REARGUARD Although the fruit turns a deep crimson colour if transported a distance, and possesses rather a sharp taste like the American 'Red Rich', it crops well in all soils. As it is sometimes troubled by mildew, it is at its best in a drier climate. The fruit is large and wedge-shaped.

EVEREST A seedling which holds it trusses high above the foliage. Where late frosts persist, this, like each of the late-fruiting varieties, will come through unharmed. It is suitable for low-lying land, cropping heavily, its round, crimson fruit being of top quality.

SPATAUS LEOPOLDSCHALL A German variety, and the latest of all the summer strawberries. It is at its best during the latter part of August when the holiday season is at its height; hence the value of all the strawberries in this section. It is a heavy cropper even in heavy soils, and is resistant to mildew and botrytis.

Autumn-Fruiting Strawberries

These, the Remontants, may be divided into two types of groups:

(a) Those which bear the whole of their crop during the latter part of the year, from August until possibly December.

(b) Those which yield two distinct flushes of fruit, the first in early summer, the second in late autumn. These are now known as the two-crop strawberries, and are especially valuable for the amateur's garden, where space is limited.

Those who have to contend with a lime-laden soil and find that their strawberry plants suffer from serious iron deficiency may be able to enjoy autumn fruit from the late crop varieties by planting in early spring. The plants are removed at the year-end after fruiting, and the runners grown on to fruit the following year.

While the true autumn-fruiting varieties may be planted in spring, the two-crop varieties should be planted early in autumn, to enable them to become established before the winter and so bear a crop in the early summer. In this way they occupy the ground only nine months, or they may be grown on for a second year if given good cultivation. It is also possible to prolong the season of the autumn-fruiting varieties by making a planting both in spring and in autumn. Those planted in autumn are then allowed to set fruit on the first flowering trusses which appear during May. The fruit should be ready early July. Where only late-summer and autumn fruit are required, those planted in spring should be disbudded until the beginning of June. There will thus be a succession of fruit from mid-summer until almost the year-end.

If the bulk of the crop is required in autumn, it is necessary to disbud until the end of May. These are perpetual-fruiting strawberries, and will continue to bear in flushes, like mushrooms, right through summer and autumn, but where heavy pickings are required in autumn, when the crop is most profitable, the plants must not be permitted to waste their energies during the early-summer period. The two-crop varieties will bear fruit in two main flushes and, unless a particularly heavy crop is required in autumn, disbudding is not necessary.

To extend the season, almost until the year-end in favourable districts, cloches or frames should be used, and this will mean making up the beds to suit the type of glass chosen. By far the best method so far tried is to use the barn-type cloche. A double row of plants is set out, spacing the rows 12 inches apart. They make large plants, and too-close planting will cause botrytis and congestion with the runners.

Methods of Cropping

From an early April planting, one method is to allow the parent plants to bear fruit in addition to runners. The runners will begin to form by mid-summer, and are left in position and allowed to root, but all blossom is removed. The plants fruit from late in August; the beds, which will be a mass of runners by mid-October, are then covered with the cloches. If situated in a warm, sunny district, the plants will continue to fruit almost until Christmas, when they may be dug up and destroyed, leaving the runners to bear the following season; alternatively the parent plants may be potted and placed either indoors or in a warm greenhouse to bear fruit for the festive season.

The following spring the runners are thinned out, keeping beds three feet six inches wide, and a fresh bed is made up. There are then two beds to bear a crop the following season, at the end of which the original bed is dug in. Where growing under cloches, the plants must be given as much fresh air as possible by removing the covers whenever favourable, for it must not be thought that the Remontants are in any way tender. Where severe weather is experienced, and in a district where late frosts persist, these strawberries will fruit abundantly when the summer fruiting varieties often fail.

It is an excess of moisture rather than cold weather which causes trouble with the Remontants. In a cold, dry climate where the plants receive a fair share of sunshine, covered plants will fruit until early December and will crop until early November without protection. In a cold, wet district the fruit may be troubled by botrytis after the end of October, whether covered or not, but where this occurs only those varieties should be grown which show resistance to the trouble.

The cloches must be protected from strong winds but plants should be given an open, sunny position. Growing too close to a hedge or wall will not only deprive the plants of much necessary moisture but also of air and sunlight, so necessary to combat botrytis and to ripen the autumn fruit. Whereas the alpines will fruit well in almost full shade, and the summer maincrop strawberries may be given partial shade, the Remontants must have a position of full sun. They also require a rich soil and clean land, for the plants may occupy the ground for two years.

Where growing on the runners in the original beds, the soil must be rich with humus and plant food if heavy crops are to be enjoyed. Plenty of moisture-holding materials are essential, so dig in decayed manure in any form, as well as spent hops, peat, shoddy or leaf-mould. And do not neglect to provide the plants with potash, two ounces per square yard on light land, and with phosphates, preferably in the form of bone meal and at the same rate, where the soil is on the heavy side.

Allow the soil to settle down before planting, for the plants like a firm bed. Early in June, after the last disbudding and when plants have made some new growth, it is advisable to provide them with a mulch of peat and decayed manure. This not only helps to retain summer moisture in the soil but also will suppress annual weeds, thus making weeding unnecessary when the runners are beginning to form. Peat is also an excellent medium for the rooting of runners. In summer the plants must never be allowed to lack moisture, for it is during the period of the warmest weather that the fruit is being formed. Because they bear such huge crops, it is essential that the plants receive all the moisture they require.

As the fruits mature, the peat mulch will act as a guard against soil splashing, but straw is not recommended, for it will interfere with the formation and rooting of runners. Instead, mats may be used around the parent plants or, better still, inexpensive special wire elevators for the heavy fruit trusses. These are pressed into the ground around the plants and removed at the end of the crop. The elevators not only prevent dirty fruit but also allow the maximum of air and sunshine to reach the trusses; this hastens ripening and does much to prevent botrytis, more troublesome with the autumn than with the summer crops.

A number of varieties will form early runners, and these may be allowed to fruit late in autumn and grown on for a second season. Late runners should be de-blossomed and the beds thinned out in early autumn, new beds being made up. The smallest runners will bear a heavy crop the following autumn, and none should be discarded. Also, those formed later in the season will come into fruit later the following season, and so every runner should be carefully used, not only for making new beds but to prolong the crop. In this way the amateur may allow the two-crop varieties to fruit early. Covering with cloches may encourage this; and by the use of runners in various stages of maturity and by de-blossoming, the plants may be persuaded to give fruit from May until December, even though pickings will be light. There will be little difference, however, in the final weight of the crop if the plants are allowed to fruit perpetually or are encouraged to give the bulk of their fruit in autumn. The varieties 'La Sans Rivale', 'Triomphe' and 'St Claude' give around one pound of fruit per plant in a single season under both methods.

After fruiting, the plants will die back completely, no foliage whatsoever being seen above ground. It is, therefore, important to discontinue cultivations and planting from Christmas until the beginning of April, otherwise the roots may be damaged and the plants may take a long time to recover.

It has been said that people usually tire of strawberries by the end of August, but the large sales now enjoyed by frozen fruit throughout the year would seem to dispel this idea. Those who have grown the autumn-fruiting varieties – which realize very remunerative prices – have learnt that well grown strawberries sell at any time and make a welcome change during the late-autumn period.

Varieties

ADA HERTZBERG A German variety which is of value to the northern garden in that it ripens its fruit into winter. The crop is large, the pillar-box red berries possessing excellent market texture.

CHARLES SIMMEN On account of its huge cropping powers and its handsome heart-shaped fruit, which is brilliant orange and richly flavoured, this is the finest of all strawberries; but only for the amateur, for it forms no runners and has to be increased by the slow process of crown division. This should be done as soon as new growth begins in April. Like 'St Claude', it crops over a long period and is highly resistant to botrytis in the dampest districts.

GABRIEL D'ARBONVILLE Like 'Charles Simmen', this variety produces no runners and must be increased by division of the crowns. It bears a large, glossy, crimson fruit of exceptional flavour, and possesses a delicate fragrance. A fine variety where space is limited, for it makes only a very small plant.

GENTO Raised by Hummel of Stuttgart, it begins to crop in June, when the fruits are small, and continues until early October, the fruits increasing in size each week. The large, wedge-shaped berries are red-fleshed and of excellent flavour.

HAMPSHIRE MAID It may be said to bridge the gap between the late-summer and autumn-fruiting varieties, but it is suitable only for light land. It bears sweet, conical fruits of deep crimson on upright trusses over a long period, but will only crop heavily if kept well watered through summer and autumn. Now the most widely planted variety for August fruiting.

KUNTNER'S TRIUMPH Often called 'Pineapple Triumph'. because of the distinct pine flavour of its rounded fruits. An Austrian variety which prefers a light soil and, like 'Red Rich', it forms copious runners. The fruit colours well into late autumn.

LA SANS RIVALE This is the heaviest cropping strawberry, producing up to two pounds of fruit per plant if given individual attention, and one pound or more when grown commercially. It makes little foliage and holds its fruit trusses well above the ground. If the plants are de-blossomed until early June it comes into bearing early September, reaching a peak throughout October. The fruits are large, wedge-shaped, sweet and of a vivid scarlet colour. They are of firm texture and transport well.

LIBÉRATION D'ORLÉANS A two-crop variety of outstanding quality which crops heavily. At its best in a heavy, humus-laden soil, the fruit possesses exceptional flavour and has a similar shape and colour to the 'Royal Sovereign', which makes it popular with the salesman.

RED RICH An American introduction, this is a genuine two-crop variety bearing the first flush in early summer, followed by a heavier crop in early autumn. The crimson fruits are very large and of poor appearance, soft in texture and possessing a sharp, acid flavour. They will be found pleasing to those who favour a refreshing fruit. It makes a large number of runners which should be thinned where growing in beds.

ST CLAUDE This variety has a longer season than any strawberry, maturing its first fruit in August and in some places continuing until November. The conical fruits are firm, rather hard in fact, and travel well. The size of the fruit is retained throughout the crop, the skin being glossy and of a dark crimson colour, sweet and with a rich fragrance. The dark green plants remain healthy while the fruit strongly resists botrytis.

ST FIACRE One of the first French Remontants, and worth growing on account of its exceptional flavour. The plants are of hardy constitution and form plenty of runners. They fruit continuously from mid-July until early November, the fruit being of a good texture.

TRIOMPHE The blunt, bright salmon-pink fruit is exceptionally sweet and rich, but its texture is soft and it should be marketed locally. It is also more suitable for the drier districts, for it suffers from botrytis in a damp climate or when planted in a clay soil. It crops heavily but the plants have an untidy habit with the fruit trusses sitting on the ground.

VICTOIRE A two-crop variety, continuing to crop very late indeed. It cloches well but suffers from botrytis unless great care is taken with ventilation. It does, however, hold its trusses above the foliage. Its richly flavoured, cerise-red fruits are the largest of all strawberries.

Upright Form

That amazing Remontant, 'Sojana', has given satisfaction. By forming its fruit on long runners, it may be grown against a wall or trellis upon which it will grow to six feet or more in height; or it may be grown along the ground like a rambler rose and covered with continuous cloches. It may also be grown in pots and trained up long canes arranged fan-wise. It should be given shelter from cold winds, and as it crops from August until late November it requires a well-nourished soil.

If growing in pots, insert them in the ground to half the height of the pots to prevent them from being blown over and to conserve moisture. A sunny position is also essential for the plants to bear well in autumn. They also require a permanent position because they are perennial, dying back in winter to come into growth again in spring; when the soil should be given a liberal dressing of decayed manure. Set out the plants three feet apart in late autumn.

As much as 14 pounds of fruit may be obtained in one season from a single plant and its runners, but they must be fed well and kept moist at the roots. The fruit is bright red with the flavour of alpine strawberries, and hangs in trusses of three or four. It is produced all the way up the stems. Where growing upright, regular attention to tying is important. There is no tedious weeding, no disbudding, no strawing to keep the fruit clean, no trouble from slugs, and its upright habit makes it possible to produce strawberries in a restricted area, or where there is no garden at all.

WORCESTER BERRY

It has the blackcurrant and the gooseberry for its parents, and possesses the characteristics of both. It makes a tall shrub, growing up to six feet where the soil is enriched with humus. Its long sturdy branches are covered in thorns like the gooseberry, but its fruit is borne in long sprigs, or trusses, like a blackcurrant. Again, the fruit combines the characteristics of the two parents, best described as being crimson-black, about the size of 'Laxton's Giant' currant, but with the true gooseberry flavour. It is an excellent plant for a windbreak, although it grows and crops better where not too exposed.

Culture

Plant in November five to six feet apart. It makes a wide bush and also makes plenty of wood each year, so it requires a deeply worked soil rich in nitrogen. Work in plenty of garden compost, hop manure or old mushroom bed compost before planting. In spring, rake in one ounce per square yard of sulphate of potash.

Prune by removing old and over-crowded wood in late autumn. The fruit is ready for picking early August but it should be allowed to hang until fully ripe, because it will not be unduly troubled by wet weather. It makes excellent jam.

Strawberry 'Royal Sovereign' ready for picking

6 Tender Fruits

TENDER FRUITS

They are native of the Mediterranean regions and the Near East and, elsewhere, should be confined to those gardens enjoying mild climatic conditions, or perhaps given the protection of a warm wall.

APRICOT

To crop well, the apricot requires a high rainfall. It requires a soil with a high lime content and should be given the shelter of a sunny wall, against which it is grown as a fan-shaped tree. The apricot suffers from die back or brown rot which will cause long-established shoots to die back entirely. Because it flowers early, the blossom is frequently harmed by frost, against which protection may be given by planting against a southerly wall to provide the warmth necessary to ripen the new wood; or by planting against the higher wall of a lean-to greenhouse.

Plant in autumn, spacing the fan-shaped trees about 18 feet apart, for they make long shoots and fruit on short spurs. The stems of the fan should be allowed to grow on without branching as far as space permits, pinching back the side shoots in summer to about one inch.

Though apricots are self-fertile, there will be a better set of fruit if the flowers are hand pollinated. This is done with a camelhair brush, with which the flowers are dusted in turn as they open. It is a necessary procedure where growing indoors.

When the fruits have set and are beginning to swell, thin them three to a cluster, and again to about four inches apart as they begin to ripen. Allow the fruit to become fully ripe before removing it when dry, and place on a layer of cotton wool to prevent bruising.

Pruning

Pruning for replacement wood is done as described for peaches. The apricot also fruits on the preceding season's growth, and when the old spurs have borne fruit for two seasons they should be removed to make way for newly formed spurs.

Varieties

ALFRED A Canadian variety, the first to mature, and a heavy bearer of large round orange-yellow fruits.

EARLY MOORPARK It makes a large oval fruit of pale apricot colouring. The flesh is orange and the first to mature, ripening towards the end of July.

HEMSKERK The best variety, bearing large crops outdoors and in pots under glass, the concical fruits being of orange-yellow, marked with red and of delicious flavour.

MOORPARK One of the latest to ripen, and one of the best, the large round fruits of orange-red being borne in quantity. Grow it under glass.

POWELL'S LATE A heavy cropper, it is the

Apricot 'Moorpark', one of the first to ripen

latest to ripen, its deep golden-yellow fruits being flushed with red. Best under glass.
SHIPLEY'S BLENHEIM A mid-season variety, it is the hardiest apricot and is a most abundant cropper, the small oval fruits being of deepest orange and of rich flavour. It is the variety most grown for canning.

CAPE GOOSEBERRY

Like the potato and tomato and other members of the Solanaceae family of plants, the Cape gooseberry originated in South America. However, it has now become so acclimatized in South Afria – where it was introduced 100 years ago – that it takes its name from Cape Province where it abounds, rather than from its native land. Cut flower growers know *Physalis franchetti*, its bright red seed pods being in great demand for Christmas decorations. The Cape gooseberry is *Physalis edulis* which grows about two feet high and, like *P. franchetti*, is perennial. It will reach maturity in a warm border in a temperate summer, or it may be grown in deep boxes of soil in a greenhouse.

Culture

It can be grown from seed, sowing in spring in a container filled with John Innes Compost, spacing the seeds about one inch apart. Cover with compost and water in, using a liquid copper fungicide to prevent 'damp off'. Place the container, which should be covered with a sheet of polythene, in the window of a sunny room, watering whenever the surface of the compost begins to dry. Germination will be in two to three weeks, when the polythene is removed. After another two weeks the seedlings will be ready to transplant to individual pots containing the John Innes Potting compost. Stand the small pots in trays on a warm inside window-sill and water sparingly but sufficiently to keep the plants growing. By early June the plants will be ready to go into their fruiting quarters, and a warm border should be selected where the soil has been deeply cultivated and well manured. The plants will benefit by incorporating plenty of peat into the soil before planting.

Plant two feet apart; if the nights are cold, cover with cloches for about ten days. By the end of June, stake the plants and begin feeding with weak liquid manure. The plants will also benefit from a syringeing with cold water during late afternoon.

By early August the flowers will have turned into green lantern-like pods which then become yellow inside; the ripened yellow gooseberry-like fruit will have formed by late September. Cut away the husks from the plant and remove the fruits by first soaking the husks in warm water. You can eat the raw fruits alone or with a little sugar.

FIG

The fig is hardier than is generally believed, and as a wall plant it grows and crops well. It is said that figs crop well growing close to the sea and where the roots are restricted. They also grow well over a chalky subsoil, and to restrict root growth it is advisable to plant over a stone or brick base made compact by ramming. This will prevent the plant from forming tap roots to the detriment of fruit. If allowed to grow rampant, a fig will make nothing but wood and foliage.

Planting

Select a south or west wall and remove the soil to about two feet from the wall and to a depth of 18 inches. At the bottom, place a six-inch layer of crushed brick or stone which is made firm. The base will be more efficient if a small quantity of sand and cement is mixed together and poured over the base to percolate among the stones. It should be allowed to set hard before planting and filling in the soil.

Figs are lime lovers; if the soil is deficient, mix in some lime rubble but no manure, otherwise the plant will make an excess of rank growth at the expense of fruit. Late autumn is the correct time to plant, making the soil compact about the roots. To restrict the roots still further, obtain pot-grown plants and plant in the pots, burying them just below soil level. Throughout summer water copiously. A mulch of decayed compost given early in June will help to retain moisture in the soil.

Figs crop abundantly when trained in the horizontal form; they also do well in the fan-shape (as for plums and peaches) and as bushes, in which form they are rarely seen. Figs may also be grown as bush trees, one each of two or three varieties of sufficient hardiness for outdoor planting. They will give worthwhile crops which will mature by early autumn.

Pot-grown bush plants, reared by specialist growers, should be planted six feet apart in a warm border in spring. The plants will eventually reach a height of six feet and grow six feet wide. They must have a sunny situation for the wood and fruit to ripen. Planting will be as described for wall plants.

The fruits should be harvested when they begin to split, not before. They should be spaced out (not touching each other) in trays, and may be kept for some little time in a cool but frost-proof room.

Pruning

Pruning calls for a degree of care. The fruit is borne on the previous season's wood, and so the only pruning to be given an established tree is to limit the shoots which will be produced from each fruit bud. The replacement shoot is stopped at the fourth leaf, and this is done at the end of July. Too-early stopping will upset the balance of the tree, as the fruit expected to mature the following summer will form too quickly at the expense of new wood. Yet, at the same time, if the shoot is not pinched back, the fruit will not fully develop, turning yellow and falling.

The fruits are formed at the axils of the leaves and begin to swell the following spring. If the extension shoots are pinched back towards the end of July, new fruitlets will form at the axil of each leaf and these will be next season's crop.

Much of the old wood and its extension shoots may remain each year. However, if the tree becomes overcrowded, some of the wood that carried the previous season's fruit will need removing. The size of the area to be covered and the vigour of the tree will decide the wood to be retained.

Should the plant make excessive growth, root pruning will be necessary, otherwise fruiting will be reduced. To keep a plant in check it may be necessary to prune the roots in alternate years. First remove the soil three feet from the stem and to a depth of 18 inches, severing the larger roots with a sharp knife. Then place some lime rubble in the trench and ram it well down. If planted in its pot, root pruning may not be necessary, although after three to four years the roots will usually have burst through the pots.

Figs growing under glass where gentle heat is used may be made to bear two crops each year. The fruits formed the previous season will begin to swell early in spring if the extension shoots are stopped at the fourth leaf. While the first fruit is reaching maturity in early May, the fruit formed in spring will ripen by September. Again the shoots formed the later weeks of summer will be those on which the fruitlets will form for the next crop.

Propagation

Figs are increased by (a) cuttings; (b) layers; and (c) suckers–the first method being that usually adopted for indoor plants. A dormant and well ripened eight-inch-long shoot is removed in January and inserted in a small pot containing a sandy compost. It should be placed in a propagating frame or on the greenhouse bench where it can be given brisk bottom heat. It will root in three to four months, and in April or May should be moved to a sunny situation outdoors to ripen.

Outdoor figs are increased from suckers detached with their roots in autumn, when may be replanted into their fruiting quarters. Or young low shoots may be layered early in summer and detached and planted in a permanent site late in autumn, by which time they should be well rooted.

Varieties

BLACK ISCHIA Hardy for outdoor planting in temperate zones, the medium-sized, purple-black fruits with crimson flesh are sweet and juicy, and are borne in profusion.

BROWN TURKEY The best all-round fig, good under glass and hardy outdoors, bearing large, purple-brown fruits of excellent flavour. It makes moderate growth and is very fertile.

BRUNSWICK Excellent under glass and sufficiently hardy for the more favourable parts outdoors, the large green fruits with their white flesh being sweet and juicy.

ST JOHN'S One of the most delicious figs and a prolific bearer under glass, its large, white-fleshed fruits being sweet and juicy.

WHITE MARSEILLES Prolific under glass and sufficiently hardy for outdoor culture, it bears large, yellowish-green fruits with white flesh, and they are sweet and juicy.

GRAPE (Vine)

The vine is hardier than the fig. It will grow and crop well against a warm wall, and in the open, too, trained horizontally along wires or as cordons.

Given suitable varieties there is no greater mistake than to treat the vine as a tender plant, for it can withstand 20° of frost and be unharmed. Outdoors, varieties of the 'Chasselas' type can be allowed to remain on the vine until early December. They will be improved in sweetness and flavour after being frosted. But harm will be done if the plants are frosted after growth begins in spring. A vine may be grown up a lath, as a single cordon, to a height of ten feet like runner beans. For this purpose 'Angevine Oberlin' and 'Chasselas d'Or' are suitable for dessert; for wine, 'Madeleine Royale' and 'Seibel 2653', a new hybrid, are reliable.

The vine requires a sunny situation, where the fruit can ripen, also the wood or canes, without which there will be little fruit the following year. It also requires a deep, loamy soil, preferably over a limestone subsoil; where lime is not present, mortar should be incorporated. It also needs nitrate or sulphur of potash, at the rate of one ounce per square yard, applied to the soil in spring. Nitrogenous manures, except the slow-acting ones, should be avoided, for they encourage soft growth and tend to cause outbreaks of mildew. Overfed vines will not fruit well. Plant in October, six to seven feet apart.

Under glass, vines may be planted in the border, or in a specially prepared border outside the greenhouse. The shoots are taken inside through an opening made at the base, from where the canes are trained up the roof. The soil should be prepared to a depth of three feet with a six inch layer of bricks or stones placed at the bottom and rammed firm as for figs. Alternatively, use boiler ash (clinker) or mortar. The soil should be a friable loam, to which is added a liberal sprinkling of bone meal and some mortar. Plant firmly.

Grapes may be grown in a cold greenhouse, but where heat is available a more reliable crop can be expected. A winter temperature of 42°F (5°C) should be maintained, and this is gradually increased to 60°F (16°C) in spring when the flowers appear. Artificial heating is discontinued with the natural warmth of early summer.

When the buds begin to 'break', a moist atmosphere should be provided to encourage them to do so, the vines being syringed frequently and the floor of the house made damp. Syringeing stops as soon as the fruits begin to colour and, if the weather is dull and cool, gentle artificial warmth should be made available.

Grapes are one of the most desirable fruits to grow

Pruning

A vine is capable of making considerable growth during a season, a young shoot often reaching a length of 20 feet or more. If this is cut back to half its growth, it is then called a rod, and on this grapes are borne the following year. Every eye may develop a shoot which will be capable of bearing a bunch or two of grapes, but, at the same time, buds appearing on the older wood or rods are also capable of bearing fruit. There should, however, be a preponderance of new wood; then those eyes formed on the old rods will not find sufficient vigour to fruit. A vine, however well grown, cannot be expected to bear fruit in plenty on both the new and old wood, so one has the choice of:

(a) Allowing one or two new shoots to make growth and restricting all other new growth. This is known as the long rod system.
(b) Allowing the plant to bear a larger number of growths, but keeping these shortened.
(c) Cutting back all new wood to the main stem to form the spur system.

The Long Rod System

With the vine, all pruning must be performed in winter, during the dormant period before the sap begins to rise. New Year's Day is chosen by the specialist growers to begin pruning, but all work should end by the first days of February. With a new vine indoors it is best to form two main stems or rods, which are trained in an outward direction and are allowed to grow at will during their first year. During this time they will make around 20 feet of growth, and at the year end one of them, the weakest, is cut back to two eyes at the base. As with fruiting trees, the important point to keep constantly in mind is the close connection between root activity and the formation of new wood, which means that the plant should be allowed to make as much leaf as can be properly maintained.

The remaining shoot should be tied to the roof, for it is on this that next season's crop will be borne, and the stronger of the two buds should be trained to bear next season's wood and crop. The original may, in turn, be cut back to two eyes, the stronger of which should be retained for growing on.

To prevent overcrowding, all laterals must be cut back to two buds, one to bear the fruit and the other, which should be stopped at two leaves, to provide the nourishment. If in excess, some foliage should be removed.

The Spur System

Not nearly so commonly used, is the short spur system. From the rod which has been allowed to grow away unchecked during the first year, alternate buds are selected on each side of the stem to produce short laterals in the following season. These bear fruit and are stopped one joint beyond. The shoots are then cut back to two buds in winter. The rod is not removed, but fruit and leaf growth will form from one of the two eyes in the following year.

But the most popular method is now the established spur system. A newly planted vine is cut back to two eyes or buds, which are trained up the roof in opposite directions. For the first year they are allowed to grow at will. The following winter they are shortened to half their length, and all laterals are cut back to two buds, one of which, as we have seen, will produce fruit, the other leaf. This will eventually build up a system of spurs similar to those of the spur-bearing apples.

All fruit bearing laterals should be stopped at the first joint after the bunch has formed; all non-fruiting laterals must be pinched back to two inches. Unwanted laterals should be removed completely.

The one drawback to the established spur system is that old vines are frequently found to be a mass of spurs, far too many for the formation of a yield of quality fruit. Where this is the case, a number of the spurs should be cut right away, using a sharp knife. On average, one lateral shoot to every foot-length of rod is sufficient. All laterals should be cut back to the first good eye or bud from the main rod.

With an established vine it frequently happens that, with the commencement of a new season, the buds at the lower portion of the rods refuse to make any growth, while those at the top are most vigorous. To even out this growth, the rods should be lowered from the roof for several weeks before being tied back again. This will persuade the lower buds to break and, at the same time, retard those at the top.

During the first season the vine should not be allowed to bear any fruit, and each lateral should be allowed to bear only a single bunch during the following two seasons.

The pinching of laterals during summer should be done over a period of several days, so as not to cause any check to the growing plant (which too vigorous defoliation may do). Then, later, all lateral growths formed from the shortened non-fruiting lateral must be pinched back as soon as they have made one leaf, so as to concentrate the plant's energies into the forming of fruit.

Although occasionally a vine is seen growing in the open against a sunny wall in the usual vertical position of the greenhouse, it is rarely seen in the horizontal form which suits it better. It requires the same treatment as for espalier pears. First a young plant is cut back during winter to the three lowest buds about 15 inches from the ground, the cut being made immediately above a bud growing in an upward direction. This is to form a leader shoot. The buds beneath should be trained, one on one side and one on the other, first in an upright position, then, when growth becomes vigorous, the rods may be tied to wires in a horizontal position. At the end of the season these rods should be shortened back, also the leader shoot. The following season other rods, spaced 18 inches above, should be trained in the same way. Each rod or arm is treated similarly, as for the indoor spur method. All buds on the lower side of the arms or rods should be rubbed out.

Vines grown in the open in the vertical position may either be grown against a wall, or trained up stakes or wires like runner beans. In this way they would follow the single rod and spur system, shortening the newly planted cane from four to five inches. After fruiting, cut back the new shoots to a single eye to provide next year's shoot.

Propagation

Vines are propagated by (a) cuttings; (b) budding; (c) grafting; and (d) layering, but the easiest method is to take cuttings. For outdoor vines, plump, well-ripened canes are removed early in spring and cut into 15-inch lengths. They are inserted four inches deep in trenches of prepared soil and made firm. To encourage rooting, they may be treated with hormone powder before being inserted into the soil. In summer they must be kept comfortably moist, and by late autumn they should be well rooted. They may then be moved to their fruiting quarters, or potted and grown on in a frame for 12 months, pinching out the side shoots and removing the tendrils. They must not be allowed to bear fruit until their fourth year, but should be encouraged to use their energy in producing plenty of strong canes.

Where heat is available, the canes are removed in January and cut into pieces three inches long, each containing a plump bud or 'eye' from which the new shoot will form. The cuttings are inserted into individual pots or squares of turf containing a sandy compost, and kept comfortably moist in a temperature of 65°F (18°C), when they will root in six months and be ready to move into larger pots to grow on, those growing in small squares of turf being planted as they are.

Bringing on the Crop

When the fruit has set it must be decided how many bunches the vine is able to bring to maturity, and this depends upon its age and size. The bunch should be of pleasing shape and the grapes as large as possible, well covered in 'bloom'. Where there is overcrowding, nip out the grapes and their stalks with a pair of pointed scissors, also any damaged fruits. At this time, those grapes growing under glass should be given ample ventilation, or they will become soft and will decay before reaching maturity. When ready to cut, a bunch of 'Black Hamburgh' should be dark crimson and globular, while 'Angevine Oberlin' will be rich yellow, like a 'Leveller' gooseberry.

Varieties

ANGEVINE OBERLIN Very early to mature, the grapes ripen to greenish-white of unsurpassed flavour.

BLACK ALICANTE Best under glass where it will ripen early and evenly, the purple-black grapes having a pronounced muscat flavour.

BLACK HAMBURGH An indoor black grape of excellent quality, being easy to grow and ripening readily even in a sunless summer.

GOLDEN QUEEN An indoor variety of outstanding flavour and excellent size, ripening early and to a deep golden colour.

HÂTIF NOIR DE MARSEILLES A large black grape which matures early and has a good muscat flavour. May be grown under glass or outdoors.

MILLER'S BURGUNDY An outdoor variety, grown in some places for its ornamental downy foliage to cover a trellis, and in France as 'Pinot Meunier' for making Burgundy. It ripens too late in Britain, except in a warm summer, for its fruit to be of any value.

MUSCAT PRÉCOCE DE SAUMUR Early to mid-season, it is a dessert variety of the highest class, ripening to rich golden yellow and with a splendid flavour.

PERLE DE CZABA Good both indoors and outside, the large white grapes possess excellent muscat flavour and are sweet and juicy.

ROYAL MUSCADINE (CHASSELAS D'OR) One of the finest of all early grapes, ripening to a translucent golden colour and being sweet and juicy.

SEVE VILLARD 23.410 It is a wine grape, bearing huge crops of small, sweet white grapes.

SIEBEL 13047 Its enormous crops of small sweet grapes ripen rosy-red and are much in demand by the French wine makers.

NECTARINE

A smooth-skinned peach, or a peach without 'bloom', it requires similar culture to the peach, that is, a soil containing lime rubble (mortar), and a position where the summer sunshine can ripen its wood. In spring, give a liberal mulching with farmyard manure, and while the fruit is swelling give copious amounts of water, although watering should cease as the fruit begins to ripen. Prune as for peaches.

Varieties

EARLY RIVERS The most reliable variety for outdoors. It is a heavy cropper, bearing in early August large brilliant red fruits of excellent flavour.

HUMBOLDT Ripe by early September, its medium-sized fruits are deep orange flushed red, and of delicious flavour.

LORD NAPIER A valuable early maturing variety bearing large, pale-green fruits flushed with red. Good for outdoor planting.

PITMASTON ORANGE A heavy bearer, its large orange fruits, flushed with brown, being of excellent flavour.

VICTORIA The latest to ripen, ready in October, its large yellow fruits being flushed with red. It is a heavy bearer.

A peach tree – just planted and watered in

PEACH

The peach will come quickly into growth, two years after planting. As in its native China, it requires protection from frost when in bloom, and needs plenty of sunshine and a long season to ripen its wood. It requires as dry conditions as possible in winter, and excess moisture about its roots will cause trouble. Under glass it is grown against the high wall of a lean-to greenhouse and in a position of full sunlight. Fan-shaped trees should planted in late autumn, 18 feet apart and in a soil containing lime (in the form of mortar) and enriched with a slow-acting nitrogenous manure such as bone meal, given at a rate of two ounces per tree. This is incorporated into the soil at planting time. Make sure as with all grafted trees, that the union is above soil level. Plant firmly and water well. During summer keep the soil thoroughly moist, and mulch with decaying manure or compost. It is essential that the trees should not lack moisture while the fruit is swelling. Peaches are self-fertile and do not need a pollinator.

Peaches are propagated by budding on to plum stocks, the Common Mussel rootstock or Pershore stock making for vigorous medium-sized trees. The peach bears its fruit on shoots of the previous season's wood. During May, new growth formed by the leaders should be cut back by about one-third, while the tips of the side growths should be pinched out during mid-summer, pinching them back when they are about two inches long. A single wood bud will be retained at the base of these shoots, to grow on as a replacement for next season's fruit; the shoot which has fruited is removed at the end of the season.

In the early years of the tree, pruning should take the same lines as the renewal system for apples; that is, while the tree is being built up, the shoot which will have borne fruit is allowed to grow on until it has reached about 18 inches. This is then fastened to the wall and the tip pinched back to a wood bud. It is the shoot formed from this bud that will bear the next season's crop.

It frequently happens, when building up a fan-shaped peach, that the branches or arms on one side are more vigorous than those on the other side. This should not be allowed to go unchecked, otherwise the balance of the tree will be completely spoilt. As it is known that the branches of the more horizontal shoots are less vigorous than those in a more vertical position, the shoots of the weaker side should be moved to a more vertical position, while those on the more vigorous side should be fastened back more horizontally. In this position they should remain until growth has become more even.

It is not a difficult matter to distinguish between blossom and wood buds: the latter are small and pointed, while blossom buds are round and fat. Where possible, select a wood bud facing the wall; an extension shoot for this will ensure a straighter shoot.

Peaches and nectarines will require more space in which to bear new wood than will either apricots or plums.

Peaches grown as bush trees should be drastically pruned back in early May each year to encourage a continuous supply of new growth. This will stimulate growth which is excessive and should be retarded by ringing round the roots and cutting back in alternate years after the establishment of the trees.

The chief source of worry is the tendency of the plant to 'bleed' or 'gum', but this will not prove troublesome if too much old wood is not allowed to form. This, when pruned, is most likely to 'gum', so it is advisable to encourage as much new wood as possible.

All shoots appearing next to a fruit should be pinched out above the second leaf. This removal

Peach 'Princess of Wales' will crop well when grown against a wall in a sunny position

of all unwanted shoots should be spread out over a period of three to four weeks early in summer.

Root pruning will also help restrict excessive growth and encourage fruiting. About five years after planting, remove soil to a depth of 15 inches about three to four feet from the main stem and, using a sharp knife, cut away all vigorous long roots before replacing the soil and treading firmly. Netting suspended from the wall and hung over the trees when in bloom will give protection from frost.

Thinning should not be done until after 'stoning'. This is a natural falling off of fruits when about the size of a walnut. Afterwards, if the plant is carrying an excess of fruits, remove others, leaving about six inches between each fruit to mature.

The fruit is ripe if it is slightly soft when gently pressed at the base. It should then be removed by placing the palm of the hand beneath it and exercising gentle pressure by moving in an upward direction. The fruit is then placed in shallow boxes or trays lined with cotton wool.

Varieties

ALEXANDER One of the earliest to ripen, it is a heavy cropper, bearing early in August medium-sized fruit of golden-yellow flushed with red.

BARRINGTON One of the best for growing under glass in temperate latitudes, it is ripe towards the end of September, the large yellowish-green fruit being marked with crimson.

DUKE OF YORK Ready early August, it bears a large yellow-skinned fruit with green flesh and is sweet and juicy.

HALE'S EARLY The first of the outdoor varieties to ripen, bearing large numbers of medium-sized fruits in mid-July; these ripen to a rich orange colour.

PEREGRINE It bears a large crimson fruit often three inches in diameter which ripens early in August, and is a heavy and reliable cropper.

ROCHESTER Ripe late in August when the golden skin will be streaked with red and the flesh will be yellow and of outstanding flavour.

ROYAL GEORGE Maturing late in August, the fruits are large, pale yellow speckled with red.

SEA EAGLE The latest to ripen, being ready in October. It is one of the largest of all peaches, of pale yellow flushed with red. Best under glass.

7 Nuts

In ancient time a hazel coppice was a valuable part of the economy of the countryside, the stakes having many uses; not the least important was for making hurdles for sheep enclosures, for fencing or for use as a windbreak. Hazel was also used for basket-making at a time when fruit, including strawberries, was carried to market in large round containers, often on the top of women's heads. Today, a hazel coppice still makes a useful price for its owner and is usually sold to the highest bidder who will divide a coppice into three parts and cut one part to ground level on a three-yearly rotation. Thus, when the last part is being cut, that cut first will be ready again the following year. The nuts are also an economic crop in those parts where the plants grow well.

HAZEL (COBNUT)

The hazel (which is the cobnut) and the filbert, of the genus Corylus, may be distinguished from each other by the length of husk; the hazel has nuts with husks shorter than themselves; the filbert has husks longer than the nuts, and it is thinner shelled. Both require similar culture, and this includes shelter from cold winds and a well-drained, gravelly soil. Plant in November, 12 feet apart, and they will make attractive hedgerow trees. They will grow well in partial shade. It will take four to five years to build up a tree and bring it into bearing. After planting, cut back the main stem to three buds, and do this each year until the trees reach a height of five to six feet, by which time they will begin to crop. To ensure satisfactory pollination, plant at least two varieties together.

The trees will thence require only the minimum of pruning, and none at all until after they have finished flowering in March, for the female flowers are borne on the old wood, and the male flowers (catkins) on the young or previous season's wood. They are fertilized by wind, and rely on dry weather during springtime for a good set of pollen and a heavy crop of nuts. For this reason they crop better in the dry parts. Cut back to three buds any vigorous shoots which have borne fruit the previous year. At the same time, remove any suckers.

Where growing for their nuts, they should be treated like any other crop. The plants will respond to a dressing with decayed manure or shoddy given early in January; in March give a two-ounce-per-tree application of sulphate of potash. This will greatly increase the nut size.

Allow the nuts to remain on the tree until quite ripe, which will be late October, by which time the husks will have turned brown. If gathered too soon, while still green, the nuts become mouldy in storage. But remove them before the winter rains.

Varieties

COSFORD Is prolific in its catkins, while the shoots

are covered with glandular hairs. It makes a large, oval nut with a thin shell, and is sweet and juicy.

DUKE OF EDINBURGH The nut is round and tapering with the husk drawn tightly around it. The catkins are plentiful, and the crop heavy.

KENTISH COB Since its introduction in 1830 it has been the most widely planted variety, for its catkins appear late and so miss the worst of the late winter weather. The nuts are large and are completely covered by the husk. It is a heavy bearer.

PEARSON'S PROLIFIC It has a dwarf habit but bears heavy crops, the nuts being large, sweet and juicy. It may be grown as a small garden hedge.

WEBB'S PRIZE A cobnut which is similar in its characteristics to the 'Kentish Cob', but the nuts appear in large bunches and are sweet and juicy.

FILBERT

It requires the same culture as described for the hazel but, if anything, the plants are rather more tender when young.

Varieties

PURPLE-LEAVED Growing six to seven feet tall, it is a most handsome tree or bush, its large round leaves being of deep coppery-purple, like those of the copper beach, while its fruit is of excellent flavour.

RED FILBERT Distinguished from the white variety in that the nuts are red skinned but have the same excellent flavour and freedom of cropping.

WHITE FILBERT With its white skin, this is one of the best filberts. The nuts are crisp and juicy.

WALNUT

Though taking at least ten years to bear fruit, walnut trees are valuable because they give light shade with their grey-green compound leaves, which are sweetly resinous when crushed. In fact, several could well be planted in parts of a large garden where specimen trees are required. As the walnut is not self-fertile, at least two trees should be planted together – though not too closely because they will eventually reach a height of almost 100 feet.

Juglans regia is the common walnut and *J. nigra* the black walnut; the latter is readily distinguished by its deeply furrowed bark. *J. regia* is the one to grow for its nuts, and the trees should be planted not less than 40 feet apart. Plant young trees, not more than three years old, for they make thick, fleshy roots as they grow older and are then difficult to re-establish.

Walnuts may be propagated from buds sown two inches deep in boxes, but the most choice fruiting varieties are grafted on to seedling stock.

Do no pruning, unless any branches have been damaged by winds, for the trees tend to 'bleed' when cut, like cherries.

Those walnuts to be used for pickling are taken from the tree late in July, but those to be eaten raw are removed from the husk late in October when they fall. The green husk is cut off and the nuts (in their shells) are placed on layers of salt in an earthenware jar until required. In this way they will keep succulent and will not become dry. Removing the husks will blacken the fingers, and the stains should be removed at once with a gentle bleach.

8 Fruit Growing in Pots and Tubs

Where space is at a minimum, apples, pears and plums may be enjoyed by growing in large pots or small tubs. It is possible to grow choice fruit round the walls of a tiny courtyard, and it is also possible to enjoy fresh fruit on a terrace or veranda, provided the trees receive some shelter from strong winds and are able to receive a liberal amount of sunshine. Apples and pears are more easily managed under these conditions of restricted planting than plums. Where town culture is required, then apples are likely to prove more reliable, and dessert apples rather than cookers on account of their size.

Method of Growing

It is usual to grow in pots in the single-cordon system; in this way the maximum number of different varieties may be grown. This will help considerably with pollination where bees and insects are generally few, besides providing the maximum weight of fruit from the minimum of room. The cordons should be supported by stout canes, which when growing against a wall will be held in position by strong wires looped round each cane and fastened to the wall at seven to eight feet intervals by strong nails.

Where a wall, especially a sunny wall, can be provided, this will prove ideal for all fruits, for not only will the trees be protected from strong and cold winds, but also the fruit will ripen and colour better than it would where growing in the open ground. If a wall cannot be provided and the plants are to grow unprotected, it will be better to grow several dwarf pyramids in tubs, for they will be better able to withstand strong winds.

Both the horizontal form for pears and the fan-shaped tree for plums may be used against a wall. Pears and apples may be grown in the single or double cordon form. Particular care must be taken in the selection of suitable pollinators. The most suitable trees will be those which form close spurs, rather than those which bear fruit on the tips of the wood, and which are of less compact habit.

Moisture Requirements

Another matter of the utmost importance is to provide sufficient moisture, lack of which is the one chief cause of failure with fruit trees in pots or tubs. Lack of moisture will prevent the fruit from reaching its normal size; without it it will lack flavour and may not store well, and it may also fall long before it is mature.

Any plant growing in a pot or tub will dry out at the roots during the period June to September, and it will do this far more quickly than will a tree growing in the open ground. The tree may be provided with a mulch to retain moisture in the soil, as well as being able to search more freely for its food and moisture. It must also be remembered that a tree in a pot or tub will have its roots subjected to the almost unprotected rays of the hot summer sun. It is therefore imperative that the maximum of protection is provided for the plants. During May, straw, strawy manure or sacking should be packed around the pots and always kept damp. This will protect the pots from the rays of the sun and so prevent a too-rapid loss of moisture from the soil.

An even better method is to fix a 10-inch board alongside, and 18 inches from, the base of the wall. This will form a trough to take the pots, the space around each pot being filled in with peat. Peat is clean to use and may be kept continually more moist than straw, or boiler ashes may be used. The pots should be placed on a two to three-inch layer of ashes or peat. Peat may also be placed over the soil of the pots to act as a mulch. An alternative mulch is one of strawy farmyard or stable manure, though this will not be so clean to handle.

Throughout the summer months the roots must be constantly supplied with moisture, a thorough watering being given almost daily, so that the moisture may reach the roots at the very bottom of the pot. The peat or straw around the pots must also be kept moist. To allow the soil in the pots to dry out for only a short period will be to cause irreparable damage for that season.

Apples and Pears for Pots and Tubs

Here is a selection of dessert apples and pears suitable for pot or tub culture:

Apples

Duchess of Oldenburg	August
Lady Sudeley	August
Ellison's Orange	September
Michaelmas Red	September
Egremont Russet	October
Sunset	November
King of the Pippins	December
Adam's Pearmain	December-January
Claygate Pearmain	December-March
May Queen	April-June

Pears

Laxton's Superb	August
Beurré Bedford	September
Gorham	September
Conference	October
Louise Bonne	November
Glou Morceau	December
Roosevelt	December-January
Winter Nelis	December-February
Santa Claus	December-February
Bergamotte d'Esperen	February-March

It was mentioned elsewhere that 'Lady Sudeley' is a tip bearer. This is correct, but it bears its fruit on very short twigs or shoots, and may be said to come somewhere between the tip and spur bearers. It is very suitable for pot culture.

Planting

A very large pot or small tub should be used, so that the roots are not unduly restricted and may be able to obtain the maximum of food from the compost. Crocks or broken brick should be placed at the bottom of each pot or tub so that the drainage holes are kept open. Over these holes should be placed a small quantity of fresh turf loam. Do not use the ordinary soil to be found in a town garden, because this will generally be sour and completely lacking in nutriment.

Then carefully remove the tap root and trim off any unduly large roots before placing the trees in the pots, spreading out the roots as previously described.

The compost should consist of turf loam to which has been added a small quantity of old mushroom-bed manure, or well-decayed farmyard manure. But do not use too much; an excess of nitrogen will cause the trees to make too much wood and foliage. But potash is important; one quarter ounce of sulphate of potash should be allowed for each pot and thoroughly worked into the compost. This should be friable so that it may be carefully packed round the roots and the pot filled to within one inch of the rim. The cane is then placed into position and immediately fixed to the wall.

It is not necessary to wait for the ending of the usual winter frosts before planting, provided the compost is made up indoors (a cellar or shed); planting may be done at any time from mid-November until mid-March, but the six weeks preceding Christmas is the best time. This will enable the trees to become thoroughly settled in their new quarters before coming into bloom late in spring.

Culture

The care of the trees will be carried out on the same lines as described for all other trees in the artificial form, but help should be given with the setting of the blossom by dusting the individual blooms with a camelhair brush during a dry day, and on several occasions during flowering time. If suitable pollinators are also planted together, there should be a heavy set of fruit.

Help may also be given the trees to satisfy their moisture requirements. This is done by frequent syringeing of the foliage from early June onwards, but if the trees are still in bloom, carry out the operation in time for the moisture to have dried off before nightfall. Damage might be done by late frosts if the blooms are wet.

The trees will also benefit from feeding once each week with diluted liquid manure water (obtainable in bottles from any sundriesman), from early July, when the fruit is beginning to swell. This should be continued until the end of September; the trees will benefit in addition to the fruit.

Where growing in a sheltered position, the fruit may be allowed to hang almost until Christmas. It is removed as required, and only that of the very late maturing varieties will need to be stored for use in the New Year. This should be removed by the third week of December, when the trees growing in pots should be repotted in alternate years into a completely freshly made up compost. Trees in tubs, which will contain a larger quantity of compost and provide more nourishment, may be allowed to remain without repotting for a number of years if systematically fed and never allowed to suffer lack of moisture. During winter the trees will require no artificial watering, but this may be necessary in April, possibly following a long period of frost and drying winds.

9 Pests and Diseases

The commercial grower of fruit becomes more and more bewildered by the constant stream of new insecticides introduced each year. Some are deadly poisonous and have caused death to their users, so that the control of pests and disease has come to be recognized as of greater importance than the actual growing of the trees. The modern chemist enjoys a national prestige while the fruit grower remains a nonentity. This is not of great importance in itself, but what does give rise to concern is the belief that many of the modern stomach upsets, ever on the increase, are in part due to the use of so many toxic chemicals which are used to control pests and disease on agricultural crops of every description. The amateur is fortunate in that he knows what has been on his fruit trees. But even he will be advised to follow a simple programme whereby the health of the trees will be maintained without sacrificing valuable pollinating insects and harming his stomach.

APPLE

Diseases

BROWN ROT It attacks apples and plums, appearing on the spurs as buff-coloured spores, and causing them to die back. The fungus also grows along the wood, causing it to decay, the apple variety 'Lord Derby' being particularly susceptible. Fruit from a tree attacked by brown rot will also be affected, turning brown in storage, although possibly appearing quite healthy at picking time. Diseased fruits must never be allowed to remain on the ground or on the tree, for in spring the spores will be dispersed by wind and may affect healthy trees. Spraying with lime-sulphur while the flower buds are green will give control.

BROWN ROT BLOSSOM WILT This is caused by the brown rot fungus *Sclerotina laxa*, and it attacks the blossom of apples, pears, cherries and plums (in another form), causing it to turn brown and die back. The fungus will then work down the flower stems on to the spurs and the branches, causing them to die back as well. A petroleum-oil wash in January, followed by a one-per-cent lime-sulphur wash just before the blossom opens (using Orthocide for the sulphur-shy varieties) should give control. With cherries, spray with Bordeaux mixture just before the blossoms open.

CANKER This fungus disease generally attacks apples, pears, plums and cherries where scab has already made its presence felt. It is the result of badly drained soil or too heavy applications of nitrogen, making for a soft tree. It is observed as reddish-coloured bodies, clustered together on parts of the wood, and this often results in a branch dying back above the canker attack. Most of those varieties resistant to scab frequently succumb to canker. 'Worcester Pearmain' may be included in the list. In those areas where the trouble is frequently seen, one of those highly resistant varieties, 'Gladstone' or 'Grenadier', should be planted.

The most satisfactory method of eradicating the trouble is to cut away the cankered portion of the wood, and then to apply a dressing of 'Medo', which penetrates the decayed tissues and so destroys the disease. With plums, Myrobolan B rootstock is resistant.

MILDEW It is prevalent on old, neglected trees, the shoots taking on a white powdery appearance. Buds which are affected often fail to develop. Spraying with lime-sulphur or Murfixtan, as for scab, will give a certain control, but the new American fungicide Karathane, used according to the maker's instructions, is efficient.

SCAB This is the most troublesome of apple diseases. It frequently attacks trees which suffer from potash deficiency, or have received too heavy supplies of nitrogen, causing a soft, sappy tree. The trouble with the disease is that it attacks all parts of the tree–buds, shoots, leaves and even the fruits, causing the formation of blackish blisters; this not only causes the fruits to rot, but also opens up the tree to a host of other diseases. Control may be achieved by spraying with a two-per-cent strength lime-sulphur solution just before the buds begin to open. Lime-sulphur should not be used on 'Stirling Castle', 'St Cecilia', 'Lane's Prince Albert', 'Cox's Orange Pippin', 'Beauty of Bath', 'Newton Wonder', 'Rival', 'Belle de Boskoop' and 'Egremont Russet', but of these varieties all except 'Cox's' and 'Newton Wonder' are highly resistant to scab.

Another method is to dust the blossom when in full bloom with sulphur dust, the time for applying the dust being governed by the flowering periods. The sulphur-shy varieties should instead be sprayed with Murfixtan, at the rate of two pints per 100 gallons of water, applying the solution just as the buds begin to burst. This is an excellent preparation for use with orchards or mixed varieties, not only where planted with different varieties of apple, but also with pears.

Pests

APPLE SUCKER The insect resembles a greenfly and lays its eggs on the spurs in autumn. In spring the insects hatch out to feed on the buds, causing them to turn brown and fall away. The eggs are readily destroyed in winter by a tar-oil or Thiol Thiocyanate wash as routine. Or spray in the green-bud stage with Lindex or liquid Malathion.

BLOSSOM WEEVIL Attacking the buds as they open during early summer, the grubs so eat into the stamens that not only do large numbers of blossoms fail to open, but many that do so prove incapable of carrying pollen. The most effective control is to spray the trees late in March with a petroleum-oil emulsion, but never use petroleum oil on 'Cox's' or 'Newton Wonder'.

CAPSID It attacks apples and currants, chrysanthemums, and dahlias, causing distorted leaves and flower buds; plant growth, too, is often stunted and sparse. For apples and currants, spray in January with DNOC, or tar-oil; or with Thiol at bud-break. With dahlias and chrysanthemums, spray with Lindex as routine from early summer. Under glass, control with Lindane smokes.

CODLING MOTH A tiny white caterpillar is responsible for the maggoty condition of matured fruit, and is really a serious pest. Its presence is indicated by a pile of brown dirt at the entrance hole of the attacked apple, and upon inspection the fruit will be found to be riddled with holes right through to the core. The moth lays its eggs during June and July following on the period of sawfly attacks, and frequently uses the skin of the young fruit for its egg-laying. Regular spraying with a Derris preparation will ensure almost complete control; this is safer to use than the older but efficient lead arsenate and white-oil emulsion, which is poisonous to humans and should not be used closer than eight weeks to the fruit maturing. Lead arsenate must never be used on 'Beauty of Bath', 'Miller's Seedling' or 'Grenadier'.

GREENFLY In this section, aphis is the most troublesome pest. It feeds on the young shoots, causing them to curl, then on the buds and even on the fruit as it is forming. Early in winter the aphis lays its eggs on the spurs, but an application of a tar-oil wash during mid-winter will quickly kill these eggs, and a repeat of the spraying the following year should rid the trees of aphis for a number of years. The spraying programme should be so regulated that control measures for red spider should take place immediately after the aphis are destroyed, otherwise the red spider will have the tree to itself and multiply accordingly.

In spring, spray with Abol X or Sybol, but do not use any insecticide based on gamma-BHC on currants.

RED SPIDER A minute red insect with spider-like legs. It attacks apples, plums, damsons, peaches, apricots, tomatoes and cucumbers under glass, and flowering plants in greenhouses and frames, especially carnations and violets. The pests cluster together on the underside of the leaves, sucking the sap and reducing the vitality of the plant while the leaves turn brown and wither. Spray apples, plums and damsons with DNOC during the dormant stage, and peaches and apricots and other plants in the open with liquid derris or Malathion, or with lime-sulphur at bud-break. Tomatoes, cucumbers and carnations under glass should be fumigated with an azobenzene smoke which is repeated after ten days. Dry conditions, indoors and out, encourage red spider attacks.

This pest is generally most troublesome with trees growing against a wall, and especially during a period of drought. Frequent syringeing of the trees during the period June to September will help to keep the pest under control. It is also more prevalent in a drier climate.

SAWFLY In its various forms, this pest appears on apples, plums and gooseberries when in bloom, feeding on the pollen. It is less than half an inch long and attacks the flower buds in spring, boring a hole through the sepals and calyx where the female deposits her egg. From this a white caterpillar will emerge after about ten days. It tunnels its way into the bud, causing a yellow liquid to drip from the hole made by the adult. The bud then turns brown and dies. The larva then falls to the ground (late in June), where it winters in a cocoon just below the surface of the soil. To prevent an attack spray the trees with Lindex solution; apples at petal fall; plums eight to ten days after; or with derris mixed with a spreader.

TORTRIX MOTH This is Shakespeare's 'worm i' the bud'. The caterpillars attack roses, apples and pears, causing the leaves to curl up at the edges and hold the flower petals in a rainproof canopy; this is made by spinning silken threads beneath which they will feast for hours, preventing the flower from opening and causing defoliation, weakening of the plant and eventually its death. They turn to chrysalids in June, and to moths by mid-July. This is one of the most destructive of garden pests, and an attack must be prevented by routine spraying with Abol X or Sybol, applied early in May each year and at monthly intervals, throughout summer. Or dust with Lindex every 14 days, although not on vines or blackcurrants.

WINTER MOTH They measure about one inch long and are green in colour. They feed first on the buds and blossom of fruit trees, then on the leaves and fruit, sometimes defoliating the trees. Towards the end of June they fall to the ground to pupate, the moths emerging in winter. The females are wingless and crawl up the trunk of the trees to lay their eggs on the branches, thus recommencing the life cycle. Grease banding the trees in October will prevent the females from reaching the branches. It is well worth taking the additional precaution of spraying the trees with tar-oil or Thiol Thiocyanate. This should be done in January, after grease banding the trees the previous October.

BLACKBERRIES

Diseases

CANE SPOT This attacks raspberries, loganberries and blackberries as purple-brown spots on the leaves and, if unchecked, it will spread to the canes, especially in cold, wet weather. Any affected canes should be cut out and burnt to prevent the disease from reaching new canes. Complete control can be obtained by spraying in spring (before the flowers open) with weak Bordeaux mixture followed by a colloidal copper preparation as used for raspberry beetle.

BLACKCURRANT

Diseases

BLACKCURRANT REVERSION A characteristic of blackcurrants caused by a virus and believed to be introduced by the 'big bud' mite, which is controlled by spraying with two-per-cent lime-sulphur. Where attacked by the virus, the leaves appear long and narrow, and the plant will not set fruit. Like the leaves, the flower trusses appear long and thin. It may be that only one or two branches are affected, and these must be removed at once and burnt. Keeping the plants free from 'big bud' mite and other pests will ensure clean stock.

CHERRY

Diseases

BACTERIAL CANKER This is a disease of cherries, affecting mostly the 'black' varieties. The yellow 'Amber Heart' and 'Governor Wood' are resistant. On others, the disease appears first as yellow circular spots on the leaves, which curl at the edges, turn brown and fall. The fungus will spread along the branches causing large areas to die back, and here it will remain over winter. As the disease is highly destructive it is advisable to give cherries a routine spraying in late autumn each year with Bordeaux mixture, at a strength of one pound copper sulphate and three quarters of a pound slaked lime to six gallons of water. Repeat early in spring before the buds open.

LEAF SCORCH When the leaves change to a mottled green and yellow colour and remain on the trees long after the period when they should have fallen, leaf scorch disease will be the cause. Fortunately, cherries will tolerate Bordeaux mixture, and an application should be given just before the buds open. The same treatment will also rid the tree of the spores of brown rot blossom wilt disease, which can cause serious damage to the culinary or acid cherries.

Pests

BLACK FLY The tiny black eggs winter on the twigs. If not killed by a January tar-oil spray they will hatch out minute grubs early in summer, and these will devour not only the leaves, but much new growth.

CHERRY FRUIT MOTH The small green caterpillars enter the buds as they open and later bore into the fruits, making them unsaleable and unfit to eat, or reducing them to a slimy mass. Later the fruits will fall to the ground and with them the caterpillars to form chrysalids. The moths emerge early in July to lay their eggs on the leaves. To prevent an attack, spray with tar-oil when dormant and dust the trees with Derris when the blossom begins to open.

CHERRY SLUGWORM The green slug is the larva of a sawfly. It emerges from the eggs which are laid in the tissues of the leaves of cherry and pear trees. It immediately begins to eat the surface tissues of the leaves, causing them to turn brown, and trees may be completely defoliated. The larva then falls to the ground and winters in a cocoon, until the sawfly emerges early in July to begin again its cycle of destruction. As routine, the trees should be dusted with Derris. This should be done every fortnight from early July until the end of August.

WINTER MOTH As described for apples, this pest

lives in the soil beneath the trees and will crawl up the trunk during the early winter months to lay its eggs on the twigs and branches. Grease banding of the trees at the end of October as for apples, and dusting the foliage with Derris in early summer, should prevent any serious attack.

Simple precautions by the amateur such as grease banding, tar-oil washing in the early winter months, and the occasional use of Derris powder should be all that is necessary.

GOOSEBERRY

Diseases

AMERICAN GOOSEBERRY MILDEW It attacks chiefly the gooseberry (occasionally black and red currants), and appears in summer as a white, mycelium-like growth on the new shoots and on the fruit. Later it turns brown and, during winter, it peels off the shoots and falls to the ground, where it remains to begin its activity again in spring. Any affected shoots must be cut away and destroyed, but it is important to ensure that the plants do not receive an excess of nitrogen, which will encourage 'soft' growth. Give each plant a quarter-ounce dressing of sulphate of potash in spring each year; this will do much to build up resistance.

To prevent an outbreak, spray or dust the plants in May with Karathane, repeating just before the fruits set. Or use colloidal sulphur; or a solution made up of four pounds of washing soda and one pound soft soap dissolved in 25 gallons of water. The latter preparation is recommended as an alternative to lime-sulphur on sulphur-shy varieties. These are the yellow varieties, e.g. 'Leveller' and 'Cousen's Seedling', which will drop their leaves and fruits if in contact with sulphur preparations.

PEACH

Diseases

LEAF CURL It is important to guard against leaf curl. This is the most common and troublesome of peach diseases, attacking the leaves which turn yellow and become crinkled at the edges. Later, the leaves take on a white powdery appearance, due to the spores of the fungus and, shortly after, they die back, causing loss of vigour in the plant. The disease usually appears during dull, wet weather, and it will spread quickly, even attacking the young shoots. There is no cure. However, spraying with lime-sulphur just as the buds begin to burst will give almost complete control. It will also destroy the troublesome pest, red spider.

Pests

MEALY BUG See under Vine.

PEAR

Diseases

LEAF SCORCH This disease causes the leaves of apples and pears to turn brown at the margins and curl up, or, with cherries, they take on a mottled green and yellow appearance. The trouble may be due to potash deficiency, and may be corrected by feeding two ounces of muriate of potash per tree. Trees troubled by leaf scorch will bear small fruits that are completely lacking in flavour.

But similar trouble may be caused by magnesium deficiency, which may be corrected by spraying the tree in foliage with a two-per-cent solution of magnesium sulphate. With cherries, spray with Bordeaux mixture just before the blossoms open.

SCAB Though the symptoms are the same, scab on pears is a totally different disease from that which attacks apples. Unlike apples, most varieties of pears will not tolerate even dilute lime-sulphur sprays, but again unlike the apple, are tolerant of Bordeaux mixture, which will control the disease if applied early in June and again when the blossoms have set. 'Fertility' and 'Doyenne du Comice' are the two varieties of pear most frequently troubled by pear scab.

Pests

MIDGE Pears are not often troubled by the sucking insects which attack the apple, but for them this is by far the most troublesome pest. Like the apple sawfly, the pest lays its eggs in the blossoms, the grubs following the same process as those of the sawfly. Both 'Laxton's Superb' and 'Conference' are among the most resistant varieties. The pest may be easily controlled by dusting with Derris when the blossom is open, and again a month later. As Derris will also control capsid, sawfly and blossom weevil, it may be considered the pear grower's great standby, as well as being effective on apples.

PEAR-LEAF BLISTER MITE The mite attacks the young leaves of the pear in spring, causing reddish-brown blisters to appear, and in these the eggs are laid. Mites, invisible to the naked eye, hatch out; later they winter in the bud scales and attack the young leaves as they appear in spring. Spraying with lime-sulphur early in spring as the buds open will prevent an attack.

PLUM

Diseases

BROWN ROT There are three serious troubles in this section:

(a) Spur blight
(b) Blossom wilt
(c) Fruit rot

Spur blight is caused by infection of the new leaves; these are attacked by spores which later travel down the spurs and on to the branches, causing decay and all that goes with it.

Blossom wilt is the same infection, only it is the blossom that is mainly attacked: the disease causes it to fall away before the fruit is set.

Both these diseases may be controlled by spraying with a one-per-cent lime-sulphur solution just before the blossom opens. A wash with petroleum-oil solution in February will also give additional control, and the two should keep down Red Spider and destroy the eggs of the leaf-curling aphis. This spraying programme given once every three years, or whenever necessary, should be sufficient to keep the plum orchard in a healthy condition, with a Derris spray immediately after petal fall.

Fruit rot. This is caused by a fungus disease which attacks the individual fruits, causing them to mummify on the trees. There is no known cure, but the trouble is not common.

CANKER The varieties 'Victoria' and 'Czar' seem most prone to the attacks which concentrate on the main stem of plums, causing the troubled area to become decayed. Should the trouble extend completely round the stem, the trees will die back and be of no further use. Myrobolan B stock has proved resistant.

CHLOROSIS This may affect all top fruits, the leaves taking on a yellowing due to lack of iron in the soil. It is a common trouble of fruits growing in a limestone soil, but it will rarely be experienced where the trees are growing in grassland. It should be corrected without delay, for otherwise the leaves cannot carry out their proper functions, and the quality and quantity of the fruit will rapidly deteriorate. The gardeners of old used to drive an iron nail through the trunk of the tree; but the modern gardener will spray the foliage with ferrous sulphate during midsummer.

CLUSTER CUP ROT This fungus occurs on plum leaves, infecting the underside of the leaves with clusters of bright orange cups, with tiny black dots appearing on the upper surface. Diseased plants seldom flower, and should be dug up and destroyed. It is, therefore, not advisable to plant anemones beneath or near plum trees, as there is no known cure for the disease.

HONEY FUNGUS It is *Armillaria mellea* which attacks, first the roots of apples, plums, and cherries, then the trunk above ground, causing the leaves to shrivel and fall and eventually the tree to die. The fungus, which appears as long black bootlace-like strands, smells of mushrooms and is persistent long after the tree is to all appearances dead. The roots and stumps of all dead trees should therefore be removed and destroyed to prevent the spreading of the fungus which may appear as honey-coloured toadstools around the base of the tree.

The disease is controlled by treating the soil around the base of the stem – and the stem itself if the trouble is observed – with the new preparation Armillatox, which will destroy the fungus not the plant.

SILVER LEAF The most dreaded of plum and cherry diseases, it enters the tree through a cut or break and, if this occurs between October and March, the tree will exude no gummy substance to heal the wound and prevent fungus spores from entering. A Ministry of Agriculture order makes it compulsory in Britain to complete all pruning by mid-July, to allow the tree time to 'gum' before mid-September. Where breakages occur at other times, treat the wound with white-lead paint as a precaution against the disease.

The symptoms of silver leaf infection are readily observed. The foliage takes on a silver-like appearance and wilts and this is followed, eventually, by the death of the tree. All prunings must be removed and burnt without delay. 'Czar' and 'Victoria' are the two most susceptible varieties; the 'Pershores' and 'Gages' are more resistant.

Pests

LEAF CURLING APHIS This greenfly causes damage to the leaves and young fruit in much the same manner as the Red Spider. The eggs are laid on the branches in late autumn and hatch out in early spring. A tar-oil wash given during December or January will kill off all eggs, so control is therefore not difficult.

PLUM MAGGOT This may prove troublesome in some seasons, the eggs being laid on the young fruit whence the grubs work their way into the centre. Fruits will either fall prematurely or will be uneatable if they mature. The best method of control is to soak the trunks of the trees with Mortegg during winter, and to dust the open blossom and young fruit with Derris.

SAWFLY The Plum sawfly lays its eggs in the flowers where the hatched grubs remain until the fruit begins to form; then they begin their tunnelling. Effective control may be had by spraying with Lindex, one ounce to two gallons of water. Immediately after petal fall.

RASPBERRY

Diseases

CANE BLIGHT The fungus attacks raspberry canes at ground level after wintering in the soil. It causes large purple cankers to form, and these may later encircle the stem and cause it to die back or to break off at the point of infection. When this occurs, the spores formed on the surface are released and may infect nearby canes. There is no known cure, although spraying with Bordeaux mixture, as for cane spot, has usually prevented an outbreak.

Pests

RASPBERRY BEETLE It is the most troublesome of all raspberry pests, and also attacks the loganberry and blackberry. The beetle is greyish-brown, about one-sixth of an inch long, and the female lays her eggs in the flowers. The greyish-white grubs feed on the fruits, making them unfit for use. To control, dust the flowers with Derris as soon as they open, and again when the fruit begins to set. This should be done as routine each year.

RASPBERRY MOTH The pest winters in the soil at the base of the canes, emerging from a cocoon in spring as a silvery-brown moth with yellow spots on the wings. The eggs are laid in the blossoms, and the small caterpillars that hatch out feed on the young fruits, causing them to die before they reach maturity. To control, soak the soil around (and the canes themselves) with tar-oil in January, and dust the blooms with Derris as they open.

REDCURRANT

Pests

CLEARWING MOTH Concentrating its activities on the redcurrant, the moth lays her eggs along the branches; upon hatching, the grubs tunnel into the stems, feeding on the sap and causing the branches to decay and die back. When once the grub enters the stems, control is difficult, but routine spraying with tar-oil in winter should ensure trouble free plants.

STRAWBERRY

Diseases

GREY MOULD (BOTRYTIS) A troublesome disease of strawberries and gooseberries, also of dahlias and anemones and of tomatoes, peas and brassicas, especially those growing under glass or outdoors under humid conditions. With gooseberries it attacks the new shoots, leaves and fruit, and the affected branch will wilt and die. It is important to remove any affected shoots as soon as the disease is observed, and strawberry and tomato plants must be dug up and burnt. Succulent and soft-wooded plants growing under glass will also be troubled if not given sufficient ventilation or if carelessly watered, and the splashing of soil will encourage the disease. It will rarely attack those plants growing outdoors which have been well supplied with potash, but an outbreak may occur where excessive nitrogen has been used, as this makes for soft growth.

With soft fruits, the disease may be prevented by dusting with Orthocide as the flowers open, and again 10 to 12 days later. But fruits used for canning or bottling should not be treated. For tomatoes, spraying with Shirlan AG as routine will prevent an outbreak.

RED CORE A notifiable disease; with many varieties it is proving troublesome everywhere. The Red Core Disease Strawberry Plant Order of 1957 (applicable to England and Wales) states that infected plants may not be sold for planting except on land already infected by the disease.

Diseased plants turn reddish brown and are stunted; upon lifting, the dead roots show a reddish cylindrical core. There is no known cure though some varieties are resistant including 'Cambridge Vigour', 'Red Gauntlet' and 'Perle de Prague', though 'Vigour' is highly susceptible to verticillium wilt.

Pests

TARSONEMID MITE A troublesome strawberry pests. The mites begin to lay their eggs in the heart of the plants where growth commences in March and, as a precaution, all plants should be given a 20-minute immersion in hot water at 110°F (43°C). It must, however, be noted that at 113°F (45°C) the plants will be killed, hence the need to take careful note of the temperature. Dusting the plants with flowers of sulphur at the end of March (also as a precaution against mildew) will give partial control, as will spraying them with a two-per-cent lime-sulphur solution.

VINE

Pests

MEALY BUG A white, wax-like insect, like a small beetle, which produces white masses, like cotton-wool, on the stems of vine, peach and apricot. It is also found on greenhouse plants, especially cacti. Vine rods should be regularly scraped to prevent the pest sheltering in the paper-like bark, and plants on which its presence is noted should be painted with methylated or surgical spirit. Vines, peaches and apricots should be sprayed with winterwash while dormant (December).

SCALE As with white scales, the insects attack peaches and apricots, figs and vines, and are to be found clustering about the stems, where they suck up the sap and lower the ability of the plant to combat disease. Spray with tar-oil wash in

December or spray with malathion in early spring.

VINE WEEVIL The larva, with its fat, cream-coloured body, attacks the roots of vines; also of auriculas and chrysanthemums, while the weevil itself hides beneath the surface of the soil by day, attacking the stems of the plants by night. The pest is exterminated by soaking the soil in spring with Lindex solution, and pot-grown plants will be kept free if a small amount of Jaypeat Compound is placed in each pot before it is filled with compost. Alternatively, add Gammexane dust to the potting compost; this will keep the soil free from the pest.

Fruit Diseases – Summary of Treatment

Apple

APPLE MILDEW *Podosphaera leucotricha*	Spray with 2% lime-sulphur at green bud.
BROWN ROT *Sclerotinia fructigena*	Spray with 2% lime-sulphur at green bud.
SCAB *Venturia inaequalis*	Spray with 2% lime-sulphur or Orthocide.

Cherry

LEAF SCORCH *Gnomoria erythrostoma*	Spray with Bordeaux Mixture before blossoms open.
BACTERIAL CANKER *Pseudomonus morsprunorum*	Spray with Bordeaux Mixture in October.
BROWN ROT BLOSSOM WILT *Sclerotinia laxa*	Spray with tar-oil when dormant with Bordeaux Mixture before blossoms open.
LEAF CURL *Taphrina deformans*	Spray with Bordeaux Mixture at bud burst.

Currants

RUST *Cronartium ribicola*	Spray with Bordeaux Mixture after fruit is gathered.
LEAF SPOT *Pseudopeziza ribis*	Spray with Bordeaux Mixture after fruit is gathered.

Gooseberry

CLUSTER CUP RUST *Puccinia pringshelmiana*	No known cure.
AMERICAN GOOSEBERRY MILDEW *Spaerotheca mors-uvae*	Spray with 1% lime-sulphur before and after flowering.

Peach

LEAF CURL *Taphrina deformans*	Spray with Bordeaux Mixture at bud burst.

Pear

PEAR SCAB *Venturia pirina*	Spray with Bordeaux Mixture before blossom.

Plum

HONEY FUNGUS *Armillaria mellea*	Treat with Armillatox.
BACTERIAL CANKER *Pseudomonus morsprunorum*	Spray with Bordeaux Mixture at bud burst.
BROWN ROT *Sclerotina laxa*	Pre-blossom spraying with Bordeaux Mixture.
SILVER LEAF *Stereum purpureum*	No known cure.

Raspberry

CANE SPOT *Elsinoe veneta*	Spray with 2½% Bordeaux Mixture at bud break.
CANE BLIGHT *Leptosphaeria coniothyrium*	No known cure.

Strawberry

GREY MOULD *Botrytis cinerea*	Dust with Orthocide.
RED CORE *Phytopthora fragariae*	No known cure..Plant resistant varieties.
MILDEW *Sphaerotheca humuli*	Spray with 1% lime-sulphur.
WILT *Verticillium dahliae*	No known cure. Plant resistant varieties.

Fruit Pests – Summary of Treatment

	Apple
Blossom	Treat in spring with petroleum-oil emulsion.
Codling moth	Spray with Derris early July.
Greenfly	Apply a tar-oil wash in mid-winter.
Red spider	Spray with lime-sulphur after blossom fall.
Sawfly	Spray with Lindex at petal fall.
Tortrix moth	Spray early May with Abol X or Sybol.
Winter moth	Grease band trees and spray with tar-oil.
Woolly aphis	Apply a tar-oil wash in mid-winter.
	Blackcurrant
Capsid	Spray in January with DNOC or tar-oil. *NOTE:* Do not use any insecticide based on gamma BHC on currants.
	Cherry
Black fly	Spray mid-winter with tar-oil.
Cherry fruit moth	Spray mid-winter with tar-oil.
Slugworm	Dust with Derris each fortnight July and Aug.
Winter moth	Grease banding and dust with Derris in May.
	Gooseberry
Greenfly	Spray in spring with Abol X or Sybol.
Sawfly	Spray with Lindex as the blooms open.
	Peach
Red Spider	Spray with liquid Derris or malathion at bud-break.
Scale	See Vine.
	Pear
Blister mite	Spray with lime-sulphur as blooms open.
Pear midge	Dust blossoms with Derris.
	Plum
Leaf-curling aphis	Wash with tar-oil in January.
Plum maggot	Treat with Mortegg in winter.
Plum sawfly	Treat with Lindex after petal fall.
	Raspberry
Raspberry beetle	Dust flowers with Derris upon opening.
Raspberry moth	Dust flowers with Derris upon opening.
	Redcurrant
Clearwing moth	Spray with tar-oil in mid-winter.
	Strawberry
Tarsonemid mite	Spray flowers upon opening with 2% lime-sulphur.
	Vine
Mealy bug	Scrape the rods and paint with surgical spirit. Spray with a winter wash while dormant December
Scale	Spray with malathion in early spring.
Weevil	Soak the soil around the base of the plants with Lindex.

Index